The Myth of Adam Smith

To Zeenet

Whose love revived me

The Myth of Adam Smith

Salim Rashid

Professor of Economics, University of Illinois

Edward Elgar
Cheltenham, UK • Northampton, MA, USA

Published by
Edward Elgar Publishing Limited
8 Lansdown Place
Cheltenham
Glos GL50 2HU
UK

Edward Elgar Publishing, Inc.
6 Market Street
Northampton
Massachusetts 01060
USA

A catalogue record for this book
is available from the British Library

Library of Congress Cataloguing in Publication Data

Rashid, Salim, 1949–
    The myth of Adam Smith / Salim Rashid.
    Includes index.
      1. Smith, Adam, 1723–1790. 2. Economics. I. Title.
  HB103.S6R37 1998
  330.15'3—dc21
                                    97–30625
                                          CIP

ISBN 1 85898 532 3

Printed and bound in Great Britain by Bookcraft (Bath) Ltd

Contents

Preface

Many years ago, as a graduate student, I began to study Anglican clergymen of the eighteenth and nineteenth centuries. My goal was to try and understand why the clergy were so ignorant of social forces and so impotent in analyzing them. To my great surprise, I found that the clergymen were in the forefront of social analysis and frequently provided the most penetrating analysis of social and economic problems. The major reason for our failure to recognize this glaring fact lay in the myth that Adam Smith erected the science of political economy. This led me to a closer study of Adam Smith and his age and this book is the result.

In the older English texts that I so love to read it is traditional to preface a few words to the "gentle reader" and I would like a similar indulgence. My aim is to provide an account of Adam Smith that is more accurate than widely used hagiographies. When I first read Adam Smith over 20 years ago I became animated and excited. I wish I could recover some of the enthusiasm of that fresh reading. Sadly, the years that followed have all gone downhill and I now have to struggle to find something nice to say about Smith. Pity me, gentle reader! Whether right or wrong, who would wish to spend 20 years and conclude that he has studied such a person!

The goal of trying to see Adam Smith in context necessarily requires me to form an opinion about what has been called Mercantilism as well as about the Scottish Enlightenment. It is impossible for me to justify here the biases I have acquired about either of these intellectual movements, but it is only fair that the reader be warned.

What has been called Mercantilism is better called Pragmatic Political Economy in order to emphasize the two most prominent features of that age. I have quoted a few authors at length and even repeated myself because experience has convinced me that the "pamphlet" literature of this age remains quite unappreciated. It was a political literature—"liberty" led to domestic free trade while foreign rivalries guided international economic policies. It is curious to see how little emphasis has been given to these features by historians of economic thought. Even scholars who have no love of Smithian hagiography, such as J.A. Schumpeter, are misled by focusing on the "leading lights" and by the closely related belief that economics is a complex "science." I have long felt that economic knowledge has the gently undulating contours of a meadow rather than the hierarchical structure of a pyramid—yet another bias that colors my account.

The Scottish Enlightenment, on the other hand, focused on psychology as the fundamental guide to social science. This important contribution was not due to any one individual, it had considerable seventeenth-century roots, many of them theological, and served as the most lasting intellectual legacy of the Scots. The world view of David Hume, or even that of Adam Smith, was not representative; they do not indicate widely accepted prejudices nor were these men generally respected leaders of opinion. Hume largely, and Smith to a lesser extent, were humored as eccentric prodigies. If one has to pick on a "representative" figure for the Scottish Enlightenment, William Robertson is appropriate for the earlier period, while for the later one it should be poor, honest Dugald Stewart, both of whom badly need appreciative biographies.

I have written largely in isolation (so much so, that I have occasionally written to scholars who died several years ago!). My attempts to correspond have been unsatisfactory. However, I must mention T.W. Hutchison, who has been very encouraging. Professor Hutchison has written a wonderful book on this theme, *Before Adam Smith*, and I am delighted at the way our views complement each other. Special thanks are due to the late Murray Rothbard, himself one of the leaders of the libertarian school, yet free from the hero-worshipping attitude of many others. Professor Rothbard has constantly encouraged and advised me and I am deeply grateful for the guidance he gave this non-libertarian. I am also particularly grateful to Larry Neal for his extensive comments on the entire first version, and to both him and Werner Baer for their continuing encouragement. Edward Elgar gave me much encouragement and Mark Blaug's enthusiasm for the manuscript was infectious.

Of the many individuals who have commented on parts of the manuscript, I must thank James Ahiakpor, Lee Alston, Royall Brandis, Hans Brems, Arthur Diamond, Charles Kindleberger, Shyam Kamath, David Levy, S. Todd Lowry, Dean Peterson, Bill Thweatt, and Paul Uselding.

The Haney Fund of Dartmouth College and the Research Board of the University of Illinois provided financial assistance for research during Fall 1976 and Summer 1986, respectively.

I regret that the pressure of circumstances has not allowed me to take account of some valuable recent literature, both articles and books—Jose Luis Cardoso, James Gherity, Ian Ross and Murray Rothbard, for example.

The Word Processing Center at the College of Commerce—Carol Halliday, Hope Cook and Debi Nimon—bore with me through many tiresome drafts and revisions.   Carol Halliday, in particular, did painstakingly valuable work on the camera ready copy. My mother-in-law, Mrs. Eileen Kuddus, kindly checked over the entire final draft and camera ready copy.

Several chapters have been published earlier, in part or in full, and I am very grateful to all the publishers for permission to use the material here. A list of relevant publishers, as well as a full citation of the original publication, is attached.

SALIM RASHID

Acknowledgements

I am grateful to the publishers of the following journals for permission to use material published earlier.

"The Policy of Laissez-Faire During Scarcities," *Economic Journal*, Vol. 90, September 1980, 493-503.

"Adam Smith's Rise to Fame: A Re-examination of the Evidence," *The Eighteenth Century*, Vol. 23, No. 1, 1982, 64-85.

"Adam Smith and the Division of Labour: A Historical View," *Scottish Journal of Political Economy*, Vol. 33, No. 3, August 1986, 292-297.

"Adam Smith's Interpretation of the History of Economics and its Influence in the 18th and 19th Centuries," *Quarterly Review of Economics and Business*, Vol. 27, No. 3, Autumn 1987, 56-69.

"Adam Smith and the Market Mechanism," *History of Political Economy*, Vol. 24, No. 1, 1992, 129-152.

"Charles James Fox and the Wealth of Nations," *History of Political Economy*, 1992, 493-98.

"The *Wealth of Nations* and Historical Facts," *Journal of the History of Economic Thought*, Vol. 14, Fall 1992, 225-243.

"The Intellectual Standards of Adam Smith's Day," *Journal of Libertarian Studies*, Vol. 11, Fall 1994, 107-116.

Thanks are also due to Donald A. Walker for permission to use "English Financial Pamphleteers of the Mid-Eighteenth Century: The Last Phase of Pragmatic Political Economy," in D.A. Walker, ed., *Perspectives on the History of Economic Thought*, Vol. 1 (Aldershot, Edward Elgar, 1989), 3-18.

Introduction

This book has been written so as to be accessible to the general reader. I have tried to maintain some independence between the chapters so that all the chapters can be read separately. For the reader who would like some sub-themes, they are as follows: Chapter 1 introduces the reader to my own prejudices. Chapters 2, 3, and 4 deal with Adam Smith's analytical and historical merits. The division of labor and the "Invisible Hand" are the most celebrated ideas connected with the *Wealth of Nations*. I begin with a historical review of the division of labor. This enables me to specify what was original to Smith and then indicate why it was of limited value. Insofar as the "Invisible Hand" is a rhetorical metaphor I discuss it at several points, particularly in the Introduction and Conclusion. If, however, the "Invisible Hand" is a concept with analytical merit, then it has to be established through a prior understanding of the market. This is the point I question in Chapter 3, "Adam Smith and the Market Mechanism." In view of the large proportion of historical and contemporary references in the *Wealth of Nations*, several scholars have argued that any deficiencies in Smith as a theorist should be counterbalanced by his superiority as an economic historian. Whether Smith used historical facts with an open mind and a desire to learn, or whether he used historical facts to illustrate his own theories, is the question raised in Chapter 4.

Chapters 5 and 6 on Public Finance and on Scarcities form the next block of chapters, intended to examine Smith's role as an applied economist. The importance of public finance for applied policy can scarcely be exaggerated, either in Smith's day or our own. Book V of the *Wealth of Nations*, which deals with public finance, is also the longest book by far in the *Wealth of Nations* and it offers us several insights into Smith's larger world view. The chapter dealing with scarcities has an importance quite disproportionate to its length. No government can afford to keep the populace hungry, and the laws guarding the price of food were among the most carefully scrutinized parts of the legal system. Smith's wholesale condemnation of these laws played no small part in Smith's own rise to fame.

Chapters 7 and 8 deal with Adam Smith's rise to fame as the "founder" of economics as a science. How a Whig-Radical would come to be the acknowledged master of all political parties is a curious story and I have tried to describe it in Chapter 7: "Adam Smith's Rise to Superior Fame."

The extent to which Smith's fame depended upon his own portrayal of other economists is the topic of the following chapter. One cannot help but have some view of the past. It was an enormous advantage for Smith's reputation that he guided people's perceptions of the past by his account of other economic systems in Book IV of the *Wealth of Nations*. Following on the theme of Smith as historian of economic thought, Chapter 9 shows that Smith should be held to proper standards because neither he nor his age was indifferent to plagiarism. The Conclusion returns to the significance of getting our picture of Adam Smith set in proper historical perspective, both for historiography and for policy.

1. Adam Smith and the Cycle of Ignorance

An inquiry into opinions which have been generally received and long established, is an undertaking that will always be sure to meet with opposition and censure; as it is not only the author of such opinions, but many of those who have concurred in them, that are apt to think themselves affected by it.

Joseph Massie, Essay on . . . Interest *(1750)*

I

To be considered great, a book must contain important ideas that are at once both true and original. A careful comparison of the *Wealth of Nations* with the literature of the seventeenth and eighteenth centuries shows that what is true is not original and what is original is not true.[1] The great fame of Adam Smith is based on false premises. Historians of economic thought have not placed Smith in context. When viewed against the long tradition of European political economy, especially the British version, as well as the developed forms of moral philosophy in the mid-eighteenth century, Smith's only virtue appears to be pedagogy.

There was widespread understanding of the workings of the market and of demand and supply well before Adam Smith wrote; furthermore, it was widely agreed that free markets should be the rule. As domestic trade did not involve the political considerations of foreign trade, Smith's predecessors had urged that the internal trade of a country should ordinarily be left free of restraint. In microeconomics, therefore, Adam Smith provided no advance over his contemporaries and his merits consist only in superior presentation of *some* issues. In macroeconomics and monetary theory, there is substantial agreement that Smith's work was behind the best of his age.

It is to international economics that we must turn to find Smith's original contribution. He provided the "first" closely reasoned argument in favor of completely free trade. While Smith's role in advocating this proposition has been widely recognized, it is worth noting two points often ignored by subsequent scholars. First, Smith frequently argues as though free trade is for the good of *all* countries and this is a proposition that cannot be established, even by modern economic theory. Secondly, if Smith's assumption that wages are bounded below by "common humanity" is taken seriously, then international economic equilibrium with full employment may not even exist. Smith's analytical contribution to economics is thus not only limited in extent, that is, to international economics alone, it is also largely counterbalanced by the fact that, on several issues, he did not see as far as several of his predecessors had done.

In the process of providing proper perspective on the *Wealth of Nations* I try to establish (actually, to re-establish) three smaller theses. First, to show by quoting contemporaries and predecessors that views often credited to Adam Smith were in fact widely advocated by contemporaries. Secondly, to show that on several occasions Adam Smith did not succeed in accepting the results already established by contemporaries. Thirdly, to argue that Adam Smith himself bears considerable responsibility for the erroneous views about the merits of the *Wealth of Nations* that have persisted for over two centuries. Several scholars have urged that I limit myself to the first proposition and then rely upon the profession's love of accuracy to do the rest. Alas, if the profession were so inclined, it could have followed up Lord Lauderdale and Dugald Stewart in 1800 or Bruno Suviranta and Jacob Viner in the 1920s. However, much as we may regret it, I see no way of denying Joseph Schumpeter's dictum that "New ideas, unless carefully elaborated, painstakingly defended, and 'pushed' *simply will not tell*."[2]

The way in which contemporary accounts simultaneously admit that Smith borrowed yet gloss over the importance of this borrowing is well illustrated by the following textbook account:

> Smith is the first of the great eclectics who wove into a harmonious whole the more important ideas of predecessors and contemporaries alike. The influence of Hutcheson and Hume is particularly in evidence; he also owed much to Turgot and the Physiocrats, especially Quesnay and such liberal mercantilists as North, Petty, Child, and Tucker. Other important ideas germinated from his disagreement with Mandeville. It is worth nothing that *The Wealth of Nations* contains remarkably few references to the writings of other authors and that Smith was perhaps less scholarly in this regard than he might have been. He knew precisely, however, what to extract from other works and how to use it to make his final product in every way unique and peculiarly his own, though many individual ideas and even illustrations are not original with him.[3]

The reader will readily give the benefit of doubt to an author who was "perhaps" lacking in fairness because he provides us with a "harmonious whole" which was "in every way unique." Now the question of intellectual priority is somewhat like the theoretical issue of the existence of evil. At an abstract level, a pinprick is just as effective as cancer in proving the presence of evil; it is the extent and pervasiveness of evil that disposes us towards accepting or rejecting the goodness of God. In the same way, to know that someone was not *entirely* original is scarcely disconcerting; to treat the issue fairly we must know how much was borrowed and how often. In the case of Adam Smith, there is no doubt that a substantial part of Smith's fame was based upon the belief that Smith was saying something radically new. The curious fact is that Smith himself is the authority for the views of his predecessors.

Jacob Viner was undoubtedly one of the finest economists to take an interest in the history of economic thought. His earlier works reflect a certain combative and polemical intent and contain some of the sharpest rebuttals to the critics of classical economics. Viner's contribution on "Adam Smith" in the *International Encyclopedia of the Social Sciences* is another matter. Having reflected carefully on the scholarship of a lifetime Viner selects three reasons for the "great importance" of the *Wealth of Nations*:

> First, it presents an impressive collection of economic data . . .
>
> Second, it was the most comprehensive and ambitious attempt to present in comprehensive and at the same time coordinated, fashion the nature of economic process . . .
>
> Third, it was an evaluating and crusading book, which sharply criticized existing society and government and argued strongly for changes in the national policy . . .[4]

Whatever Smith's merits as a data collector and as a lobbyist, the first and third reasons given by Viner, neither will lead us far into his abilities as an economist. This can only be considered in the second point, where Viner is careful to refer only to Smith's "attempt" and not to his success. When he does come to discuss Smith's original contributions, it is the moderation of Viner's assessment that rings out loudly:

> Smith's main merits as an "analytical" or "scientific" theorist, to use modern eulogistic terms for "pure" economic theory, lie in his eclectic spirit. While deliberately resorting to abstraction, he very much doubted that abstraction could provide either understanding of the real world or, by itself, safe guidance for the legislator or statesman. On specific points of economic analysis some predecessors did better than Smith, and he failed to absorb fully some of the genuinely valuable analytical contributions of Hume, the physiocrats, and Turgot. If "analytical" as an eulogistic term is to be interpreted strictly in terms of degree of rigor, internal consistency, and close analogy to abstract mathematical operations, Schumpeter's verdict that "the Wealth of Nations does

not contain a single analytical idea, principle, or method that was entirely new in 1776" . . . is difficult to challenge, and not merely because valuable ideas that are "entirely new" are hard to spot in any area of intellectual endeavor.[5]

Of all the supporters of Adam Smith, perhaps no one matches Viner in being deeply versed in the primary literature of the seventeenth and eighteenth centuries. Viner's refusal to challenge Schumpeter's charge could suffice to indicate that Smith's originality is not an easy fortress to defend. The undocumented nature of Schumpeter's charge against Adam Smith is perhaps due to Schumpeter's early death, but the flat assertion that Smith's work did not contain a single new analytic idea or principle has actually been somewhat unfortunate. As it stands, this notorious charge has only served to set tongues wagging. Detailed parallel quotes are nowhere provided, not even for Schumpeter's insistence that Smith's basic ideas followed the Natural Law doctrines of Grotius and Pufendorf. That Schumpeter's knowledge of Mercantilist pamphlets was limited largely to those available in modern reprint (in 1945) also seems clear. Whether or not Schumpeter is correct (I believe he is largely correct), the reader has no way of deciding.

The pages that follow rely upon the works of many scholars. Indeed, I have often felt that a simple juxtaposition of all the existing criticisms of Adam Smith, many of them by Smith's professed admirers, would suffice to condemn the *Wealth of Nations*. A long hagiographic tradition has resisted the piecing together of existing sources by developing a "yes, but" methodology: "*Yes*, Adam Smith made mistakes, *but* they do not affect his greatness." In the decade or so that I have been trying to develop my critique of the *Wealth of Nations* I am happy to report that some eminent scholars have been kind enough to praise my work as "properly critical," "of course right" and to label the existing state of affairs as "something of a cover-up." However, such critical opinions are not available in print. There appears to be considerable historical precedent for keeping criticisms private:

> When I had the privilege many years ago of living in [Alfred] Marshall's house and talking quite intimately and unreservedly about the doctrines of the various schools, I found that in private conversations he was quite ready to express, in a far more vigorous way than in his published writings, his dissent from a number of contemporaries. Very much the same is true of Pareto, who did not hesitate to speak out his mind very frankly as to the short-comings of famous and distinguished economists, both living and dead, both at home and abroad.[6]

Whether such a tradition of public silence is good for an academic profession is a topic worthy of discussion.

II

The monograph is as concerned with Adam Smith as with the inability of historians of economics to appraise his works in rigorous fashion. After a century of adulation, indirect criticism of Adam Smith began in the 1870s with the studies of national unification.[7] For the next 50 years criticism of various aspects of the *Wealth of Nations* and its doctrines began to be voiced. In 1926, Jacob Viner, an admirer of Smith, wrote that "On every detail [of economic doctrine], taken by itself, Smith appears to have predecessors in plenty. On few details was Smith as penetrating as his predecessors."[8] So Smith did not, according to Viner, contribute any new economic ideas, nor did he bring into sharp focus all the best ideas he used. If only Viner had documented these points carefully, how one would have to cheer! This incipient criticism of Smith left a bad taste and was not incorporated into the standard textbooks. By 1976 economists seemed to have decided that a suitable synthesis of historical research with the axiom of Smith's greatness was impossible and so there has been a calm return to the old verities. Since the bicentennial of 1976, criticizing Smith has been like calling the bride ugly. As a result, we now read praise of Smith that is just a variant of the nineteenth-century panegyrics. There is an important difference. The nineteenth-century hagiographers wrote without the advantage of a careful examination of the literature prior to Adam Smith; contemporary scholars can scarcely live in such bliss. The literature our ancestors wrote in ignorance of, we appear determined to ignore.

Even those sympathetic to a critique of Adam Smith have trouble believing that the case against him can be as transparent as it really is. As I noted earlier, "Why then is he so famous?" is the immediate question that follows. There appears to be an implicit belief in the survival of the fittest in the world of ideas. If Smith is famous, then, *ipso facto*, he is a great economist. Since the primary way of judging Smith's merits is by examining the relevant sources, such objections have little to do with the main argument but it is useful to say a few words about it. For the majority of economists, it is simply much too inconvenient to rethink the issue about Smith versus his predecessors. Smith is so readable and so quotable while those other authors were not even academics! As for sheer length, even though the five books of the *Wealth of Nations* may have deterred some readers, it is at least of a reasonably finite length; the microfilms of the pre-Smithian literature, on the other hand, number over a thousand reels. Who in his right mind would give up the former for the latter?

There are also strong forces aiding this wishful ignorance of the majority. Lovers of liberty seem to feel that their cause needs heroes, and having long since established Smith as a saint, they bristle at the thought of any blemish on his character. Someone should remind them that it is a very fragile ideology that hinges on the virtue of a "founding father." Paradoxically, Marxists too feel a special love for Smith. Did he not belong to the Scottish Historical School and speak on occasion of the labor theory of value? Did he not sneer at the virtues of public-spirited merchants and condemn their secret combinations? One may wonder at the consistency of someone who can draw praise from such opposing quarters; but nonetheless, their happy conjunction has permitted Smith to continue as a crowned monarch.

There is a final species of ignorance that is perhaps the hardest to deal with. Many people make a virtue of inertia and argue that our energies should be focused only upon current policy issues. On being told that freedom of trade was considered a virtue in Britain well before Adam Smith, they typically reply, Who cares? Is anyone *truly* original anyway? Is not all Western philosophy, in Whitehead's words, a series of footnotes to Plato? It seems to be a somewhat irresponsible procedure to encourage others to accurate scholarship and yet refuse to consider carefully the fruits of such efforts. In view of the large volume of favorable commentary on Adam Smith, what the inertia argument amounts to *practically* is a plea for the preservation of current prejudices: "Where ignorance is bliss, 'tis folly to be wise." At the risk of offending current attitudes, I have begun by taking a moralistic attitude and claimed that it is simply *wrong* for us to continue to be so casual about historical scholarship. In the Conclusion, I shall try to be more utilitarian and point out some of the consequences of our willful ignorance.

Panegyrics on Adam Smith continue unabated.[9] Surprisingly, distinguished historians of economic thought join in such accolades. Joseph J. Spengler is not content with William Letwin's assessment that Smith incorporated "everything useful" from his predecessors and "everything worth doing that they left undone, he accomplished." To this already heroic achievement, Spengler adds:

> Smith's great work did more . . . Smith set in motion an engine of analysis that made individual man temporarily victorious in his millennia-old struggle to be free of exploitation at the hands of those who control the apparatus of state.[10]

Perhaps this extravagant language is explicable by the occasion for their delivery—the bicentennial of the *Wealth of Nations*.

In order to prevent misunderstanding about a rather simple methodological issue, it should be made clear now that my aim is not to point out a few inconsequential errors in the *Wealth of Nations*. It is hard enough writing a long essay without making errors; to write a thousand-page book without blemish is well-nigh impossible. What does bear highlighting is the fact that Smith makes repeated errors, both on facts and on theory. He does not even stick consistently to the very issues his admirers would like to claim for him, such as the benefits of free choice by consumers. On some issues where one cannot be said to be strictly right or wrong, such as the measure of value, Smith's approach is backward compared with his predecessors. If we examine only one aspect of Smith, it is easy enough to be critical about that particular issue and feel that Smith's greatness must be based on "something else." It is only when we run from chapter to chapter in disappointment that it finally strikes us that we are perhaps staring at the emperor's new clothes.

If we identify economics with the use of the concepts of "demand and supply," then Adam Smith never did become an economist. Much of the inconsistency and meandering of the *Wealth of Nations* becomes readily explicable once we consider such a hypothesis. The simplest explanation for Adam Smith's whimsical treatment of what *we* would consider economics lies in the conjecture that Smith came to economics only in order to justify certain philosophical conclusions. Unusual though the conjunction of views might appear, this is consistent with the admiration of George Stigler:

> Smith had an overwhelmingly important triumph: he put into the center of economics the systematic analysis of the behavior of individuals pursuing their self-interest under conditions of competition . . . The proposition that resources seek their most profitable uses, so that in equilibrium the rates of return to a resource in various uses will be equal is still the most important substantive proposition in economics.[11]

Stigler is careful not to make any claims for Smith's originality so the above quote does not really address the criteria used here. That such praise of Smith has no historical foundation (in suggesting that the movement of economic resources due to profitability was original to Smith), I hope the subsequent pages will establish. For now, let it be noted that this "fundamental contribution" nowhere and nohow is based upon the use of the demand-supply apparatus. Greed tells us that resources will wish to move to more profitable uses; liberty permits the move to be made and for rates of profit to be equalized.

Belief in a system of liberty, already widely prevalent, gripped Smith's imagination at an early age and made him determined to show that this system was also applicable to economics. He could only succeed, however, by speaking to his contemporaries as an economist; that is, he too would have to speak of demand and supply. Probably by 1751 Smith had a clear realization of what he would have to do in order to convince others of conclusions to which philosophy had led him. Till the end of his life, this aim motivated his actions. Conscious that he had come to the principal conclusion—the applicability of freedom to economics—all by himself, Smith became obsessed with the idea of establishing his claim to have discovered this new intellectual world. This accounts for the persistent churlishness and jealousy found in Smith's writings. More worrisome, however, is the fact that Smith never did quite learn how to use demand and supply. Frequently, when faced by a concrete policy issue, Smith appears to have dipped into the literature until he found something to his liking and then paraphrased that pamphlet. This *ad hoc* borrowing continued for almost 25 years. Finally, even Smith had no heart for correcting and unifying the disjointed notes of a quarter-century. As a result, the *Wealth of Nations* is marvelous if one resolves to read no more than 20 pages at a time. Those who try to read more and to reason upon what they read soon find themselves wondering why Smith seldom treated logical consistency as a virtue. It is not that Smith could not be logical and consistent on other issues; demand and supply, however, eluded his grasp till the end of his life, and so he has left us in the *Wealth of Nations* some streaks of good philosophy accompanied by large patches of questionable economics.

In choosing "Adam Smith and the Cycle of Ignorance" as the title of this chapter I wished to emphasize the fact that much of what I have to say is not new: people have simply chosen to ignore facts which were known in the 1790s. I shall refer later to the works of such Scots as Dugald Stewart, Francis Horner and Lord Lauderdale; in concluding this chapter I wish to indicate several features of the obituarial biography that appeared in *The Times* on 6 August 1790, some two weeks after Smith's death. The accuracy of this account is not the point, the attitude towards Smith is.[12]

Adam Smith is described as being "in his youth a hard student" given to airs of vacancy by his absentmindedness. Smith's Oxford days are described principally with reference to the better beef available at Balliol College. After graduating from Oxford, Smith dallied for want of a profession: "The Church seemed an improper profession, because he had early become a disciple of Voltaire in matters of religion." Finally, Smith opened a class for teaching rhetoric at Edinburgh. *The Times* notes that Smith's fluency in English was coupled with knowledge of and admiration for the French Encyclopedists and David Hume, as well as a distaste for Dr Samuel Johnson. *The Times* then comments:

> Such opinions, or rather prejudices, which then prevailed very generally in Scotland, being embraced by a man, from whose English education they could not naturally have been expected, contrived with Dr Smith's merit in rendering him a very fashionable Professor.

Of Smith's tenure as Professor of Moral Philosophy at Glasgow, *The Times* singles out Smith's connections with the merchants:

> The College was torn by parties, and Dr Smith embraced that side which was more popular among the people of condition: That is, the rich merchants of the town, among whom he was well received, and from those conversations, particularly that of Mr Glassford, he learned many facts necessary for improving his Lectures; for being in a commercial town, he had converted the chair of Moral Philosophy into a professorship of trade and finance.

The last sentence conveys an unflattering picture, and this attitude continues when we are told of Smith's lectures that:

> A man who is continually going over the same ground will naturally smooth it. Dr Smith's lectures gradually acquired greater improvement and higher celebrity.

These lectures are said to have attracted the attention of Charles Townshend, who subsequently engaged Smith, "by very liberal terms," to act as a travelling tutor for his stepson, the Duke of Buccleuch. In showing a tannery to Charles Townshend, Smith slipped and fell into the tanning pit:

> He was dragged out, stripped, and carried with blankets, and conveyed home on a sedan chair, where, having recovered of the shock of this unexpected cold bath, he complained bitterly that he must leave life with all his affairs in the greatest disorder; which was considered an affectation, as his transactions had been few and his fortune was nothing.

The account goes on to commend Smith's repayment of students' fees before departing—perhaps the most engaging anecdote of Smith's life—as well as the appointment of a student to read the remaining lectures:

> This accordingly took place; tho' the Doctor was in general extremely jealous of the property of his Lectures; and, fearful lest they should be transcribed and published, used often to repeat, when he saw anyone taking notes "that he hated scribblers."

After his travels with the Duke, Smith worked on and published the "justly celebrated work on the Nature and Causes of National Wealth." The initial popularity of the book is ascribed to the praise of Charles Fox in Parliament, and the notice concludes by saying

> Dr Smith's system of Political Economy is not essentially different from that of Count Verri, Dean Tucker and Mr Hume; his illustrations are chiefly collected from the valuable collection *Sur les arts et métiers*; but his arrangement is his own; and as he has both carried his doctrines to a greater length, and fortified them with stronger proofs than any of his predecessors, he deserves the chief praise, or the chief blame, of propagating a system which tends to confound National Wealth with National Prosperity.

The absence of an admiring tone scarcely needs to be further emphasized. Smith is seen as an eccentric professor, jealous of his lectures, and noteworthy as the creator of a "system." While the principles of the system were not new, Smith had argued for it at greatest length. It was a system which tended to confuse "national wealth" with "national prosperity"—a clear indication that Smith's new system was seen to hold economic prosperity as the primary ingredient of national well-being. The disassociation of international economics from foreign politics is perhaps Smith's most important legacy.

The freedom with which I describe the bias and errors of others should not be taken to imply that I am myself unbiased or unimpeachably correct. I have made every effort to avoid historical or logical errors, but so too, I am sure, does everyone else. Not believing in the possibility of being unbiased, I can only offer as a defense the following words of a historian, J.B. Bury, whose world view is quite alien to my own:

> It seems to be always assumed as self-evident and universally admitted that impartiality and freedom from bias are indispensable qualifications in every historians' ideal of how history should be written. Here I totally disagree. I do not think that freedom from bias is possible, I do not think that it is desirable . . . Is there any event or transaction worth investigating or writing about on which the writer can fail to have a definite bias if the subject really engages his interest?[13]

NOTES

1. In *The Crisis of Keynesian Economics* Henry Hazlitt makes the identical charge against John Maynard Keynes. I am grateful to several members of California State University, Hayward, for pointing this out, as well as for making clear the implicit premise that the ideas are also significant.
2. Joseph Schumpeter, *History of Economic Analysis* (London: Allen & Unwin, 1954), 464. This remark is not made with reference to Smith, although Schumpeter's general portrayal of Smith is fairly critical.

3. I. Rima, *History of Economic Analysis* (New York: Irwin, 1986), 75. For a more detailed assessment of this type, see W. Letwin, *The Origins of Scientific Economics* (London: Methuen, 1963), 221-8.
4. J. Viner, "Adam Smith," in *International Encyclopedia of the Social Sciences* (1968). Reprinted in J.C. Wood, ed., *Adam Smith: Critical Assessments* (London: Croom Helm, 1984).
5. *Ibid.*
6. E.R.A. Seligman, "Pareto and Pantaleoni: Personal Reminiscences of Two Italian Economists," *Political Science Quarterly* (1930), **XLV**, 343.
7. Of course there had been much earlier criticism, e.g., the works of John Rae and Friedrich List, but, in the English-speaking world at least, these critiques had only a slight impact.
8. Jacob Viner, "Adam Smith and Laissez-faire," in J.M. Clark et al., *Adam Smith 1776-1926* (Chicago: 1928), 118.
9. At a "textbook" level, the following careful construction of Smith's achievement is indicative:

> The birth of economics as a science is usually placed at 1776, the year Adam Smith wrote *The Wealth of Nations*. It is no accident that economics was born the same year that Americans declared for freedom. Europeans had had a long experience with government oppression and regulation, and only a little experience with freedom. How would a free society work? Would order emerge out of natural liberty? If everyone pursued his own interests, would the social system hold together, or would it degenerate into chaos? Adam Smith undertook to answer these questions, and in so doing forged a new science—economics.

Jack High, review of Paul Heyne's *The Economic Way of Thinking in American Economics Texts: A Free Market Critique* (Reston, Va.: Young America's Foundation, 1980), 189.

10. J.J. Spengler, Introduction to Milton Friedman *Adam Smith's Relevance for 1976* (IIER Occasional Paper no. 5, December 1976), 1-2. Friedman's own assessment of Adam Smith is more guarded and realistic. Perhaps the occasion is also responsible for Kenneth Boulding's equally extravagant opening words in his Frank E. Seidman Lecture (Memphis, Tenn.: P.K. Seidman Foundation, November 1976):

> There is occasionally an extraordinary rightness about coincidence, even in names. There is something peculiarly delightful in the fact that Adam Smith is both the Adam and the Smith of economics, the father and the forger. THE WEALTH OF NATIONS is indeed seminal work. It contains within it the seed of almost everything that happened in economics since it was published.

11. G. Stigler, "The Success and Failures of Professor Smith," *Journal of Political Economy* (December 1976), **84**(6): 1199. Stigler is one of the few admirers of Smith to uphold uniform standards for judging all economists, famous or not. I am grateful to Professor Stigler for pointing out that his quote does not actually make claims for originality, as I had originally assumed.
12. The entire account is quoted by C.R. Fay, *Adam Smith and the Scotland of his Day* (London: Cambridge University Press, 1956), 32-5.
13. "The Late Professor J.B. Bury," *Cambridge Historical Journal* (1927), 196.

2. Adam Smith and the Division of Labor: A Historical View

It has been said of the first chapter of the *Wealth of Nations*, which deals with the division of labor, that it is "beyond all comparison, the most popular chapter in the *Wealth of Nations*; no part of the work has been so often reprinted . . . no part of it is so commonly read by children, or so well remembered by them."[1]

The seeming unanimity of opinion regarding the brilliance of Adam Smith's analysis has perhaps precluded attempts to place Smith's ideas in its eighteenth-century context as well as to record subsequent criticisms of Smith's views in the early nineteenth century. This is not to suggest that the existence of either predecessors or critics is unknown. Indeed, the edition of the *Wealth of Nations* by Edwin Canaan as well as that of R.H. Campbell and A.S. Skinner both contain several relevant footnotes on this issue.[2] What is missing in the literature, however, is a connected account of the issues. It is the aim of this chapter to help to fill the lacuna.

In order to judge the analytical merits of Adam Smith's ideas the following points need consideration: first, a description of Smith's own ideas and an assessment of their internal consistency; secondly, the state of knowledge prior to the *Wealth of Nations* must be noted, with special emphasis on the possible sources from which Smith may have borrowed. Even if Smith was not completely original, it is nonetheless a considerable contribution to clarify existing ideas or to give them a new emphasis: this is the third item to be examined. These three heads thus amount to an evaluation of Smith's consistency, originality and good judgement. Finally, it is necessary to step back for a moment from the focus upon the eighteenth century and ask ourselves whether, in the light of our current knowledge, the particular formulation provided by Adam Smith was in fact a worthwhile one.

We are emphatically told in Chapter 1 of Book I that the division of labor is the most important reason for greater production and is the primary force leading to prosperity:

The greatest improvement in the productive powers of labour, and the greatest part of the skill, dexterity and judgment with which it is any where direct, or applied, *seem to have been the effects of the division of labour.*

. . .

It is the great multiplication of the production of all the different arts, *in consequence of the division of labour*, which occasions, in a well-governed society, that universal opulence which extends itself to the lowest ranks of the people.[3]

The example of pin-making is used to provide illustrative proof of the productivity of the division of labor. A competent pin-maker, we are told, could not make more than 20 pins a day, whereas, upon dividing the tasks into 18 operations, such as drawing, cutting, grinding, etc., ten men can make over 48,000 pins in a day. On average, therefore, each individual's productivity is increased 240-fold. Truly a momentous force. It is important to note that this example is especially interesting because the productivity increase involves *no* change in technique: it is purely a case of applying existing knowledge more efficiently.[4]

Three reasons are given why a concentration of effort upon a single task increases efficiency. First, the skill of individual workers is much improved by specialization; secondly, workers save the time and effort involved in having to switch from one operation to another; and finally, the division of labor facilitates the invention of machinery. The three reasons are most applicable only in manufacturing and Smith notes that agriculture is not suited to the division of labor, with the implication that not much growth could be expected in that sector. The emphasis laid upon the division of labor is not a little curious and is very much original to Smith. It is the division of labor that is the major cause of the observed inequality in individual talents: "the very different genius which appears to distinguish men . . . is not upon many occasions so much the cause, as the effect of the division of labour."[5] And it is the common worker who, in attempting to modify machinery in order to ease himself, invents most new machinery. Smith is so taken with this idea that he even recounts a story, now considered mythical, of a boy inventing a new valve in order to be free to play with his fellows. The makers of machines and philosophers are also given credit for inventing some machines, but their role appears to be secondary.[6]

If the division of labor is indeed such a potent source of wealth, what hinders its fullest development? The title of Chapter 3 of Book I clearly enunciates the fundamental principle "That the division of labour is limited by the extent of the market." No one would wish to be more productive if they could not exchange the surplus products of their industry. This capacity to exchange is but another name for the market. Hence, where there are extensive markets it pays to subdivide labor greatly since all the increased output can be sold. To make his point, Smith uses the homely but effective example of a porter, who can find constant employment only in great towns. In a somewhat abrupt jump, Smith then goes on to point out that better transportation widens the effective market for products and is thus a great stimulus to the further division of labor.[7]

II

In turning to the British predecessors of Adam Smith on the division of labor, it is useful to divide the subject into two heads: first, how far the productivity of a suitable division of labor was recognized; and secondly, whether the relationship of this division to the extent of the market was noted. The increase of output and the improvement in quality upon specialization is remarked upon by several authors, beginning with Sir William Petty. In the *Political Arithmetic* we are told that:

> Cloth must be cheaper made, when one Cards, another spins, another Weaves, another Draws, another Dresses, another Presses and Packs; than when all the operations above-mentioned were clumsily performed by the same hand.[8]

Petty goes on to point out that, in much the same way, the Dutch are able to convey goods cheaply by sea because each ship is specialized for a specific function. In another place, Petty goes on to give a more striking example of the division of labor in the manufacture of a watch:

> If one man shall make the Wheels, another the Spring, another shall Engrave the Dialplate, and another shall make the Cases, then the Watch will be better and cheaper, than if the whole Work be put upon by any one Man.[9]

Petty's writings appear to have been fairly widespread because we find the same three examples recurring in the *Considerations on the East-India Trade*, a pamphlet which earned the highest praise from both J.R. McCulloch and Lord Macaulay. We shall return to the *Considerations* in treating the relationship of the division of labor to the market, so let us move on and observe that in Mandeville's *Fable of the Bees* there is a distinct reference to the benefit of subdividing tasks, where the example of ships is used yet again.[10] What has not been observed in the literature yet, however, is the fact that the Anglo-Irish economists clearly noted the productivity of dividing tasks. In a brilliant pamphlet urging the erection of a bank in Ireland, Henry Maxwell, an Irish Member of Parliament, pointed out in 1721:

> Those, either Spinners or Weavers, that betake themselves to spin one Sort of Thread, and weave one sort of Cloth will become greater Proficients in their several kinds, and work both better and quicker, and consequently cheaper, than if each of them attempted to spin every sort of thread, or weave every sort of Cloth .... As an extended Manufacture cannot be carry'd on without this Variety of choice, so this Variety of choice requires a populous Country.[11]

In the *Weekly Observations* of the Dublin Society, a series of letters written in 1737 to provide practical guidance for the economic development of Ireland, the Reverend Samuel Madden attacked the practice of letting farmlands to weavers. This absence of specialization, he claimed, ruined both farming and weaving:

> The readiness and neatness of the execution depend so much in every art upon daily repetitions of the self-same motions, that the least interruptions are pernicious, much more, where those interruptions, from one business, are filled up by attending one another, which requires different motions.[12]

It may be noted that Adam Smith owned a copy of the *Weekly Observations* in his library.

The next 20 years saw two other economists refer directly to the productivity of divided labor. Joseph Harris does so in his *Essay upon Money and Coins* in 1757, and so too does the Reverend Josiah Tucker in his unpublished but privately circulated *Elements of Commerce*. In Tract I of his *Four Tracts*, published in 1774, two years before the *Wealth of Nations*, Tucker emphatically noted the benefits of the division of labor. This is a tract that had considerable circulation. As it consists of a polished version of a controversy in which Tucker had engaged with David Hume, it is not unlikely that Smith may even have seen the original version as early as 1758:

> In the richer Country, where the Demands are great and constant, every Manufacture that requires various Processes, and is composed of different Parts, is accordingly divided and subdivided into separate and distinct Branches; whereby each Person becomes more expert, and also more expeditious in the particular Part assigned him. Whereas in a poor Country, the same Person is obliged by Necessity, and for the Sake of getting a bare Subsistence, to undertake such different Branches, as prevent him from excelling, or being expeditious in any.[13]

While the improvements, in both quantity and quality, obtained by the division of labor were thus quite widely recognized, the recognition of the dependence of such division upon the market is not so explicit. Petty has only a concluding sentence stating that the Dutch provide cheap freight because "they can afford a particular sort of Vessel for each particular Trade."[14] The *Considerations*, however, is much more exact on this issue; in the cases of both watch-making and shipping the benefits of the division of labor are described only *after* we have been told that: "If the Demand of Watches should become so very great as to find constant employment for as many Persons as there are Parts in a Watch,"[15] and the same qualification is stated, almost verbatim, for the case of shipping. Josiah Tucker is equally explicit on the role of the market in permitting specialization.

Henry Maxwell touches upon the role of the market in his statements regarding populous countries, and follows his discussion of the division of labor immediately by a statement on the necessity of having nearby markets:

> The next thing necessary to increase a Manufacture, is, Nearness and Number of Market Towns, where the Manufacturer may have choice of Markets, and those not at a great distance.[16]

It may be noted that both Maxwell and Harris deal indirectly with the market, by referring to population and arguing thereafter as though larger populations necessarily implied richer markets.[17]

A review of the state of knowledge accessible to Adam Smith therefore suggests that Adam Smith definitely introduced crispness into treatments of the division of labor by his statement that "The division of labour is limited by the extent of the market." This is short, it is entirely correct, and it makes explicit something that could be read in earlier authors but may well not have struck the attention of most readers. One would also like to be able to say that Adam Smith introduced a similar sharpness of analysis in discussing the reasons for increased productivity. Unfortunately, not only does the example of pin-making appear to have been taken from the French *Encyclopédie* but also the three advantages of the division of labor are also distinctly stated there.[18] Why Smith should have chosen to borrow without acknowledgement from such a widely read source is unclear but it seems that several contemporaries were well aware of the source. When Adam Smith and Adam Ferguson fell out in the 1760s and 1770s, Smith appears to have accused Ferguson of plagiarism; to which Ferguson justifiably replied that he had only dipped into the same French source as Smith![19] On the whole, Smith's treatment of the division of labor shows some definite improvement in formulation and clarity but is disappointing in its treatment of possible sources.

However, it would be a mistake to leave the issue at this stage. Even if Smith had accepted all the details of his contemporaries, he nonetheless gave the subject a new look by his heavy emphasis upon the division of labor as the major reason for increased production. In the words of Joseph Schumpeter:

> nobody, either before or after A. Smith, ever thought of putting such a burden upon division of labour. With A. Smith it is practically the only factor in economic progress.[20]

A decisive change of emphasis certainly deserves to be considered an original contribution, and in assessing the overall merits of Smith's first three chapters, this point will have to be considered. Schumpeter's statement of this point is particularly forceful:

> Classical scholars as well as economists . . . are prone to fall into the error of hailing as a discovery everything that suggests later developments, and of forgetting that, in economics as elsewhere, most statements of fundamental facts acquire importance only by the superstructures they are made to bear and are commonplace in the absence of such superstructures.[21]

III

Before turning to an assessment of the merits of Smith's analysis as well as the justification of the extraordinary emphasis he put upon the division of labor, it is necessary to realize that, in a broad sense, the division of labor had been an integral part of social theory for many centuries. It is clearly noted by Plato, who emphasizes the adaptation of individual talents to tasks as a primary benefit of the division of labor. It is even more forcefully stated by Xenophon in the *Cyropaedia*, with a strong economic emphasis:

> In large cities, however, because many make demands upon each trade, one [trade] alone is enough to support a man, and often less than one: for instance, one man makes shoes for men, another for women . . . Of necessity he who pursues a very specialized task will do it best.[22]

This passage was later stated by Dugald Stewart as a source to which Adam Smith was probably indebted and, by implication, to which Smith should have drawn attention.[23]

The general tone of remarks upon the division of labor in earlier centuries is not so much in terms of the narrow productivity gains as described by

Smith, but in the much wider sense of providing for an effective and comfortable social life. This viewpoint is traceable from the Greeks through Aquinas and Luther down to the eighteenth century. Francis Hutcheson, for example, writes:

> Again, 'tis plain that a man in absolute solitude, tho' he were of mature strength, and fully instructed in all our arts of life, could scarcely procure to himself the bare necessaries of life, even in the best soils or climates; much less could he procure any grateful conveniences.[24]

This observation leads Hutcheson directly into the desirability of living in large, complex societies:

> Larger societies have force to execute greater designs of more lasting and extensive advantage. These considerations abundantly show the necessity of living in society, and obtaining the aid of our fellows, for our very subsistence; and the great convenience of larger associations of men for the improvement of life, and the increase of all our enjoyments.[25]

This "global view" of the benefits of the division of labor as the attraction and the cement of larger complex societies is very much a commonplace in the eighteenth century and forms part of the meta-economic scaffolding upon which the house of Smithian economics was built. It is indicative of the singular peak Adam Smith was placed upon that every "anticipation" of Smith's ideas once called forth extended comment. The above quote from Hutcheson does not show any unusual perceptiveness, yet a careful scholar like W.R. Scott felt obliged to explain:

> In this passage Hutcheson anticipates Adam Smith's claim for the advantages of Division of Labour in the separation of employments and the increase of dexterity, while the growth of invention and the distinction between simple and complex cooperation are also implied. What is new in Smith's *Lectures* is the direct application of the principle to existing industrial conditions.[26]

Scott's generous attributions to Hutcheson are as notable as his attempt to find originality in Smith's "direct application" to industry.

In assessing the merits of Adam Smith's treatment of the division of labor, it is useful to begin by noting that Smith completely ignored the traditional view of the division of labor as permitting individuals to perform those tasks that were most suitable to them. In the words of Harris: "Men are endowed with various talents and propensities, which naturally dispose and fit them for different occupations."[27] Why Smith would choose not only to ignore this obvious factor, but indeed, to insist on the contrary is by no means clear. Of his predecessors, Mandeville is the only author who insisted that the division of labor required only ordinary talents and capacities, and perhaps Smith is carrying Mandeville's argument to its extremity:

> [It is] almost inconceivable to what prodigious Height, from next to nothing, some Arts may be and have been raised . . . tho' none but Men of ordinary Capacity should ever be employ'd in them. [The] Task [of constructing a] First-Rate Man of War . . . would be impractical, if it was not divided and subdivided into a great Variety of different Labours; and it is as certain, that none of these Labours require any other, than working Men of ordinary Capacities.[28]

The actual merits of Adam Smith's analysis of the division of labor was most sharply disputed by one of his admirers, Dugald Stewart, in the latter's lectures on political economy at the University of Edinburgh. We recall that Smith gave three reasons for the increased productivity consequent upon specialization: first, the increased dexterity of the worker; secondly, the saving of time in not having to move from one job to another; and finally, the tendency of the division of labor to encourage the invention of machinery. Stewart criticized each point in turn. That a workman gains in dexterity by concentrating on one task, Stewart has no doubt, but the efficiency gains thus obtained he considers to be quite limited. Indeed, so slight are the gains from this source that much work in pin-making was done by children:

> Hence I am led to conclude, that though one of the advantages of the division of labour be to increase the rapidity of manual work, yet this advantage bears so very small a proportion to that which is gained in the last result, that it is by no means entitled to stand at the head of the enumeration; and certainly goes a very little length in accounting for that minute division and subdivision of labor which has been introduced into some of the most prosperous manufactures of this country. On this head, therefore, I entirely agree with a remark of Lord Lauderdale in his *Inquiry into the Nature and Origin of Public Wealth*, where he observes, that even in the trade of the pinmaker, without the use of machinery to supersede the work of the hand, no great progress could have been made in the rapidity with which pins are formed.[29]

Secondly, while it was perfectly true that a worker saved time by not having to change jobs, "the economy of time gained in this way must plainly bear a still more inconsiderable proportion than the former, to the magnitudes of the effect which it is brought to explain." If then the division of labor is to explain the productivity of labor it must be by its influence upon the invention of machinery. Smith's example of a boy improving the steam engine in order to play longer with his friends Stewart finds "extremely unsatisfactory." Without disputing the fact, he considers such incidents improbable on grounds of self-interest because the effect of such improvements would not be to shorten the workday for the inventor and indeed might even lead to his being unemployed. More importantly, the effect of the division of labor was to fix attention on one simple operation while the improvement of machinery required a knowledge of a great variety of operations:

> In confirmation of this reasoning, it may be worth while to remark, that among the many complicated machines which the manufactures of this country exhibit, while many of them may be traced to men who never entered the workshop, but in order to gratify a mechanical curiosity, hardly one can be mentioned which derives its origin from the living automatons, who are employed in the details of the work.[30]

Dugald Stewart did not deny that the division of labour stimulated the invention of machinery but the way it did so was by acting "not on the inventive powers of the workman, but on those of his employer, or of the speculative observer." (Stewart is not entirely fair to Adam Smith, since Book I, Chapter 1 does contain some discussion of the role of the philosophical inventor.)

A closer analysis virtually stands the Smithian analysis on its head:

> The obvious effect of the division of labour in any complicated mechanical operation is, to analyse that operation into the simplest steps which can be carried on separately. Of these steps, there may probably be some which can only be performed by the human hand, while others, either in whole or in part, admit of the substitution of machines. *Now, it is only by resolving an operation into its simplest elements, that this separation can be made, so as to force on the attention of the mechanist, in their simplest forms, those particular cases where his ingenuity may be useful.* It is thus, too, that the advantages arising from the aid of machinery become so apparent and palpable, as to excite the efforts of inventive genius; a machine which supplies the labour of the hand, superseding of course a particular description of workmen, and thereby exhibiting the utility of the invention on a scale proportioned to the number of individuals whose labour it supersedes. While thus it enables one man to perform the work of many, it produces also an economy of time, by separating the work into its different branches, all of which may be carried into execution at the same moment.[31] (Emphasis added)

Stewart has here made two very significant innovations. In the first place, his analysis of production has focused upon the separation of tasks into the simplest ones, those most capable of mechanical duplication, and the gain in time and dexterity followed as a corollary of this attempt to gain simplicity. Secondly, the entrepreneur and not the worker is put at the center of the stage. It is the capitalist who is driven by the lure of profits to improve his machinery continually, and Smith's picture is thus misleading.

Charles Babbage provided a succinct account of the technological reason for the link between invention and the division of labor, a point also raised earlier by the Stewart-Lauderdale critique:

> That the master manufacturer, by dividing the work to be performed into different processes each requiring different degrees of skill and force, can purchase exactly that precise quantity necessary for each process; whereas, if the entire work is executed by one workman, that person must possess sufficient skill to perform the most difficult, and sufficient strength to carry out the most laborious of the operations into which the art is divided.[32]

Andrew Ure looked at the same point through the employer's eyes and noted how important the subdivision is to the social control of industry. The function of science now is to mechanize every "difficult" process so as to reduce the bargaining power of skilled workers:

> On the contrary, wherever a process requires particular dexterity and steadiness of hand, it is withdrawn as soon as possible from the "cunning" workman who is prone to many kinds of irregularities, and it is placed in charge of a particular mechanism, so self-regulating that a child could supervise it.[33]

Several nineteenth-century economists, including some of Smith's professed admirers, made considerable modifications to Smith's original doctrine. Richard Whately pointed to the fact that it was just as easy to deliver a single letter as to deliver a whole parcel and that this benefit was *not* dependent upon the acquisition of skills; the origins of the division of labor must therefore be sought in such tasks. E.G. Wakefield, who has already been quoted, made the far-reaching criticism that every successful division of labor must be accompanied by a plan for its subsequent combination: "The division of employments which takes place in a pin-factory, results from, and is wholly dependent on, the union, generally under one roof, of all the labour by which the pins are made." Smith's one-sided emphasis Wakefield found to be "not only very deficient but also full of error." William Stanley Jevons largely followed Wakefield on this issue.[34]

IV

In comparing Smith with his British predecessors, E.A.J. Johnson was struck by the fact that most attempts to increase labor productivity either consisted of exhortations to work harder or demands that the workers accept lower wages.[35] This fact may be most easily explained by noting that Smith's predecessors, with only a few exceptions, wrote with the explicit intention of influencing some immediate policy change. Now the extent to which labor is to be subdivided in any manufacture cannot be specified beforehand; only the individual entrepreneur can judge the extent to which it is proper by an estimate of expected sales. Profit maximization ensures that he will neither try for more subdivision nor settle for less. In this sense, then, the division of labor is not a variable that pamphleteers could influence and they were therefore content to leave it alone. With his more philosophical aim of trying to *understand* the nature of productivity, Smith of course felt no hesitation about dealing with factors which he could not influence.

Later generations have used the division of labor as the paradigm for the gains from international trade. This is a feature upon which Smith himself laid little stress and the argument is based on an abuse of language. The phrase "division of labor" can be used for any activity where there is some specialization. When this phrase is used in international trade to suggest that trade between two countries is beneficial in allowing two countries to specialize, this is not at all the same phenomenon that occurs in the pin-factory. The gains here typically arise from the *different endowments* of the two countries (and reflects a point raised for centuries on the beneficence of Providence). The fact that international trade was soon—that is, in the nineteenth century—explained on the basis of the division of labor is more a tribute to the persuasive impact of the first three chapters of the *Wealth of Nations* than an accurate analytical extension.

An overall assessment of Adam Smith's contribution to the economic theory of the division of labor must begin by noting the clarity Smith brought to this issue by relating it directly to the extent of the market. Furthermore, there is little doubt that his unique emphasis upon the division of labor makes his doctrine substantially an original one. These positive points, however, fade when set against Smith's deficiencies. From the scholarly point of view it must be regretted that (a) he neglected the fairly extensive British tradition of viewing the division of labor as *a* factor in productivity; and (b) he failed in elementary courtesy towards the *Encyclopédie*.[36] Viewed in a wider framework, Smith's treatment of the division of labor was not only rather narrowly focused, as emphasized by Dugald Stewart, it also distracted attention from both the role of machinery and the activity of the entrepreneur. Smith's original emphasis has been misleading.

As the division of labor has long been considered, along with the case for free trade, as the most original and important contribution of Adam Smith, it is worth going into both issues in greater detail, particularly with respect to the state of knowledge when the *Wealth of Nations* was written. Anton Tautscher claimed, and Charles Kindleberger has supported him, that a complete anticipation of Smith's views on the division of labor can be found in E.L. Carl, *Traité de la richesse des princes* (Paris, 1722).[37] Tautscher also felt that Smith knew of Tautscher either directly or through some intermediate source. Jacob Viner treats Tautscher's views lightly, but I feel more credence should be given to Carl, especially since a popular author of the 1730s and 1740s, Noel Antoine Pluche, provides a likely intermediary.

A Catholic priest, who had to live by teaching because his Jansenist leanings got him into trouble with the authorities, Pluche wrote the most successful theodicy of the eighteenth century, *La Spectacle de la nature*. Published in eight volumes between 1732 and 1750, there were some 57 French and 17 English editions. In an inventory of 500 private libraries of the period, the *Spectacle* was found in 206 of them. An English translation of the work was first published in 1739, so there is good presumption that Adam Smith would have come across the work in his youth. Today Pluche is discussed only as a minor figure in the history of sciences. This appears to be most unfortunate as it will lead economists who come across references to the *Spectacle* simply to ignore the volume.

The last three volumes of the *Spectacle* were published in 1746 (Volumes 6 and 7) and 1750 (Volume 8). These are most concerned with man and society. Already in Volume 5, however, we find Pluche interested in economic issues. In the chapter "Of Sciences" (an unlikely place to be sure), we find him discussing (a) whether Sparta or Carthage had the better social system; (b) whether monopolies are desirable; and (c) whether workers should be kept poor, etc. On each of these issues Pluche takes the viewpoint later adopted by Smith. What is more remarkable is that Volume 6 has a clear reference to (a) the Invisible Hand and (b) the corn model of an economy (commonly, but mistakenly, called the Ricardian model).

Pluche uses needles, not pins, as his primary example. I quote at length from this inaccessible piece so that readers familiar with the *Wealth of Nations* can make the comparison for themselves:

> The smallest of our Coin is too high a Price for a Needle: Which is astonishing, when we come to consider through how many Hands it has passed before it was fit for Use. In the first Place, this Needle is a Bit of good Iron, which has been

beat on the Anvil into a clumsy Cylinder, and then drawn successively through several Holes of a Wire-drawing Iron of less and less Bores, so as at last to become almost imperceptible; and for each of these Operations it must have been heated in the Fire. This Iron Wire is afterwards cut into proper Lengths, and each Bit is flatter at one End, and then on an Anvil punched through on both Sides. Another Workman, with another Punch, clears the Hole of a Bit of the Metal that remained in it. It is then passed to another Workman, who rounds the Head with a File. It is pointed by another File: And a third makes the Channel in each Side of the Eye for lodging the Thread. A fourth File is employed in taking off all the Roughness. This Needle is then put to heat red-hot on a flat Iron in the Fire, and thence with a Number of others thrown into cold Water to harden. It goes into the Fire the eighth or tenth Time; and then from the forge it is brought to the Anvil, where it is hammered strait. [Followed by a description of polishing, sorting and smoothing.]

Such are the numerous Preparations of that feeble Instrument, to which we are indebted for the inestimable Invention of Sewing, and the Ornaments of Embroidery. (Noel Antoine Pluche, *La Spectacle de la nature*, 1746, Vol. 6, Dialogue XII, pp. 318-19)

Two of the three advantages of the division of labor follow, and a discussion of the merits of "mechanical engines" comes immediately after:

Most Manufactures owe their chief Profits to this Method of distributing the different Parts of a Work among different Workmen, so that each Hand sticks constantly to his particular Part. Thus he is not obliged to seek his Work: But his Work comes to him. He neither changes Place nor Tools. Works would go on very slowly and expensively, if one Hand was to go through the whole; because he must frequently change Tools, and take up a new Manner of working. (Ibid.)

Whether both Smith and the *Encyclopédie* drew upon Pluche or not, the clear adumbration of the "Invisible Hand" in Pluche's *System* is notable:

It is with all Mankind as with the Inhabitants of a populous Town. The latter will, all of them, tell you that they are of such and such Professions. The Majority of then are even used to rost up their Names and respective Arts. Doubtless they all work for themselves, and yet they are all of Service to the whole Body of Society. One offers you a Pair of Shoes: Another makes you a Hat. This Man will sell you some Fish, or a Piece of Cloth, and another will bring some Fruits or Drinks of all Kinds to you. All the Sign posts of *London and Paris* are so many Offers of Service. In these Cities as well as elsewhere, every one thinks he works for himself: Nor is he in that at all mistaken. But Things happen to be so ordered and disposed from one End of the Earth to the other, as if every Inhabitant had no other View but the Service of Society. What is done for Society is done for me, and for every individual Member of it. I ought then to thank God for the Diversity he has introduced into the Conditions of Men, in Order to maintain an Exchange of Helps among them, and for having rendered these Helps infallible and certain, by animating every private Man by the Spur of Want and Necessity. (Ibid., pp. 90-1)

Smith's analysis would be really valuable if the division of labor could be shown to be one of the major features of modern economic growth. Since the studies of Kuznets, Kendrick and Solow, it has been widely agreed that technological change is the primary source of economic growth. This would appear to be close to the viewpoint of Dugald Stewart and especially to that of Lord Lauderdale. By contrast, the role of science is considered to be an adjunct of the division of labor in the *Wealth of Nations*.[38] Adam Smith's single-minded emphasis upon the division of labor cannot be said to have had forward-looking qualities. Smith cast much light on one aspect of the productive process but at the expense of casting a shadow over those features of production, such as the contributions of inventions, machinery and management, which have proved of greater longer-run significance. Adam Smith's presentation of the division of labor was a great rhetorical triumph but it is doubtful if his analysis was genuinely perceptive.[39]

NOTES

1. E.G. Wakefield, editorial note in his edition of the *Wealth of Nations* (1843), I, 1. In the questions Sir John Herschel, the famous scientist, set for schoolmasters at the Cape, we find that political economy is represented by the division of labor.

   Political Economy
   By what arguments is it shown that the division of labour is beneficial. What circumstances limit the application of these arguments—to what sort of labour are they least applicable—How do they apply to intellectual labour. (*Sir John Herschel and Education at the Cape*, ed. W.T. Ferguson and R.F. Immelman, Cape Town: Oxford University Press, 1961, 69)

2. E. Cannan, ed., *The Wealth of Nations* (New York: Random House, 1937). R.H. Campbell and A.S. Skinner, ed., *The Wealth of Nations* (Oxford: Oxford University Press, 1976). Referred to hereafter as *WN*. For a careful study of this topic from an internal point of view, see R.L. Meek and A.S. Skinner, "The Development of Adam Smith's Ideas on the Division of Labour," *Economic Journal* (December 1973), **83**, 1094-1116.
3. *WN*, I, 13, 22 (emphasis added).
4. T.S. Ashton makes this point: "Adam Smith was anxious to isolate the results of the application of his celebrated principle from those of the use of machinery and power. The pin trade employed only simple appliances, it was almost ideal for his purpose" (*An Economic History of England: The 18th Century*, London, 1955, 103).
5. *WN*, I, 17, 28.
6. Ibid., 20-1.

7. Ibid., 31-2. There is implicit in Smith's treatment of the idea that the products being discussed face inelastic demands. With elastic demand, the cheapness consequent upon the division of labor may well suffice to sell the additional output profitably.

8. W. Petty, *Political Arithmetick* (1690), in *The Economic Writings of Sir William Petty*, ed. C.H. Hull (London: Cambridge University Press, 1899), I, 260. Several predecessors of Adam Smith are noted in the editions both of Cannan and of Campbell and Skinner.

9. W. Petty, *Another Essay in Political Arithmetick* (1683) in Hull (1899), II, 473.

10. *WN*, I, 13.

11. H. Maxwell, *Reasons offered for erecting a bank in Ireland . . .*, 2nd edn (Dublin, 1721), 31.

12. Dublin Society, *Weekly Observations* (1738), 170. This view appears to be repeated by Adam Dickson, *Small Farms destructive to the Country* (Edinburgh, 1764), 15-16.

13. J. Tucker, Tract I of *Four Tracts* (1774). Harris is quoted by Campbell and Skinner in *WN*, I, 13, fn. 1.

14. Petty, *Political Arithmetick*, 261.

15. *Considerations on the East-India Trade* (1699), 591. C. McLeod has recently identified Henry Martin as the author: "Henry Martin and the authorship of the Considerations upon the East India Trade," *Bulletin of the Institute of Historical Research* (Nov. 1983), **LVI**, 134, 222-9.

16. Maxwell, *Reasons offered . . .*, 33.

17. If demand is indeed inelastic, as suggested in fn. 7, then population is a good proxy for market size.

18. This point is distinctly noted by Cannan, and subsequently by Campbell and Skinner.

19. R. Hamowy, "Adam Smith, Adam Ferguson, and the Division of Labour," *Economica* (August 1968), 249-59.

20. J.A. Schumpeter, *History of Economic Analysis* (London: Allen & Unwin, 1954), 187.

21. Ibid., 53.

22. Quoted by M.I. Finley, *Economy and Society in Ancient Greece* (London: Chatto & Windus, 1981), 186. Professor Finley discounts Xenophon's importance.

23. D. Stewart, *Lectures on Political Economy*, Vol. 8, of *The Collected Works of Dugald Stewart*, ed. Sir W. Hamilton (Edinburgh, 1858-78), 311.

24. F. Hutcheson, *System of Moral Philosophy* (Glasgow, 1755), I, 287.

25. Ibid., 290.

26. W.R. Scott, *Francis Hutcheson* (Cambridge: Cambridge University Press, 1900), 237.

27. J. Harris, *An Essay upon Money and Coins* (London, 1757), I, 16.

28. B. Mandeville, *The Fable of the Bees*, ed. F.B. Kaye (Oxford: Oxford University Press, 1924), II, 142.

29. Stewart, *Lectures on Political Economy*, 315.

30. Ibid., 318.

31. Ibid., 319.

32. Charles Babbage, *On the Economy of Machinery and Manufacturers* (London, 1832), 137-8. Babbage also claims that needle-making is more illustrative of the division of labor than pin-making.

33. Andrew Ure, *The Philosophy of Manufactures* (London, 1835), 19.

34. R. Whately, *Introductory Lectures* (London, 1834), 134. Wakefield, editorial note to *Wealth of Nations*, 25 and 33.

35. E.A.J. Johnson, "Land and Labor," in his *Predecessors of Adam Smith* (Englewood Cliffs, N.J.: Prentice-Hall, 1937), 244.

36. C. Kindleberger, "The Historical Background: Adam Smith and the Industrial Revolution," in *The Market and the State*, ed. T. Wilson and A. Skinner (Oxford: Oxford University Press, 1976), 1.

37. I have not seen the original work by Carl, but rely on the account provided by Jacob Viner (see n. 38) and by T.W. Hutchison in *Before Adam Smith* (Oxford: Blackwell, 1988).

38. There is some ambiguity in the *Wealth of Nations* about the importance of the scientist in invention but the *Lectures on Jurisprudence* simply defines away the issue:

> But he who contrived that the outer wheel should go by water was a philosopher, whose business it is to do nothing, but observe every thing. They must have extensive views of things, who as in this case bring in the assistance of new powers not formerly applied. Whether he was an artizan, or whatever he was who first executed this, he must have been a philosopher. (*Lectures on Jurisprudence*, ed. R.L. Meek, D.D. Raphael and P.G. Stein, Indianapolis: Liberty Classics, 1982, 492)

This appears to sharpen an earlier formulation, op. cit., *Lectures*, 351.

39. Samuel Hollander writes that Smith's "true originality lies in the attempt to account for sub-division of labour within plants in terms of plant size and also raw material and seasonal characteristics, and for the dispersion of processes between plants in terms of industry size" (*Classical Economics*, New York: Blackwell, 1987, 166). Hollander's evaluation virtually repeats that of Jacob Viner in Viner's *Introduction* to the reprint of John Rae, *Life of Adam Smith* (New York: Riley, 1965), 105. Since the bulk of the Viner-Hollander claim is based on inferences from various illustrations given by Adam Smith, rather than on anything Smith directly said, the assertion is misleading. Neither Hollander nor Viner seem aware that the Reverend Josiah Tucker had provided penetrating observations on the role of the division of labor which anticipated both Dugald Stewart and Charles Babbage. These observations are contained in Tucker's privately printed *Instructions for Travellers* which Tucker circulated for comment, a copy of which was owned by Adam Smith.

3. Adam Smith and the Market Mechanism[*]

The correct way to read Adam Smith is the correct way to read the forthcoming issues of a professional journal.

George Stigler

I

One of the sharpest critics of the *Wealth of Nations*, Joseph Schumpeter, felt forced to concede the merits of Adam Smith's price theory:

> The rudimentary equilibrium theory of Chapter 7, by far the best piece of economic theory turned out by A. Smith, in fact points towards Say and, through the latter's work, to Walras. The purely theoretical developments of the nineteenth century consist to a considerable degree in improvements upon it.[1]

Schumpeter's judgement has been widely accepted, all the more readily because of Schumpeter's little-disguised aversion to Smith. No one, however, appears to have asked how far such a characterization serves to indicate Smith's *contribution*. It may well be true that Chapter 7 is the best analytical effort of Smith and that it was very influential in the century to follow. But was it an improvement over what was available in the latter half of the eighteenth century?

In 1901, Hannah Sewall had already provided an accurate forecast of what was to be established by subsequent research:

> So much was done [in the seventeenth and eighteenth centuries] that there is scarcely any proposition of importance in the modern discussion of value which was not either stated or suggested by the writers of this first period of economic

[*]An early version of this chapter was presented at the Atlantic Economic Society Meeting in London, April 1987. I am grateful to Mark Blaug, T.W. Hutchison, H.C. Recktenwald and W. Thweatt for comments.

science, and which had not been discussed before Adam Smith made political economy a world study.[2]

In discussing Adam Smith's contributions to the theory of value Paul Douglas expressed some embarrassment at the sesquicentennial of the *Wealth of Nations* in 1926:

> The contributions of Adam Smith to the theory of value and of distribution were not great, and in commemorating the publication of *Wealth of Nations* it might seem to be the path of wisdom to pass these topics by in discreet silence.[3]

How is it that within 25 years this judgement would be quite reversed, by Schumpeter, and subsequently by other scholars?

To avoid misunderstanding, it should be emphasized that I am not concerned with the labor theory of value or the measure of value, a topic satisfactorily discussed in the above essay by Douglas; or with Adam Smith's curious rules for the allocation of capital, an issue which Smith's latest editors have considered one of the weakest points of the *Wealth of Nations*; nor with the roles of self-interest, the Invisible Hand or the beneficence of *laissez-faire*, where detailed studies by Myers and Hamowy exist; nor even with Adam Smith's much publicized criticism of the Mercantilists on foreign trade: it was explicitly stated by such "typical" Mercantilists as Malachy Postlethwayt that foreign trade was to be considered a political problem, and it is therefore not very meaningful to compare Smith and his predecessors on this issue.[4]

Until quite recently, Adam Smith's price theory drew praise largely because it was seen as the starting point of meaningful economic analysis. Alec Macfie notes and regrets the emphasis of the first two books of the *Wealth of Nations*:

> The theory of static equilibrium there so carefully sketched has grown into an analytic system and method which has for long dominated English-speaking universities, and our universities today control our theory as never before in modern times.[5]

What Macfie, in common with most other scholars, fails to do is to note whether and how far Adam Smith's analytics in Books I and II of the *Wealth of Nations* were in fact advances on contemporary opinion.

In recent years the merits of Adam Smith's analysis of the market have been most forcefully (and independently) argued by Marian Bowley and by Samuel Hollander.[6] It is notable that neither scholar gives careful attention to the eighteenth-century pamphlet literature. Hollander's chapter has no direct references (presumably he considers sufficient the references given in an earlier chapter) while Bowley provides direct comparison only with the Scholastics and with Cantillon. Even if such a comparison were accurately done it would be most unfair to the rich pamphlet literature arising since 1660. One needs to go no further than J.R. McCulloch's *Selected Tracts* to find that considerable awareness of the workings of self-interest in the market is shown by Daniel Defoe in *Giving Alms No Charity* or by the anonymous author of *An Apology for Pawnbroking*.[7] It will be shown below that my interpretation of what Adam Smith actually said does not differ from Bowley or Hollander on many occasions; that my evaluation nonetheless differs is perhaps largely attributable to the context within which I place Smith. In section III several of Smith's pretty applications are considered and an explanation offered for Smith's success in providing such nice illustrations of market phenomena.

The failure to grasp the sophistication of eighteenth-century micro-economics is perhaps the greatest defect in the existing literature. Jacob Viner dropped a significant hint when he wrote that: "On every detail, taken by itself, Smith appears to have had predecessors in plenty. On a few details was Smith as penetrating as the best of his predecessors."[8] The extent to which Smith failed to climb to the level of his predecessors is an issue deserving more careful consideration. *It is not claimed that the eighteenth-century understanding of the market was complete—only that Smith had nothing to add to what already existed.* He never went ahead of, and frequently stayed behind, the best views of his predecessors. It will become clear that I take the modern neoclassical version of microeconomics to be "correct" and pass judgement on earlier writers by the degree to which they approach "correct theory." Since the goal is to judge Adam Smith's merits as a price theorist this seems an appropriate procedure.

One important methodological point, which guides the criticism of this chapter, needs to be cleared at the outset. Trite though it may sound, theorists must *theorize* and be judged for their theories. To provide us with a wonderful array of anecdotes, stories and facts as well as a fund of insightful observations is no doubt a contribution—but it is not theorizing. It is up to the theorist to tell us the essence of the matter—the crux of his theoretical insight—and it is illegitimate for modern scholars to *extract* such ideas out of other, non-theoretical parts of a book. The enormous size of the *Wealth of Nations* has encouraged an unfortunate methodology whereby the explicitly theoretical portions are given equal weight with observations and historical facts. Scholars range at will and show us that the theory explicitly proposed is not fully representative of Adam Smith's "general" view.[9] This procedure forgets that it was Smith's responsibility to do his own theorizing.

II

The famous opening of the *Wealth of Nations* concerns the division of labor. It is well known that Smith held the division of labor to be the prime reason for increases in productivity, and hence for economic growth. Whether such a view is true or not, it has no bearing on this book because the division of labor is a technological feature and its adoption is something internal to a firm, while we are concerned primarily with markets and prices. Hence the nature of the division of labor is not something to be directly explained by "economics" (as we understand it) but the extent to which the division of labor is practiced leads us directly to the market.[10]

Since the division of labor is regulated by the extent of the market the first requirement for a deeper understanding of economic prosperity lies in describing the working of the market. This is attempted by Adam Smith in Chapter 7 of Book I, entitled "Of the Natural and Market Price of Commodities." As the title indicates, Smith distinguishes between "Natural" and "Market" price and the former is clearly the more fundamental of the two. What then determines natural price?

Smith begins by telling us that in every society, at any given time, there exists an ordinary or average rate of wages, profits and rent which are determined by circumstances which have little to do with the price of individual commodities. These average rates for each factor of production Smith calls the natural rate and defines the natural price as the sum of the natural rates of wages, profits and rents. This price is distinguished from the market price, which is merely another name for whatever price reigns in the market at any given time: "The actual price at which any commodity is sold is called its market price. It may either be above, or below, or exactly the same with its natural price."[11]

Those individuals who are willing to pay the natural price of a commodity have a special role to play. Their demand constitutes what is called the "effectual demand" and market price is said to arise out of the interplay of the *actual* supply and the desires of the *effectual* demanders: "The market price of every particular commodity is regulated by the proportion between the quantity which is actually brought to market, and the demand of those who are willing to pay the natural price of the commodity." The explicit theoretical construct thus consists of juxtaposing a *point* supply and a *point* demand.[12] This is an awkward way of formulating the market pricing process, especially since Smith's subsequent description makes it clear that in cases of excess supply new buyers enter the market and in cases of deficient supply some effectual demanders have to "leave" the market.

If, however, we gloss over the location of equilibrium, that is, the natural price, and ask instead how Smith describes what happens when we are not in equilibrium, the treatment is excellent:

> When the quantity of any commodity which is brought to market falls short of the effectual demand, all those who are willing to pay the whole value of the rent, wages, and profit, which must be paid in order to bring it thither, cannot be supplied with the quantity which they want. Rather than want it altogether, some of them will be willing to give more. A competition will immediately begin among them, and the market price will rise more or less above the natural price, according as either the greatness of the deficiency, or the wealth and wanton luxury of the competitors, happen to animate more or less the eagerness of the competition. [13]

Smith then treats of the opposite case, that is, when supply exceeds effectual demand, and shows just as clearly that an excess supply will cause price to fall and lead to a restriction in supply. The general tenor of Smith's argument regarding adjustments of price is quite modern and leads to the conclusion that: "The natural price, therefore, is, as it were, the central price, to which the prices of all commodities are continually gravitating." [14]

Given the centrality of natural prices in Smith's schema, what we need is an adequate theory of natural prices. Since natural price is defined as the sum of natural wages, profits and rents, this requires an explanation of the natural rates of wages, profits and rents. However, Smith's statement of the most important features determining the natural rates does not seem to have any role for microeconomics:

> There is in every society or neighbourhood an ordinary or average rate both of wages and profit in every different employment of labour and stock. This rate is naturally regulated, as I shall show hereafter, partly by the general circumstances of the society, their riches or poverty, their advancing, stationary, or declining condition; and partly by the particular nature of each employment.
>
> There is likewise in every society or neighbourhood an ordinary or average rate of rent, which is regulated too, as I shall show hereafter, partly by the general circumstances of the society or neighbourhood in which the land is situated, and partly by the natural or improved fertility of the land.
>
> These ordinary or average rates may be called the natural rates of wages, profit, and rent, at the time and place in which they commonly prevail.
>
> When the price of any commodity is neither more nor less than what is sufficient to pay the rent of the land, the wages of the labour, and the profits of the stock employed in raising, preparing, and bringing it to market, according

to their natural rates, the commodity is then sold for what may be called its natural price.[15]

So the natural rates are set, first, by the macroeconomic health of the economy, and secondly, by various technical and sociological features of different employments. Smith has provided us with a dichotomy between factor pricing and goods pricing. *If* it could be sustained, this would be an important contribution.

The next step is to specify each of the natural rates that serve to constitute the natural price. Chapter 8 of Book I attempts to determine the natural rate of wages. A careful reading of this chapter, however, shows that, amidst a great many digressions, all that is established is the existence of a lower bound on real wages; this lower bound is set by the condition that workers should be enabled to reproduce themselves. In a rather terse version of the Malthusian argument Smith points out that if wages do not permit reproduction, labor supply will fall and force wages to rise, while if wages are more than adequate for reproduction, labor supply will increase and call wages to fall:

> It is in this manner that the demand for men, like that for any other commodity, necessarily regulates the production of men; quickens it when it goes on too slowly, and stops it when it advances too fast.[16]

It will be noted that this mechanism must take at least a dozen years, since a new generation has to be raised, and nothing specific is said about the rate of wages in the interim.

Smith lays emphasis upon the fact that wages rise, not in countries which are rich, but in countries which are growing richer. The increased demand for labor in such growing economies always succeeds in keeping ahead of the reproductive cycle and so wages can keep on rising. This is most spectacularly seen in North America, the fastest-growing part of the world:

> Labour is there [American colonies] so well rewarded that a numerous family of children, instead of being a burden, is a source of opulence and prosperity to the parents. The labour of each child, before it can leave the house, is computed to be a hundred pounds clear gain to them.[17]

This observation is certainly accurate, but it leaves Smith's analytical structure incomplete. Both Europe and North America are stated to be growing economies, the former much more slowly than the latter. In neither continent can wages be at their natural level. At what level then are they set?

The same difficulty faces us in the next chapter, on profits. Once again we have several digressions, some of which are highly interesting, but we look in vain for a clear-cut paragraph which will tell us what the natural rate of profit is at any given time and place. Instead, what we are told is that the natural rate of profit declines as a country becomes richer. While wages rise as a country continues along its course of growth, profits do just the opposite. The argument is based on an analogy between the trade for a single commodity and the trade of the entire economy:

> When the stocks of many rich merchants are turned into the same trade, their mutual competition naturally tends to lower its profit; and when there is a like increase of stock in all the different trades carried on in the same society, the same competition must produce the same effect in them all.[18]

This explanation is expanded a little later, where the increased competition of traders is attributed to the gradually increasing difficulty of finding "a profitable method of employing any new capital." Once again we are provided with some interesting observations, but no help in determining natural profits. Without an explanation for its two principal components, wages and profits, the analytical structure of market price is left hanging in mid-air. Mark Blaug's comment is entirely appropriate:

> A cost-of-production theory of the value of a commodity is obviously empty and meaningless if it does not include some explanation of how the prices of productive services are determined. But Adam Smith had no consistent theory of wages and rents and no theory of profit or pure interest at all. To say that the normal price of an article is the price that just covers money costs is to explain prices by prices. *In this sense, Adam Smith had no theory of value whatever.*[19] (Emphasis added)

Blaug can find theoretical merit only in Smith's treatment of resource movements under the profit motive. It will be argued later that such a claim has no historical support, if it is meant to imply that Smith's original contribution lay in pointing out that economic resources follow high profits.

There is a pause in the continuity of the argument while Smith deals with the causes of the inequalities in wages and profits across various occupations. In Chapter 11 of Book I Smith turns to the rent of land. In earlier chapters he occasionally refers to average rents, and speaks of rents as though rent is another component of price, on all fours with wages and profit. This loose language is shed in the first half of this chapter and we have an excellent exposition of rent which left Malthus and Ricardo little to improve upon:

Rent, it is to be observed, therefore, enters into the composition of the price of commodities in a different way from wages and profit. High or low wages and profit, are the causes of high or low price; high or low rent is the effect of it. It is because high or low wages and profit must be paid, in order to bring a particular commodity to market, that its price is high or low. But it is because its price is high or low; a great deal more, or very little more, that it affords a high rent, or no rent at all.[20]

After such a clear exposition of the price mechanism one is surprised to find a quite different story told later in the chapter. A different set of principles, it appears, governs the rents of coal mines:

The most fertile coal mine regulates the price of coals at all the other mines in its neighbourhood. Both the proprietor and the undertaker of the work find, the one that he can get a greater rent, the other that he can get a greater profit, by somewhat underselling all their neighbours. Their neighbours are soon obliged to sell at the same price, though they cannot so well afford it, and though it always diminishes, and sometimes takes away altogether both their rent and their profit. Some works are abandoned altogether; others can afford no rent, and can be wrought only by the proprietor.[21]

Immediately after this extraordinary passage Smith correctly notes that the cost of production at that mine which pays no rent must be a good indicator of the lowest price at which the commodity be sold!

That Smith was unclear in his own mind as to the role of rent may be seen by turning to his treatment of rent in an earlier chapter. When supply is deficient, we are told, some component of natural price must be above its natural level. So far so good. Smith, however, chooses rent as an example of a return that can exceed its natural rate.[22] Not only does this contradict his own observation that rents are less affected by fluctuations of market prices than wages or profits, it also disguises the more plausible sequence whereby high profits are earned on the limited supply, the high profits thereafter leading to a greater cultivation of lands and eventually to higher rents. A little later, Smith points out that natural causes may keep the market price above the natural price for long periods of time. To illustrate this, Smith refers to commodities such as special French wines, which require land of such singular quality that the entire supply of such land is inadequate to meet the "effectual demand":

Some natural productions require such a singularity of soil and situation, that all the land in a great country, which is fit for producing them, may not be sufficient to supply the effectual demand. The whole quantity brought to market, therefore, may be disposed of to those who are willing to give more than what is sufficient to pay the rent of the land which produced them, together with the wages of the labour, and the profits of the stock which were employed in preparing and bringing them to market, according to their natural rates. Such commodities may continue for whole centuries together to be sold at this high price.[23]

Not only is it difficult to find an adequate definition of "effectual demand" in such cases but the fact that market price could exceed natural price "for whole centuries together" should give one pause to consider whether the distinction between natural and market prices is even worthwhile in such cases.

The most recent editors of the *Wealth of Nations* have praised Smith's treatment of the determination of market price: "This section of Smith's work is perhaps among the best from a purely analytical point of view, and is quite remarkable for the formality with which the argument unfolds." The subsequent discussion by Campbell and Skinner fails to make clear that Smith's analytical apparatus is based upon a dichotomy between product and factor markets and that its effective use requires us to know the natural rates of wages, profits and rents; that Smith fails to give us any guidance as to the level of natural wages in any country that is not stationary, of natural profits in any country at all, and provides an account of natural rents in a way that would confuse any careful reader. If, however, we accept that there is such a thing as natural price, to which market price must tend, then the process of adjustment is very clearly described.

It can scarcely be claimed that Smith taught his contemporaries about the market mechanism, in the sense of being the first expositor of such ideas. This suggests the thought that those students of the *Wealth of Nations* who believed they understood the functioning of the market after reading Book I probably had a sufficient understanding of the market mechanism when they began, so that they were able to find their way through Smith's confusion. When Francis Horner reviewed Canard's prize essay for the National Institute of France in 1803 he noted how Canard had depicted labor embodied as the measure of exchangeable value:

> This notion, which is certainly incorrect, is far from being peculiar to M. Canard: it is much employed in the treatise of Smith on the Wealth of Nations, and has the effect of involving, in very great obscurity, all the observations which that profound author has delivered on the analysis of price.

The multitude of English sources which dealt capably with the price mechanism need not be repeated, but it will help to quote a Scottish intellectual, Lord Kames, the one-time patron of Adam Smith, whose

Sketches were published in 1774, and who shows a competent knowledge of the forces determining prices:

> Where the quantity exceeds the usual demand, more people will be tempted to purchase by the low price; and where the demand rises considerably above the quantity, the price will rise in proportion. In mathematical language, these propositions may be thus expressed, That the price is *directly* as the demand, and *inversely* as the quantity.

Lord Lauderdale is said to have "worshipped" Smith in his youth, but Lauderdale's *Inquiry* shows itself to be a lineal descendant of Kames' *Sketches* and not of Smith's *Inquiry*.[24]

III

If Adam Smith's analytics are of little use then perhaps it was his shrewd illustrations that served to educate future generations? There is certainly considerable truth in such a claim. There are many instances in which Adam Smith provides us with convincing illustrations of opportunity cost and of the equalization of returns in different uses. Chapter 10 of Book I deals with "Wages and Profit in the Different Employments of Labour and Stock." It is a beautiful exercise in tracing, for example, differences in money wages to differences in the prestige of different jobs, or of differences in profits to differences in the risk associated with different activities. Despite some occasional lapses from clarity, it well deserves the praise bestowed upon it by Wakefield in 1843: "This, one of the most admired and most admirable chapters in the *Wealth of Nations*, is allowed on all hands to be free from error, and to contain, even now, the only complete account of the subject to which it relates."[25]

Nor is Smith's use of such reasoning limited to this famous chapter. There is a fine development of this theme in the discussion of the relative profitability of tillage versus pasture:

> Corn is an annual crop, butcher's-meat, a crop which requires four or five years to grow. As an acre of land, therefore, will produce a much smaller quantity of the one species of food than of the other, the inferiority of the quantity must be compensated by the superiority of the price. If it was more than compensated, more corn land would be turned into pasture; and if it was not compensated, part of what was in pasture would be brought back into corn.[26]

The same point of view is also developed later:

> When the price of cattle, for example, rises so high that it is as profitable to
> cultivate land in order to raise food for them, as in order to raise food for man,
> it cannot well go higher. If it did, more corn land would soon be turned into
> pasture.[27]

And in an extended discussion of the profitability of raising cattle, which
is too long to be quoted in its entirety, Smith notes both the problems of
joint costs and how it affects the allocation of land:

> Whatever regulations it tends to sink the price either of wool or of raw hides
> below what it naturally would be, in an improved and cultivated country, have
> some tendency to raise the price of butcher's-meat. The price both of the great
> and small cattle, which are fed on improved and cultivated land, must be
> sufficient to pay the rent which the landlord, and the profit which the farmer
> has reason to expect from improved and cultivated land. If it is not, they will
> soon cease to feed them. Whatever part of this price, therefore, is not paid by
> the wool and the hide, must be paid by the carcase. The less there is paid for
> the one, the more must be paid for the other. In what manner this price is to be
> divided upon the different parts of the beast, is indifferent to the landlords and
> farmers, provided it is all paid to them.[28]

The examples chosen, and to a certain extent the reasonings used, bear a
likeness to those used by the Reverend John Smith in the *Chronicon
Rusticum* (1747). While the *Chronicon* deals with this issue at several points,
the following comment on a pamphlet of 1581 is most instructive because
it illustrates the continuity of the pamphlet literature. John Smith is
describing the contents of the pamphlet, which consists of a dialogue:

> The Doctour, who appears to be the Moderator in this Dialogue, resolving the
> Original of these advanced Prices of things into the Alteration of the Value of
> Coin, discourses very sensibly upon the Subject of Money; and accounts for
> Wool being dearer in Comparison than Corn, from the former being allow'd to
> be exported, the latter too much restrained in that respect; says, that reversing
> the Measures would produce just the contrary Effect; and wisely argues, that by
> giving an equal proper Liberty to both; in that Case, notwithstanding Inclosures,
> the Balance would be preserved; for that the Farmer would shift from Sheep to
> Corn, and vice versa, as he was likely to find his Account best, in the one, or
> the other.[29]

What is creditable in Smith's presentation is the care and forcefulness with
which known ideas are developed. It is a familiar characteristic of Smith to
develop a commonplace fact into a carefully elaborated illustration of a
theory. These are much desired virtues in a pedagogue.

Even though Adam Smith did not provide any explicit theoretical guidelines that are particularly valuable, one cannot fail to ask: What principles *did* guide Smith in making the perceptive and accurate observations provided above? The views expressed on the Law of Settlements for the poor perhaps give us a clue. The law itself was believed by Smith to have restricted the mobility of labor and Smith therefore ascribed to the law not only the great differences in the price of labor in contiguous areas but also indignantly exclaimed that:

> There is scarce a poor man in England of forty years of age, I will venture to say, who has not in some part of his life felt himself most cruelly oppressed by this ill-contrived law of settlements.[30]

This strong assertion has drawn the critical attention of several of Smith's editors. Campbell and Skinner make a pointed remark regarding Smith's indifference to providing factual details to support his assertion: "The general principles, the opposition to restrictions damaging to the free allocation of resources, were held so strongly that there seemed no case to answer."[31] This observation is pregnant with consequences which have not been developed.

If Smith indeed began by assuming that any violation of natural liberty was both morally wrong and economically harmful, how far could such a position take him into analytical economics? First, Smith's procedure needs to consider the absence of competition on only one side of the market. In the case of the Law of Settlements, for example, Smith did not proceed to ask whether masters might not find it profitable to find ways of evading the law. This is just what later critics, such as Sir F.M. Eden, contended.[32] Secondly, if we assume that a market reaches a stable equilibrium, then the belief in one-sided competition alone suffices to provide several analytical results. For example, in the version of Ricardian rent theory espoused by Piero Sraffa, the same final outcome is reached whether only farmers compete (for land) or only landlords compete (for farmers). This one-sided analytical procedure works best when there are constant returns to scale, and the assumption of fixed proportions, used on several occasions by Smith, is perhaps a consequence of his analytical method.[33]

It is my belief that Smith thoroughly appreciated—and made his readers appreciate—the fundamental fact that a genuinely competitive market leads to zero profits. This observation is repeatedly and successfully applied to such fields as the choice of occupations, the preference for pasturage over tillage, or the determination of joint prices. It will even suffice to move us towards the "natural price," wherever that might be. This is a form of argument that is quite easy to learn and is independent of the more intricate demand-supply apparatus. Both forms of argument give the same conclusions when we deal with completely unobstructed trade; once we add taxes or tariffs to the problem this is no longer so, and the works of Smith's predecessors are harder to follow and often worth the extra effort. If one re-examines Smith's concepts, for example "natural" price or any of its components, it is evident that the concepts are so *defined* that any deviation implies the existence of a profitable venue of activity—and hence encourages resource movements in a free economy. The fundamental principle was widely known and appreciated, as may be seen from the two pamphlets earlier referred to, Defoe's *Giving Alms No Charity* and *An Apology for Pawnbroking*. (These examples can be readily multiplied.) The repetition of fundamentals is, however, the principal tool of good pedagogy. Smith's exposition undoubtedly contributed to the wider understanding of the market mechanism.[34]

Apart from the wide extent and deep appreciation for the market visible in the general run of economic pamphleteering, it is instructive to contrast Smith with Sir James Steuart. The common knowledge of an age is most evident when individuals with the most divergent views employ the same ideas. An examination of Steuart and Smith on the workings of competition clearly shows that Steuart was as knowledgeable as Smith.[35] This should not surprise us. Steuart was concerned with telling an intelligent statesman how to devise rules which would move a free economy in desired directions. In modern terminology, Steuart's statesman was a Stackleberg leader and it is elementary that such an agent has to know the reaction functions of the followers—in this case the competitive market.

If, then, Adam Smith is to be credited with providing us with an understanding of the market mechanism, the case must rest *not* on his *theoretical* treatment, but rather on the process of adjustment to equilibrium and on the many insightful examples that he presented. Given the weakness of Smith's own analytical constructs, in assessing the merits of this achievement it is necessary to spend only a little space on the theory and to focus instead on the application of the price mechanism by Smith's predecessors.

IV

In reviewing the literature prior to Adam Smith it is possible to take a European view, as Schumpeter did, and find antecedents for Smith's ideas in the works of the Scholastics and the Natural Law philosophers. Due to limitations of space, this is the only group to be directly quoted here. Max

Beer provided a striking example from the thirteenth century in Richard of Middleton, who formulated a rudimentary two-country, two-good model to explain the benefits of trade:

> Now, it is natural for the business of trade and commerce to equalize supply. The merchant, then, buys corn cheap in country A and sells it at the higher market price that is ruling in country B, or he buys wine cheap in country B and sells it at the higher market price that is ruling in country A, so that in reality the consumer is not in the least overcharged, for he pays for each commodity the normal price, the just price, which is ruling in his respective country. *The Exchanges are equal, yet the merchant earns his profit, and he does so rightfully, for, far from having injured either country, he brought benefit to both.*[36] (Emphasis added)

The value of scholastic economic thought has subsequently been impressed upon us by Marjorie Grice-Hutchison, Raymond de Roover, Barry Gordon and, most recently, Odd Langholm.[37] Azpilcueta's statement of the quantity theory of money provides an explicit *ceteris paribus* clause and goes on to use the comparative historical method to illustrate the theory:

> other things being equal, in countries where there is a great scarcity of money, all other saleable goods, and even the hands and labour of men, are given for less money than where it is abundant.[38]

Finally, Juan de Lugo writes very clearly in 1642 that price fluctuates because of the subjective desires of the majority in the market:

> not because of the intrinsic and substantial perfection of the articles—since mice are more perfect than corn, and yet are worth less—but on account of their utility in respect of human need, and then only on account of estimation; for jewels are much less useful than corn in the house, and yet their price is much higher. And we must take into account not only the estimation of prudent men, but also that of the imprudent, if they are sufficiently numerous in a place.[39]

While the manner of secular writers in the early modern period may have been more attractive, they did not show any considerable advance in economic principles over the best scholastics.[40]

Be that as it may, the point to be made here concerns not just influence, in the sense of glimpsing the mountain peaks reached by the best minds, but rather the sort of influence imbibed simply by being part of a common culture. The same situation appears in a reprinted letter in the *London Magazine* (May 1753, 218-19). It begins by asserting that the domestic circulation of money makes a nation "neither richer nor poorer," therefore foreign trade only will be considered. Trade is said to be "the bartering of goods; money being no more than pieces of goods," showing reliance on real analysis. The definition of natural and artificial prices that follows is significant, both for substance and language:

> Natural prices arise from three causes. 1. Quantity of goods; as in corn, good or bad harvests make it cheap or dear. 2. Demand; as in silks, old or new patterns are cheap or dear. 3. Plenty or scarcity of money; as in fine wines, which bear no prices in poor villages, but are current in rich cities.
>   Artificial prices are super-additions to natural prices, by taxes and monopolies.[41]

Cheapness of price is stated to be the cause of fluctuations in trade, and the remarkable feature is the self-conscious manner in which this point is demonstrated:

> —All men want and buy some sort of goods; with money men buy; therefore, all men want money: And because the less money men part with for one want, the more they have left for other wants, all buyers will flock to the cheapest sellers; therefore, cheapness of price is the cause of trade.

From this simple but pointed demonstration a conclusion of far-reaching significance is drawn:

> From hence may be laid down an universal rule to judge of all schemes relating to trade—Do they tend to add artificial prices to goods? Whatever pretenses they are covered with, they are destructive—Do they tend to reduce goods to their natural prices? They are beneficial.

The extremely commercialized nature of British society has been ignored by economists. In the sense which is most germane to the thesis proposed here, it is readily documented that

1. Monopoly was carefully defined by the English in the late sixteenth century and its detriment to social welfare clearly observed. Adam Smith's casual hyperbole that "The price of monopoly is upon every occasion the highest which can be got" is a step backwards.[42]
2. The paradox of value or the diamonds-water paradox had been both posed and solved by several economists, such as John Law.[43]
3. The use of competition as a standing if implicit assumption was widespread and the notion of short run and long run clearly emphasized by such famous economists as John Locke.[44] As for Smith's explicit

analytical apparatus, consisting of a point demand and a point supply, this also shows little advance on John Locke:

> Unlike a modern price theorist, Locke did not see price as the result of the interaction of two functional relationships which are defined for a given moment in time. Instead, he always describes price as an exchange ratio which is determined by a set of proportions involving the quantity of a good (the stock available) and its vent (a flow).[45]

4. "Demand" and "supply" (in the loose, pre-Marshallian sense) were widely and correctly used—indeed, the workings of this mechanism were treated as a truism; for example, Dudley North says:

> as corn, wool &c. when they come to market greater quantities than there are buyers to deal for, the price will fall; so if there be more lenders than borrowers, interest will also fall.
>
> As more buyers than sellers raiseth the price of a commodity, so more borrowers than lenders will raise interest.[46]

Note that North takes the mechanism completely for granted for the case of goods and seeks to explain its workings in the case of interest rate.[47]

5. The ahistorical approach used hitherto is exemplified in the way "natural price" is seen as prescient of capitalist society. Before Smith, the notion of a short-run equilibrium price around which day-to-day fluctuations would occur was already well established. The *New Whole Duty of Man* says:

> So long as you keep within the lattitude of lawful gain you may use your skill against another man in driving a bargain: *for in an ordinary plenty of commodities there is an ordinary price*, which those that deal with them know and understand.[48] (Emphasis added)

By the 1750s economists such as Joseph Massie and Malachy Postlethwayt (and the anonymous author of the *London Magazine* piece quoted earlier) were already using the word "natural" to qualify words like "interest" or "price" without being self-conscious.[49] Adam Smith's use of the word "natural" is somewhat peculiar because he appears to focus upon a relatively stable long-run quantity, which is an odd context because his primary concern is with economic *growth*. Richard Cantillon uses "natural" somewhat in Smith's sense, but Cantillon's usage was not general. Since Smith's views on the allocation of resources also follow Cantillon closely, this is almost surely Smith's source. It is a pity that

Schumpeter did not live to complete his *History*, since it is hard to reconcile the praise for Smith's analytics (earlier quoted) with the following:

> Cantillon paid much attention to the problem of market price as distinguished from normal price—exactly as did A. Smith later on. One feature of his treatment is worth noting because it persisted practically to J.S. Mill. Like all "classics" of the nineteenth century, Ricardo especially, Cantillon never asked the question *how* market price is related to normal price and precisely *how* the latter emerges—if indeed it does emerge—from the supply and demand mechanism that produces the former. Taking this relation for granted, he was led to treat market price as a separate phenomenon *and to restrict the supply and demand explanation to it*. Thus emerged the superficial and, as the later development of the theory of value was to show, misleading formula—normal price is determined by cost, market price is determined by supply and demand.[50]

Thomas Pownall was quite worried by the sharp distinction Smith drew between "market price" and "natural price." Given the highly favorable connotations of "natural," Pownall felt that one could be led to assume that interventions against the "market price" and in favor of the "natural price" might be needed. By the 1820s, T.R. Malthus could only provide a lame justification for Smith's peculiar use of natural price.[51]

6. There is no suggestion in the literature prior to Adam Smith that factor prices were somehow different in nature from goods prices. By emphasizing this point Smith served to turn economics into a blind alley for almost a century. Malthus, one of Smith's greatest admirers, realized Smith's deficiency by the time he came to write his *Principles*, and asked why demand and supply could not determine natural price (or the long-run cost of production) as well as the market price. Such words fell on the deaf ears of the Ricardians, and Ricardo replied defiantly:

> The author forgets Adam Smith's definition of natural price or he would not say that demand and supply could determine its natural price. Natural price is only another name for cost of production. When any commodity sells for that price which will repay the wages for labour expended on it, will also afford rent, and profit at their then current rate, Adam Smith would say that commodity was at its natural price. Now these charges would remain the same, whether commodities were much or little demanded, whether they sold at a high or low market price.[52]

It was not until the Marginal Revolution that the ill effects of Smith's dichotomy could be left behind.

V

From the time of publication of the *Wealth of Nations* in 1776 until the middle of the twentieth century, Adam Smith has been viewed primarily as the source of *laissez-faire* ideas. The benefits of economic freedom can be argued on the basis of three axioms:[53]

1. Individuals desire to maximize their wealth.
2. Individuals know better than governments how to maximize their own wealth.
3. National wealth is the sum of individual wealth.

This is an effective argument for free trade and it never really requires an understanding of the microeconomics of demand and supply.

It is quite unfortunate that, in recent years, economists have tried to claim that Smith was not only a vigorous advocate of free trade but also an economic theorist of some merit. The strong claim that Smith was prescient about modern capitalism not only founders on his treatment of contemporary facts, it also makes one wonder how such quaint rules for the allocation of capital could be espoused by an appreciator of capitalism or why he would support the legal regulation of interest rates, having provided very good grounds for leaving them free.[54]

It has been argued in this book that even the weaker claim that Adam Smith synthesized and improved contemporary understanding of the market is dubious. Lord Keynes was generally appreciative of the "macro-economics" of Mercantilism but he seriously misled his readers when, with reference to the basic tools of economics, he wrote that "before Adam Smith this apparatus of thought scarcely existed."[55]

That Smith doubted the mutually beneficial nature of the worker-capitalist relation, as is clearly noted in the previously cited essay by Douglas, is surely suggestive. More serious charges from the analytical point of view can also be made. Smith failed to appreciate the role of utility and demand, and he confused issues on the measure of value. He introduced a new concept of "natural" price, one that was less useful than that used by his contemporaries, and he thrust upon his readers the dichotomy between goods markets and factor markets. For nearly two centuries Adam Smith was praised for his doctrine of economic freedom and for having pointed to labor as the primary source of value.[56] This praise had at least the merit of being well-grounded in the text of the *Wealth of Nations*. It is high time that the modern revision, which views Adam Smith as also being an analytical economist, be questioned.

NOTES

1. J. Schumpeter, *History of Economic Analysis* (London: Allen & Unwin, 1954), 188-9. Criticisms of various aspects of the *Wealth of Nations* abound, e.g., E. Cannan, *Theories of Production and Distribution* (London, 1893) or Paul Douglas, "Smith's Theory of Value and Distribution," in *Adam Smith 1776-1926* (Chicago: University of Chicago Press, 1928). The examination of Schumpeter's praise for Smith's treatment of markets and prices, however, appears to be new.

2. Hannah Sewall, *The Theory of Value before Adam Smith* ([1901]; reprinted New York: Augustus Kelley, 1968), 124. An excellent chronological account of the growth of economics in the seventeenth and eighteenth centuries is to be found in T.W. Hutchison, *Before Adam Smith* (Oxford: Basil Blackwell, 1968). For some aspects not covered by Hutchison, see S. Todd Lowry, "Lord Mansfield and the Law Merchant: Law and Economics in the Eighteenth Century," *Journal of Economic Issues* (1973), **VII**, 605-22. A brief, readable account of Lord Mansfield can be found in "Borrowing from Scotland," by Lord Denning (Glasgow: Jackson, 1963), 1-18.

3. Paul Douglas, "Smith's Theory of Value and Distribution," in his *Adam Smith 1776-1926*, 77. A referee has pointed out that the only criteria used to judge Adam Smith's microeconomics are those of modern neoclassical microeconomics and asked whether such an approach does not unduly distort the insights to be gained from the *Wealth of Nations*. I fully concede that neoclassical microeconomics should not be the only criteria to use when judging the overall merits of an economist. Whatever Adam Smith's merits considered from this wider standpoint, they are not considered here and this constitutes a definite limitation of this book. A good example of the wider viewpoint, provided by the referee, is M. Norton Wise and Crosbie Smith, "Work and Waste: Political Economy and Natural Philosophy in Nineteenth Century Britain," *History of Science*, 3 parts (1989-1990); 27(3), 264-301; 27(4), 391-449; 28(1), 221-61.

4. Adam Smith, *An Inquiry into the Nature and Causes of the Wealth of Nations*, ed. R.H. Campbell and A.S. Skinner (London: Oxford University Press, 1976), 32 (hereinafter *WN*); M.L. Myers, *The Soul of Modern Economic Man* (Chicago: University of Chicago Press, 1983); R. Hamowy, *The Scottish Enlightenment and the Theory of Spontaneous Order* (Carbondale, Ill.: Southern Illinois University Press, 1987). A brief but penetrating critique of Adam Smith as a supporter of free individual choice is made by Roger W. Garrison, "West's 'Cantillon and Adam Smith:' A Comment," *Journal of Libertarian Studies* (Fall 1985), **VII**(2), 287-94.

5. A. Macfie, *The Individual in Society* (London: Allen & Unwin, 1967), 20-1.

6. M. Bowley, *Studies in the History of Economic Theory before 1870* (London: Macmillan, 1973); S. Hollander, *The Economics of Adam Smith* (Toronto: University of Toronto Press, 1978).

7. J.R. McCulloch, ed., *Select Tracts* (London, privately printed, 1856). As to the weak spots visible in the earlier authors, let it be noted that Smith also made some peculiar assumptions about economic behavior, such as the independence of the volume of savings and the rate of return to savings (Bowley, *Studies*, 193; Hollander, *Economics*, 169).

8. J. Viner, "Adam Smith and Laisser-Faire," in Douglas, *Adam Smith 1776-1926*. I have discussed the strength of eighteenth-century microeconomics in "Smith, Steuart and Mercantilism: Comment," *Southern Economic Journal* (January 1986), **52**(3), 843-52, and

developed the theme further in "The Financial Pamphleteers of the Eighteenth Century," in *Perspectives on the History of Economic Thought*, ed. D.A. Walker (Brookfield, Vt.: Edward Elgar).

9. While Samuel Hollander is not the only scholar to adopt such a liberal method, Hollander's treatment of Adam Smith on utility and demand as well as Smith's rules for the allocation of capital come particularly to mind. Of course one can disagree about what constitutes theory. For example, I consider Smith's observation that wages are sometimes set by bargaining to be only an observation—albeit a perceptive one—and as such is ignored.

10. See Chapter 2.

11. *WN*, I, 73.

12. Ibid., 73.

13. Ibid., 73-4.

14. Ibid., 75.

15. Ibid., 72. If one is not careful, a reading of widely used texts such as Mark Blaug, *Economic Theory in Retrospect*, 4th edn (Cambridge: Cambridge University Press, 1985), 42, can easily mislead.

16. *WN*, I, 98.

17. Ibid., 88.

18. Ibid., 105.

19. Ibid., 352-3. Blaug, *Economic Theory*, 39. See Cannan, *Theories of Production*, on this point.

20. *WN*, I, 162.

21. Ibid., 184. The coal cartels of 1771 may well have provoked this section of the *Wealth of Nations* (H. Levy, *Monopoly and Competition*, London: Macmillan, 1911, ch. 6). Smith's difficulty with composition is well known. As a result, it appears that when he came across new and interesting facts he simply tacked them on, without being overly concerned about consistency. Mountifort Longfield's appropriate comment was:

> Adam Smith appears not to have possessed much taste or capacity for long or subtle trains of reasoning. The "Wealth of Nations" is written with very little attention to system, and this circumstance has probably tended to increase its utility. It prevented any error from infecting the entire work. (*Lectures on Political Economy*, 1834, Dublin: Milliken, 262)

22. *WN*, I, 75.

23. Ibid., 78.

24. R.H. Campbell and A.S. Skinner, Introduction to *WN*, 25; *The Economic Writings of Francis Horner*, ed. F.W. Fetter (London: London School of Economics, 1957), 60; Lord Kames, *Sketches of the History of Man* (London: Strahan & Cadell, 1774), 111. R.F. Teichgraber's claim in *"Free Trade" and Moral Philosophy* (Durham, N.C.: Duke University Press, 1986) that Adam Smith somehow established the "new paradigm" of the market is not well founded.

25. E.G. Wakefield ed., *Wealth of Nations* (1843), I, 328.

26. *WN*, I, 165.

27. Ibid., 237.

28. Ibid., 238.

29. Ibid., 251. The pamphlet being commented upon is *A compendious or briefe examination of certayne ordinary complaints* (1581), now believed to be by Sir Thomas Smith. The

great merit of this pamphlet led to its being reprinted in Glasgow in 1751 by the brothers Foulis.

30. Ibid., 157.

31. *WN*, Introduction, 54. If the consequences of this viewpoint are consistently followed up, they show that many of Adam Smith's "facts" are traceable to authors who shared his views on natural liberty, and on other occasions they are actually claims of "what should be" if the system of natural liberty were true. Samuel Hollander has argued that Ricardo did not deviate from Smith's method of "strong" theory. On the above reading, Hollander is entirely correct and Ricardo is distinguished only by his abrupt directness. S. Hollander, *The Economics of David Ricardo* (Toronto: Toronto University Press, 1979).

32. F.M. Eden, *The State of the Poor*, ed. A.G.L. Rogers (London: Routledge, 1928), 53. Eden was followed by David Buchanan in his edition of the *Wealth of Nations* (Edinburgh, 1814), I, 235-36. Smith underestimated the conflict between individual liberty and the maintenance of competition (W.R. Cornish and G. de N. Clark, *Law and Society in England 1750-1950*, London: Sweet & Maxwell, 1989, 269).

33. P.A. Samuelson, "Wages and Interest: A Modern Dissection of Marxian Economic Models," *American Economic Review* (Dec. 1957), **47**(6), 884-912. In the Introduction to the Penguin edition of the *Wealth of Nations*, Andrew Skinner considers the main contribution of Smith's price theory to lie in enabling us to see the conditions of equilibrium in the economy as a whole. The fact that the entire equilibrium concept is based on the *definition* of natural price as that price which provides no excess returns is not noted by Skinner (*The Wealth of Nations*, ed. A. Skinner, Harmondsworth, Middx: Penguin, 1982, 55-6). In the immediately preceding pages, Skinner has to bring out Smith's "implicit" assumptions on several occasions.

34. Schumpeter's remarks on Smith's expositional powers are worth rereading (*History*, 185-6). A simple but striking example of the appreciation of competition is given by the pamphleteer of 1712 who defends high duties thus: "Whoever lives a few years will probably see many more undertakers of these works, who, by striving to undermine one another, will always keep prices low" (quoted by Levy, *Monopoly and Competition*, 97).

35. See Rashid, "Smith, Steuart and Mercantilism." Although it is not so explicitly stated, this point can also be read out of Andrew Skinner's Analytical Introduction to Sir James Steuart, *An Inquiry into the Principles of Political Economy* (London: Oliver & Boyd, 1966). I have also profited from an unpublished M. Phil thesis of A. Karayiannis, "Sir James Steuart (1713-1780), On Methodology, Political Economy, Value and Distribution" (University of Dundee, 1988).

36. Quoted in M. Beer, *Early British Economics* (London: George Allen & Unwin, 1938), 42.

37. R. de Roover, *Business, Banking and Economic Thought in Late Medieval and Early Modern Europe*, ed. V. Kinshner (Chicago: University of Chicago Press, 1974); B.J. Gordon, *Economic Thought before Adam Smith: Hesiod to Lessius* (New York: Barnes & Noble, 1975); M. Grice-Hutchison, *Early Economic Thought in Spain* (London: Allen & Unwin, 1975); O. Langholm, "Economic Freedom in Scholastic Thought," *History of Political Economy* (Spring 1982), **14**(2), 260-83. The extracts are from Grice-Hutchison, 104, 101.

38. Grice-Hutchison, 104.

39. Ibid., 101.

40. Thus Pufendorf, whom Adam Smith knew well, wrote that the "natural price" was that set "by the common judgment and estimate of men, together with the consent of the parties" (Sewall, *Theory of Value*, 41).

41. It is not unlikely that this letter was linked with the efforts of the third Lord Townshend to provide for freer trade. See S. Rashid, "Lord Townshend, Moral Philosophy and

Laissez Faire," *Journal of Libertarian Studies* (Winter 1986), **8**(1), 69-74. *London Magazine* (May 1753), 218-19.

42. Indeed it seems to reproduce the very wording of the Malynes-Misselden period of the early 1600s (Levy, *Monopoly and Competition*, 65).

43. Douglas, *Adam Smith*. The footnotes provided by Campbell and Skinner in their edition of the *Wealth of Nations*, 44-6, should suffice for this point.

44. This point was clear to the Physiocrats but has been inadequately drawn out by modern commentators; see, e.g., Karen Vaughn, *John Locke* (Chicago: University of Chicago Press, 1980).

45. Ibid., 27.

46. D. North, *Discourses upon Trade* (London, 1691), 5.

47. W. Thweatt, "Origins of the Phrase Supply and Demand," *Scottish Journal of Political Economy* (1983), **30**(3), 287-94.

48. Quoted by H.W. Robertson, *Aspects of the Rise of Economic Individualism* (London: Cambridge University Press, 1933).

49. A careful reading of such seventeenth-century writers as Sir Josiah Child and Charles Davenant shows that they used the phrase "intrinsic" value in similar fashion. The Cantillon-Smith usage, on the other hand, appears to follow Sir William Petty. This, in turn, probably grew from the belief in an objective "intrinsic" value, noted by Sewall, *Theory of Value*, 51. According to the rules for market transactions under Judaism, it would appear that the concept of a "normal price" is of very long standing (Meir Tamari, "Judaism and the Market Mechanism," in W. Block and J. Hexham, eds, *Religion, Economics and Social Thought*, Vancouver: Fraser Institute, 1986).

50. Schumpeter, *History*, 220.

51. Thomas Pownall, *A Letter to Adam Smith . . .* (London, 1776); T.R. Malthus, *Principles of Political Economy*, 2nd edn (London, 1836), 78-9.

52. "Notes on Malthus," in D. Ricardo, *Collected Works*, ed. P. Sraffa (London: Cambridge University Press, 1951-67), 6, 46.

53. This is most clearly argued by Wesley Mitchell, *Types of Economic Theory* (New York: Augustus Kelley, 1967), I, 61-4.

54. C. Kindleberger, "Adam Smith and the Industrial Revolution," in *The Market and the State*, ed. T. Wilson and A.S. Skinner (Oxford: Oxford University Press, 1967), 1-25. There is a tradition that Jeremy Bentham converted Adam Smith on the interest rate issue but this has not been confirmed.

55. Introduction to H. Henderson, *Supply and Demand* (Cambridge: Cambridge University Press, 1922).

56. S. Rashid, "Adam Smith's Version of the History of Economics and its Influence in the Eighteenth and Nineteenth Centuries," *Quarterly Review of Economics and Business* (Autumn 1987), **27**(3), 56-69. Reproduced here as Chapter 8.

4. The *Wealth of Nations* and Historical "Facts"

Though beauty of diction, harmony of periods, and acuteness and singularity of sentiment, may captivate the reader, yet there are other qualifications essentially necessary. . . . Fidelity, accuracy and impartiality are also requisite.

Joseph Towers, Observations on Mr. Hume's History *(1778)*

I

In looking back at the *Wealth of Nations* during the Adam Smith Centennial in 1876 commentators were agreed that close attention to facts and the inductive nature of the *Wealth of Nations* clearly distinguished it from all its successors. This opinion has only been reinforced in subsequent years by a host of commentators, whether they be economic historians such as C.R. Fay and W.R. Scott, or historians of economic thought such as T.W. Hutchison and Jacob Viner.[1] D.D. Raphael provides a convenient summary of this viewpoint in his biography:

> [Adam Smith] did not, however, simply assume that the facts would conform to a preconceived idea. Adam Smith never approached his inquiries in that sort of spirit. He was an empiricist, a thinker who began with experienced fact and then produced a hypothesis to explain the facts. . . . In all his work Smith followed the method of empiricism, of taking the facts of experience as the basic data and reaching general propositions by induction from them.

This orthodoxy has been challenged by Philip Mirowski in a careful study, which appears to be the only recent examination of its kind, of Adam Smith's views on the rate of profit in eighteenth-century England. At a more general level, skepticism had been expressed earlier by R.H. Campbell and A.S. Skinner in their Introduction to the bicentennial edition of the *Wealth of Nations*:

> Smith's desire to devise a major intellectual system determined the use he made of historical and factual material. No one of his intellectual eminence would distort the facts, even if only because refutation would thus have been infinitely

52

easier, but, even when facts were not distorted, they may still have been used in such a subordinate and supporting role to the dominating systematic model that their use for any other purpose needs qualification.

Campbell and Skinner refer to the Poor Laws and colonial trade to support their claim that:

> On contemporary issues his writing verges on propaganda, he uses evidence in ways which are not wholly convincing to those not committed to his system, and he presses interpretations of contemporary events to more extreme conclusions than may well be warranted.

However, this condemnation is immediately modified in the next paragraph when we are told that such defects "must not be stressed unduly," that the "stretching of empirical data" did not discredit the main thesis, and even that "the analysis, both systematic and institutional, was largely applicable in Britain." How did Smith manage continually to stretch the evidence and yet maintain relevance? Campbell and Skinner are only the latest editors to query several of Smith's facts. Many other students of the *Wealth of Nations* have expressed doubts about various parts. The collective impact of these separate queries has yet to be assessed. A closer look at the "facts" presented in the *Wealth of Nations* would appear to be warranted.[2]

In order to evaluate the role played by "facts" in the *Wealth of Nations* a variety of issues have to be addressed. What facts did Smith know of? What sources did Smith utilize? How critical was he in his use of these sources? Did he search carefully for the best source among those available? What facilities did he possess for acquiring knowledge of facts? How does Smith's use of facts and sources compare with the practice of contemporaries? Once we are in a position to judge the care and discrimination with which Smith arrived at his facts, the more interesting question arises as to what use Smith made of the facts he presented. Did he actually try to learn from them, as an economic historian "should," or did he merely use them to illustrate his theories when they were suitable and to deny their relevance otherwise?

The popular view of Smith as a factual economist is no doubt strengthened by Smith's own words, which often suggest a careful, scholarly consideration of sources and facts. He refers us to the Postscript to the Universal Merchant as follows:

> This Postscript was not printed till 1756, three years after the publication of the book, which has never had a second edition. The postscript is, therefore, to be found in few copies. It corrects several errors in the book.

And in referring to the sums earned by turnpikes he says:

> Since publishing the two first editions of this book, I have got good reasons to
> believe that all the turnpike tolls levied in Great Britain do not produce a neat
> revenue that amounts to half a million; a sum which, under the management of
> Government, would not be sufficient to keep in repair five of the principal roads
> in the kingdom. I have now good reasons to believe that all these conjectural
> sums are by much too large.

Nonetheless, a careful look at the *Wealth of Nations* shows us that Smith's
acute statements appear limited to direct observations or to what may be
called a cultivated person's "general knowledge." Direct observations
establish only the lowest level of familiarity with facts; a second level is
reached when these comparative accounts are combined at a point in time
with the evolution of the economy over time. Smith was not perceptive of
aggregate or of systematic historical changes; not only was Smith not
farsighted, he was not even more perceptive than many of his
contemporaries. The importance of facts to an economist appears most
clearly if we see how facts influence him in forming views on economic
policy. When we examine how Smith deals with the most important issues
of economic policy there is a great deal of evidence to support the view that
Smith's writing "verges on propaganda" rather than possessing any
institutional features which made it "largely applicable in Britain."[3]

II

That there has been some ambiguity about the historical facts used in the
Wealth of Nations because of something called "conjectural history" has
long been recognized by scholars. Conjectural history is defined in the
earliest perceptive commentary on the *Wealth of Nations*, by Dugald
Stewart, who is led to this topic by asking how mankind achieved
civilization: "By what gradual steps the transition has been made from the
first simple efforts of uncultivated nature, to a state of things so wonderfully
artificial and complicated." Many of the queries that guided Stewart deal
with what we would now call the "pre-history" of a subject. His resolution
of the problem is most ingenious:

> In this want of direct evidence, we are under a necessity of supplying the place
> of fact by conjecture; and when we are unable to ascertain how men have
> actually conducted themselves upon particular occasions, of considering in what
> manner they are likely to have proceeded, from the principles of their nature,

and the circumstances of their external situation. . . . When we cannot trace the process by which an event *has been* produced, it is often of importance to be able to show how it *may have been* produced by natural causes.

Stewart explicitly noted that the strict accuracy of such conjectural history was not important because of his guiding belief that nature, that is, God, had guided man to civilization. Applying the same Providentialist belief to Adam Smith requires more careful justification and it is, in any case, inapplicable to historical events. W.P.D. Wightman is the most severe critic of conjectural history and writes of its practitioners that they leave us "in doubt as to where the 'fact' ended and the fiction began . . . where evidence was lacking they supplied a likely story." While there are some topics where the conjectural aspect is most likely, particularly in Book III of the *Wealth of Nations*, it is not at all clear which facts we should simply ignore because they are part of conjectural history. When W.P.D. Wightman asks: "How, for instance, could Smith *know* that 'wonder and not any expectation of advantage' was the *first* 'principle' to prompt mankind to the study of philosophy" he has focused on an issue where a "rational reconstruction" is evidently the basis for Smith's view. The same point can also be made when Smith attributes the division of labor to a "propensity in human nature . . . the propensity to truck, barter and exchange one thing for another."[4]

Campbell and Skinner have pointed out the difficulties created by this method because the difference between historical fact and conjectured fact is not always obvious. Campbell and Skinner, however, provide too much latitude to Adam Smith in their presentation. When Adam Smith claims that the inflation due to the influx of American silver ended in the 1630s (a point highly praised by Earl Hamilton) how are we to know whether he had some factual basis for this claim or whether it was an inspired guess?

When Adam Smith attributes the decline of feudalism to the greed of the feudal lords for trinkets, there is nothing obviously conjectural in his account. If Smith's account is indeed historically based, then it is surely a powerful illustration of Smith's beloved thesis that men achieve outcomes which are no part of their intentions. We cannot give Smith credit when he is right, but ignore the issue as conjectural history when he is not. Since Adam Smith himself made no distinction between the two classes of facts in the *Wealth of Nations*, I will use all "facts" stated in the *Wealth of Nations* as indicative of Adam Smith's method of study, while keeping in mind the different significance of the two types of "fact."[5]

There is one class of "fact" that requires some preliminary remarks. Several editors of the *Wealth of Nations* have been surprised at the many inaccuracies in the references. Some of these are quite innocuous, such as the failure to quote *verbatim* some statutes on pages 261 and 262; others indicate an absence of mind, as the claim on page 218 that 1759 was a cheap year for corn although he quotes a lower figure for 1761. Smith is somewhat less careful in representing his sources and there seems to be no parallel in Bernier, Smith's purported source, to support the account of public works in India (pp. 729-30): Smith's representation of the overall views of individuals can be quite misleading; Edwin Cannan remarks of Smith's account of Locke on the precious metals with annoyance: "There is very little foundation for any part of this paragraph." A more minute search might provide further grounds for cavil about the references provided by Smith. For example, one could ask for the sources used by Smith to claim that there was no recorded evidence of the existence of sharecropping in England. But these are not points of great significance by themselves and serve only to make small changes to the existing list of comments of editors like Cannan or Campbell and Skinner. Some indication of the location of these inaccuracies, about 90 in number, is provided in an appendix. It is not a small list. Considering the size of the *Wealth of Nations* and the enormous range and variety of facts quoted therein it is not a very long list either. Their significance is mainly negative. What they establish is that Smith was *not* a painstaking scholar. He had every opportunity and ample resources to see to it that every fact and reference in the *Wealth of Nations* was accurate, but made no visible effort to ensure accuracy. (Why, for example, does Smith leave the 1775 figures for the gross product of the excise on liquors in all later editions?) Inattention to detail is not the greatest failing for someone who paints on a great canvas. It is only when this minor defect is added to more weighty issues that it can serve to corroborate a substantive point. The significance of facts must be judged with respect to Smith's larger purposes in writing the *Wealth of Nations*—namely, the establishment of the theory of political economy on a sound footing and the reform of economic policy.[6]

There are several types of economic fact to be considered in assessing the *Wealth of Nations*. First, there are Smith's personal observations and those facts he obtained from his conversations. In contrasting the differences in diet between England, Scotland and Ireland, Smith decisively uses his own observations of the common people. Thus Scottish oatmeal is seen to be inferior to English wheat:

> In some parts of Lancashire it is pretended, I have been told, that bread of oatmeal is a heartier food for labouring people than wheaten bread, and I have frequently heard the same doctrine held in Scotland. I am, however, somewhat doubtful of the truth of it. The common people in Scotland, who are fed with oatmeal, are in general neither so strong nor so handsome as the same rank of people in England, who are fed with wheaten bread.

Irish potatoes, however, are a different story:

> But it seems to be otherwise with potatoes. The chairmen, porters, and coal heavers in London, and those unfortunate women who live by prostitution, the strongest men and the most beautiful women perhaps in the British dominions, are said to be, the greater part of them, from the lowest rank of people in Ireland, who are generally fed with this root.

Many economic historians, such as C.R. Fay and R.M. Hartwell, have been struck by the quality of Smith's personal observations and several other instances of charming factual detail are to be found in the *Wealth of Nations*. The multiplication of such instances, however, is unsatisfactory because they serve to establish nothing of significance about the larger purposes of the *Wealth of Nations*. And they fail to do so because such observations are largely independent of any theoretical content.[7]

In addition to those facts bearing directly on economics, there are others, which bear on wider issues and add considerable charm to the *Wealth of Nations*. The claim that agricultural workers cannot combine easily because they are dispersed is noteworthy:

> The inhabitants of the country, dispersed in distant places, cannot easily combine together. They have not only never been incorporated, but the corporation spirit never has prevailed among them. . . . Country gentlemen and farmers, dispersed in different parts of the country, cannot so easily combine as merchants and manufacturers, who being collected into towns, and accustomed to that exclusive corporation spirit which prevails in them, naturally endeavour to obtain against all their countrymen, the same exclusive privilege which they generally possess against the inhabitants of their respective towns. They accordingly seem to have been the original inventors of those restraints upon the importation of foreign goods, which secure to them the monopoly of the home-market

while the description of robotization by the division of labor has long since become a classic:

> In the progress of the division of labour, the employment of the far greater part of those who live by labour, that is, of the great body of the people, comes to be confined to a few very simple operations; frequently to one or two. But the understandings of the greater part of men are necessarily formed by their ordinary employments. The man whose whole life is spent in performing a few simple operations, of which the effects too are, perhaps, always the same, or very nearly the same, has no occasion to exert his understanding, or to exercise his invention in finding out expedients for removing difficulties which never

occur. He naturally loses, therefore, the habit of such exertion, and generally becomes as stupid as it is possible for a human creature to become.

While these examples are of great importance—and the academic division of labor has unfortunately led sociologists and political scientists to be more appreciative of these passages than economists are—it is surprising that no empirical instances are given to corroborate the penetrating thesis about the alienation of the worker. Was Smith making this point more from his knowledge of human nature than from observation of facts?[8]

Dugald Stewart made some very perceptive remarks on Adam Smith's modes of thought in his biographical *Account*:

> In Mr Smith's writings, whatever be the nature of his subject, he seldom misses an opportunity of indulging his curiosity, in tracing from the principles of human nature, or from the circumstances of society, the origin of the opinions and the institutions which he describes.
>
> The same turn of thinking was frequently, in his social hours, applied to more familiar subjects; and the fanciful theories which, without the least affectation of ingenuity, he was continually starting upon all the common topics of discourse, gave to his conversation a novelty and variety that were quite inexhaustible. Hence too the minuteness and accuracy of his knowledge on many trifling articles which, in the course of his speculations, he had been led to consider from some new and interesting point of view, and of which his lively and circumstantial descriptions amused his friends the more, that he seemed to be habitually inattentive, in so remarkable a degree, to what was passing around him.

It will be noted that this procedure makes facts a convenient vehicle to carry one's theoretical views. If indeed Stewart is right, then we should find Smith making little effort to search out all the authorities in a given field and judge their respective merits. One set of reasonably accurate facts will suffice. What is of more importance to Smith is the scaffolding erected on these facts. As the facts are meant to illustrate, the potency of contrary facts will be denied, while the minuteness and accuracy of Smith's knowledge continue to amaze the reader.[9]

When Smith is dealing with general issues he uses his knowledge most persuasively, as in the influence of inheritance laws on land distribution in the colonies:

> First, the engrossing of uncultivated land, though it has by no means been prevented altogether, has been more restrained in the English colonies than in any other. The colony law which imposes upon every proprietor the obligation of improving and cultivating, within a limited time, a certain proportion of his

lands, and which, in case of failure, declares those neglected lands grantable to any other person; though it has not perhaps, been very strictly executed, has, however, had some effect.

Secondly, in Pennsylvania there is no right of primogeniture, and lands, like moveables, are divided equally among all children of the family. In three of the provinces of New England the oldest has only a double share, as in the Mosaical law. Though in those provinces, therefore, too great a quantity of land should sometimes be engrossed by a particular individual, it is likely, in the course of a generation or two, to be sufficiently divided again. In the other English colonies, indeed, the right of primogeniture takes place, as in the law of England. But in all the English colonies the tenure of their land, which are all held by free socage, facilitates alienation, and the grantee of any extensive tract of land generally finds it for his interest to alienate, as fast as he can, the greater part of it, reserving only a small quit-rent.

No data or references are given, and it is entirely plausible that none would have been necessary to Smith's contemporaries.[10]

An examination of the National Debt and the East India Company serves to illustrate one aspect of the *Wealth of Nations*. We find Smith repeating a familiar pattern: reliance on a single work for his facts and, in some cases, for several of his interpretations. James Postlethwaite is the source of his facts on the National Debt. Smith says nothing very unusual in his section on the National Debt, except to express profound distrust of its growth. Typically, he tries to explain why the different modes of financing the debt in England and in France reflect the societies of their respective capital cities. And when he finds the British economy to have grown despite the increasing debt, Smith concludes with a counterfactual claim:

> Great Britain seems to support with ease, a burden which, half a century ago, nobody believed her capable of supporting. Let us not, however, upon this account rashly conclude that she is capable of supporting any burden; nor even be too confident that she could support, without great distress, a burden a little greater than what has already been laid upon her.[11]

In the case of the East India Company, Smith produces virtually no facts. He relies on general descriptions of the East India Company, of the sort that any newspaper reader would have been aware of, such as the monopoly position of the East India Company, their adaptation to the role of sovereigns and the private trading of Company employees. Knowledge of human nature suffices to inform Smith that, when placed in such a situation, the Company and even more its officials will engage in fraud, abuse and rapine. He appears to have found such a description of the Company in the book of William Bolts and accordingly condemned the Company:

The public trade of the company extends no further than the trade with Europe, and comprehends a part only of the foreign trade of the country. But the private trade of the servants may extend to all the different branches both of its inland and foreign trade. The monopoly of the company can tend only to stunt the natural growth of that part of the surplus produce which, in the case of a free trade, would be exported to Europe. That of the servants tends to stunt the natural growth of every part of the produce in which they chuse to deal, of what is destined for home consumption, as well as of what is destined for exportation.

Smith's description of the nature of the East India Company's government will strike a welcome chord in the heart of every Bengali:

It is a very singular government in which every member of the administration wishes to get out of the country, and consequently to have done with the government, as soon as he can, and to whose interest, the day after he has left it and carried his whole fortune with him, it is perfectly indifferent though the whole country was swallowed up by an earthquake.

It is not clear that a close knowledge of historical facts is at all necessary for pronouncing such judgements.[12]

III

Economic historians have long argued with historians of economic thought over Adam Smith's relation to the "Industrial Revolution." The merits of Adam Smith's observations on the contemporary economy have most recently been debated by Charles Kindleberger and Ronald Hartwell in one of the volumes appearing at the bicentennial of the *Wealth of Nations*. Hartwell is right in pointing out that the use of "Industrial Revolution" in this context has been unfortunate because there is considerable debate on whether there was such an event in the eighteenth century, and if so, when did it occur? It is more fruitful to ask: How aware was Smith of the economic changes that were occurring around him? Several examples can be given of Smith's recognition of the fact that the contemporary economy was growing and, indeed, that it had been growing since the time of Elizabeth I. But these quotes also show that Smith's awareness was of a rather vague sort and very much in line with a multitude of earlier and contemporary authors who praised Elizabeth for starting England on her present course.[13]

Simply to establish Smith's awareness of economic growth is to settle for a watered-down proposition. One would like to focus on those features of the eighteenth century that were to lead to the palpably obvious "Industrial Revolution" of the nineteenth century. Richard Koebner has noted that because the Industrial Revolution was followed by a widespread belief in the vigor and productivity of free enterprise so it was only natural to provide Smith with prescience and to claim that he had blessed the Industrial Revolution before it began. Nonetheless, Koebner insists:

> This was an artificial construction for which not a single line of his writing, if read in its context, could provide any evidence. Much more than that—apart from having no inkling of many technical innovations which lay ahead and of the forms of organization by which they were to be exploited—Adam Smith had been rather unfavourably disposed towards those elements of society who were to organize mechanised production and to divert it into the channels of commerce.

Koebner points out that the innovation in production and business organization which were to add up to the Industrial Revolution had been matters of discussion for several decades and that careful observers such as Josiah Tucker in 1757 and Edmund Burke in 1769 had already provided several instances of the spirit and enterprise of British merchants in the Midlands. Nonetheless, Birmingham is for Adam Smith—even in the third edition—a city of "toys." Adam Smith had ample opportunity to study the changes in English industry, not only between 1767 and 1775, when the first edition was being written, but also down to the significant revision of the third edition of 1783:

> The passages which could be taken as testifying to Smith's interest in recent technical progress are very sparse and rarely explicit. The hints, if there are any, are very casual, and *betray none of that eagerness to be exactly informed* on the most various aspects of contemporary economic life which he shows in his expositions of money transactions, labour conditions, soil conservation, and the corn trade. . . .
>
> One possible answer is, of course, that his systematic search for principles of economic behavior did not impose on him the obligation of offering opinions on individual contemporary experiments. To concede this is, however, not to dispose of the question why did not any of these new features stimulate his thought. *He need not have described them; yet they could have animated his theoretical outlook. If they failed to have such effect this must be thought to be characteristic of the workings of his mind.* (Emphasis added)[14]

Charles Kindleberger has sharpened these points in his review of what he calls an "open and shut" case against Adam Smith's recognition of the Industrial Revolution:

There is virtually no mention of cotton textiles, only one reference to
Manchester in a list of cities, nothing on pottery, nothing on new methods of
producing beer. Canals are dealt with under public works, but illustrated by the
canal of Languedoc, finished in 1681, rather than with the Bridgewater canal
of 1761, which initiated the spate of canal building and improvement in Britain
culminating in the canal mania of the 1790s. Turnpikes are referred to without
notice of the fact that travel times were falling rapidly.

Samuel Hollander has challenged Koebner's view but Kindleberger
satisfactorily demonstrates the inadequate and partial nature of Hollander's
argument by showing that Smith does not discuss the spread of coal in
industrial use but primarily for space heating; that Smith failed to appreciate
the significance of substituting coke for charcoal or the dynamic interaction
of coal use and transportation costs; or even that James Watt influenced
Smith. The central issue relates to quantitative orders of magnitude. What
were the major growth sectors and was Smith aware of them? Nothing that
the supporters of Smith have noted comes close to appreciating the force of
Koebner's critique that Smith's writing betrays "none of that eagerness to
be exactly informed on the most various aspects of contemporary economic
life." Kindleberger's observation on the substantially revised third edition of
the *Wealth of Nations* is decisive:

> A detailed and up to the minute discussion in the 3rd edition of 1783 concerns
> not industrial output but the impact of the herring bounty on the catch.[15]

If Adam Smith was not really in tune with the pace of contemporary
economic change, we would expect this to appear as much in his
appreciation of personalities as of events. When we turn to Adam Smith's
portrayal of the human beings involved in the process of economic growth
we find this suggestion confirmed. The active, restless, creative entrepreneur
not only gets no praise, Smith classifies such individuals with the derogatory
class of "projectors." The projectors are the subject of considerable sarcasm.
They are those who have devised "expensive and uncertain projects . . .
which bring bankruptcy upon the greater part of the people who engage in
them." The older term "adventurer" is also sometimes used by Smith to
indicate someone who takes great risks, but his references to this group have
no contemporary significance.[16]

When Smith comes to describe the activities of the businessman—those
who live by profit—he is almost condescending:

> The profiles of stock, it may perhaps be thought, are only a different name for
> the wages of a particular sort of labour, the labour of inspection and direction.

They are, however, altogether different, are regulated by quite different principles, and bear no proportion to the quantity, the hardship, or the ingenuity of this supposed labour of inspection and direction. They are regulated altogether by the value of the stock employed, and are greater or smaller in proportion to the extent of this stock.

In other words, those who have money can make more in their sleep, as it were. As a result, Smith goes on to suggest that this routine work is frequently left to a clerk, and there is a hint of exploitation in Smith's description of how the clerk is paid for his efforts:

> In many great works, almost the whole labour of this kind is committed to some principal clerk. His wages properly express the value of this labour of inspection and direction. Though in settling them some regard is had commonly, not only to his labour and skill, but to the trust which is reposed in him, yet they never bear any regular proportion to the capital of which he oversees the management; and the owner of this capital, though he is thus discharged of almost all labour, still expects that his profits should bear a regular proportion to his capital. In the price of commodities, therefore, the profits of stock constitute a component part altogether different from the wages of labour, and regulated by quite different principles.

At various other points in the *Wealth of Nations* Smith refers to the undertaker having to face risk and uncertainty, to plan their activities and to organize production. These are all made in contexts that do not dwell upon entrepreneurship *per se*, and if read in context do little to correct the abrasive picture he paints when he does focus upon the role of the businessman.[17]

The prudent individual whom Smith does admire has all the attributes of a philosopher-trader:

> In the steadiness of his industry and frugality, in his steadily sacrificing the ease and enjoyment of the present moment for the probably expectation of the still greater ease and enjoyment of a more distant but more lasting period of time, the prudent man is always both supported and rewarded by the entire approbation of the impartial spectator. . . . The man who lives within his income, is naturally contented with his situation, which, by continual, though small accumulations, is growing better and better every day. . . . He does not go in quest of new enterprises and adventures, which might endanger, but could not well increase, the secure tranquility which he actually enjoys.

Mercifully, this individual does not disturb the tranquility of his mind by invading the *Wealth of Nations*. On the whole, it is a very mild assessment to state that Smith provides an "overall neglect of the entrepreneurial function."[18]

That conjectural deductions were really Adam Smith's forte is further corroborated by Smith's failure to observe the turmoil brewing in France. John Rae's defense of Adam Smith on this issue is revealing:

> McCulloch has expressed astonishment that for all his long stay in France Smith should have never perceived any foreshadowings of the coming Revolution, such as were visible even to a passing traveller like Smollett. But Smith was quite aware of all the gravities and possibilities of the situation, and occasionally gave expression to anticipation of vital change. He formed possibly a less gloomy view of the actual condition of the French people than he would have heard uttered in Quesnay's room at Versailles, because he always mentally compared the state of things he saw in France with the state of things he knew in Scotland, and though it was plain to him that France was not going forward so fast as Scotland, he thought the common opinion that it was going backward to be ill founded.

Rae does not see that these observations do not approach the makings of a "Revolution." This is a good illustration of Koebner's point that sensitiveness to rapid economic change was not "characteristic of the workings of his [Smith's] mind."[19]

The same point reappears in Smith's account of the fall of the feudal system:

> What all the violence of the feudal institutions could never have effected, the silent and insensible operation of foreign commerce and manufactures gradually brought about. These gradually furnished the great proprietors with something for which they could exchange the whole surplus produce of their lands, and which they could consume themselves without sharing it either with tenants or retainers. All for ourselves, and nothing for other people, seems, in every age of the world, to have been the vile maxim of the masters of mankind. As soon, therefore, as they could find a method of consuming the whole value of their rents themselves, they had no disposition to share them with any other persons. For a pair of diamond buckles, perhaps, or for something as frivolous and useless, they exchanged . . . the maintenance of a thousand men for a year, and with it the whole weight and authority which it could give them . . . and thus, for the gratification of the most childish, the meanest and the most sordid of all vanities, they gradually bartered their whole power and authority.

This graphic illustration of a society in transition is surely extraordinary for anyone who considers economic determinism to have some merit.

The issue itself was not a new one in English history, since several historians had considered the pivotal role of Henry VII in lowering the status of nobility and raising that of the commons. David Hume gave some importance to the general growth of prosperity even while accepting the considerable consequences that flowed from Henry VII's law permitting the nobility to alienate their estates. Smith's emphasis on the hidden hand is unique among his contemporaries. The partiality for a conjectural history, under Providential guidance, is considerably in evidence.[20]

IV

One of the principal questions that should be, but has rarely been, asked is whether Smith's observational abilities and capacity to marshal facts is superior to that of his contemporaries. Since perceptive Englishmen would observe a more advanced economy than Smith, it seems more fair to use two Scotsmen: Adam Anderson, who lived largely in England, and a "pure" Scot, the Reverend Thomas Hepburn.

Adam Smith used Anderson's *Historical . . . Account* and referred to the "sober and judicious" Anderson. What are some of the notable aspects of Anderson's historical treatment of commerce? First, he is well aware of the interplay of politics and economics:

> 1509. This year is also remarkable for the death of Henry VII. King of England. We may therefore, with Mr Echard and others before him, justly remark, that several laws made in his reign, and by his influence, were very conducive to the advancement of agriculture and commerce; . . .
>
> "By gradually," says Echard, "putting stops to the power of the nobility, who had "lately raised such storms in the nation;" that is, particularly against himself, leave was granted, as we have seen, to all freeholders at pleasure, without fines for alienation. Which was a good means to make land estates change proprietors the more easily and frequently, as the commerce and wealth of the nation gradually increased. He wisely enough considered the old maxim, *dominium sequitur terram,* and that King John's Barons were often too hard for him, because most of the lands were possessed by them, or by their vassals; and that as he himself had been raised by the nobility, he might possibly be cast down by them.

While quoting the Acts of Parliament frequently, Anderson is often critical of the motives which led to the passage of various laws as well as of the representativeness of Parliamentary Acts in describing their own age:

> Whoever will attentively consider the gradual increase of the trade, manufactures, and people of England, must, at the same time, acknowledge, that in some of our acts of Parliament of old, the true condition and increase thereof

was far from being fairly or justly stated; being often egregiously misrepresented either in the preamble, or in the main bodies of such statutes; *sometimes probably to answer the temporary and sinister purposes of men in power, and perhaps sometimes only from mere inadvertency and ignorance.*

. . . In several other acts of Parliament of old, we find the pewterers, clothworkers, &c. companies of London, and other towns, in their complaints against non-freemen, among other things confidently asserting, that a multiplicity of artists "causes the enhancing of the price;" the contrary of which is long since known to be invariably true. Neither is the other accusation against a multiplicity of workmen always true, viz. that of making slight goods, since such a multiplicity will as often strive to excel in goodness and ingenuity as in cheapness. (Emphasis added)

He is equally careful in using the Acts of Parliament as a source of data:

1535. We may have already observed, that since the accession of King Henry VIII. there was not only a great increase of the woollen manufacture of England, but likewise of its foreign commerce, and also many other marks of increasing riches. Nevertheless, any one entirely unacquainted with the circumstances of England at that time, would be led to imagine quite the contrary, by only perusing the preambles of certain acts of Parliament of the twenty-sixth and twenty-seventh years of that King's reign.

The Acts of Parliament were by no means the only sources Anderson consulted. Rymer's *Foedra* appears to be most frequently used and this is supported by the best contemporary authors as necessary. For the period between 1600 and 1650, for example, John Wheeler, Gerald Malynes, Edward Misselden, Thomas Mun, and Lewis Roberts are supplemented with an unpublished and highly interesting account by Sir Robert Cotton. Adam Smith cannot be said to show any improvement over Adam Anderson in the critical use of historical documents.[21]

When James Boswell published the account of his trip to the Highlands of Scotland with Dr Samuel Johnson, many readers noted the perceptive comments on economic development. Since Dr Johnson is known to have been more than ordinarily knowledgeable about economics, it is more instructive to look at the comments of an ordinary clergyman, the Reverend Thomas Hepburn, on the economic condition of the Orkneys. Hepburn begins *A Letter to a Gentleman from his friend in Orkney, containing the true causes of the poverty of that country (written in 1757)* by noting that "In a free country like ours," poverty can result only from natural causes or a want of effort:

In a free country like ours, the poverty of any particular district must be owing to one or more of the following causes, *viz.* the climate, soil, situation, want of improvement in agriculture, neglect of manufactures and fisheries, destructive and illegal trade, luxury, that species of oppression which eludes the force of law, or, *lastly* faction.

A survey of Orkney's situation shows no physical reason for poverty, and Hepburn reviews in succession the backward nature of tillage, grazing and planting, of which it will suffice to quote one example:

The progress of agriculture, you know, sir, depends in a great measure on the landlords: The flourishing state of agriculture in *England* is much owing to the humanity of the landlords; most part of our *Orkney* lairds seem to be absolutely devoid of this divine principle; they crush the spirit of improvement in the farmers, by short leases, grassums, numerous unlimited services, and many other hardships; all the rents are payable in kind, and high prices are demanded for deficiencies, which happen often; so that two good crops are scarce sufficient to make up for one bad crop: they are entirely ignorant of the art of keeping their grounds clean, and in good order; hence their crop is frequently choked with weeds, is ill to be won, the grain is small, hungry, and often unwholesome; they sow no grain but small rough bear, and black oats, alternatively; their plow has but one stilt, the plowirons are so clumsy and short, that the furrow is very shallow and unequal, and most often be delved with spades; their harrow is small, light, and timber-teethed; they use no wheel-carriages, nor oxen plows, though their horses are but of the ordinary shelty kind; they never fallow their corn lands, but near the hills they lay them lee for one year. How rude must agriculture be in that country, where they winnow all their corns through their fingers, instead of sieves, riddles, or fanners? What sort of farmers must they be, who fleece fine meadow grounds, to lay on their corn lands?

After describing in some detail the poor practices of the farmers and the utter lack of interest in the landlords, Hepburn goes on to discuss the possibilities of manufacturing and laments the want of attention to Orkney's comparative advantage in fishing:

Only one kind of manufacture is carried on in *Orkney*, that of the spinning of linen yarn, which was ill received at first, as all innovations are, by rude and ignorant people; but the commonality are now reconciled to it, and no wonder, for it brings to numbers of them yearly a pound for every shilling they were formerly possessed of: Several persons who deal in this manufacture, pay the spinners in spirits and *Dutch* tobacco. I had almost forgot to tell you, that many *Orkney* landlords and their wives exact intollerable and burdensome services of spinning from their tenants: Little lintseed is sown in *Orkney*, tho' the soil is very proper for it. Whoever has a-mind to try any manufacture in *Orkney*, will meet with this encouragement, that the price of labour is not high.

But the chief neglect in *Orkney* I take to be that of fishing, which might be here, as in the neighbouring islands of *Zetland*, the staple commodity of the country; but *Orkney* is so divided, the prejudices of the inhabitants so many, and almost incurable, that the union of any number of them, considerable enough for promoting this, or any other publick spirited scheme can hardly be expected.

Smuggling and luxury are next to attract Hepburn's attention:

Smuggling, or illicit trade, the bane of every society where it prevails, falls next to be considered; this mischief, I am sorry to inform you, has made a rapid progress in *Orkney* for thirty years past; it is now at such an height, that the value of *Dutch* gin, *Dutch* tobacco, *French* brandies, wine, rum, tea, coffee, sugar, &c., yearly imported by smuggling, is equal, at a moderate computation, to two-thirds of the yearly rent of the country.

. . . I am sure there is more tea, punch, and spirits of all kinds drunk, more silks, velvets, cambrics, and other fineries, used in *Orkney*, in proportion to the wealth of the country, than in the richest countries in *Scotland*.

Hepburn is not opposed to consumption, provided it is supported by industry, but in the Orkneys he finds it "imported like any idle fashion" and he goes on to provide a sociological explanation for the prevalence of fashion:

In these confined islands, almost all of the families of any standing are related to one another by the ties of blood. A stranger would readily fancy all the gentle people a family of cousins; nor would his fancy be wrong. Hence as relation is more permanent than fortune, there must be many unequal marriages. Now, whether the odds of fortune is on the side of the man or the woman, it is certain that they don't fix the rate of living according to the returns of their industry. They rather incline to imitate, in some measure, in every article of life, the manners and fashions of their rich relations. This makes luxury more general here, than in most places on the continent of *Scotland*.

Having suggested in the beginning that oppression is a ground for poverty, Hepburn makes some perceptive observations on the bad influence of custom in a free country:

Oppression is of two kinds: either such as is directly against the laws of the land, and consequently punishable by them, or such as arises from antient usages, prejudices, and customes, from avarice, inhumanity, or other causes which elude the force of law. Instances of both kinds in *Orkney* could be adduced, tho' the first is rare, and feeble in its effects, when compared to the second, which is common over all *Scotland*, and more violently exercised in some northern countries than even in *Orkney*. This species of oppression consists of particulars already mentioned; such as short tacks, rents payable in every product of industry, entry-monies or grassums, numerous, and what is worse, undetermined services. These forever retard improvement, and keep the husbandman in such poverty, and so slavish a dependance, that he is continually subjected to a thousand nameless hardships. It is indeed impossible to enumerate every particular oppression which springs from these sources, or the various mischiefs occasioned by them.

Where in the *Wealth of Nations* is there a superior description of underdevelopment?[22]

V

The role played by "facts" in Adam Smith's economic philosophy can be most clearly demonstrated by his approach to the major policy issues of his day. The range of facts that he could personally observe or see as a Customs commissioner is slight compared with those he would have to marshal to make his case for economic liberty in the *Wealth of Nations*. How did Smith search out his facts? How did he choose his authorities from the available sources, and what use did he make of them? In order to provide some system to this inquiry it is useful to proceed by considering those issues dealt with in the *Wealth of Nations* that were of considerable contemporary significance. In the domestic economy the most important issues would be the Poor Laws and the inland corn trade; the corn bounty and the wool trade are of equal importance to both domestic and foreign affairs; while joint-stock overseas companies and the Methuen Treaty serve to illustrate all major issues of foreign trade.

In the course of the *Wealth of Nations*, Adam Smith expresses his opinion on many topics of interest—several of which have attracted considerable attention because they involve substantial historical interpretation even though they involve much more than "facts" in the narrow sense used in most of this chapter. One of the most important of these views is Smith's claim that economic policy was based on the self-interested advice of merchants. However desirable it might be, a detailed defense of this presumption by Adam Smith can scarcely be expected. But the existence of the presumption must be noted because it can be expected to influence Smith's choice and interpretation of facts. Modern economic historians, such as Charles Wilson, have pointed out that the explanation leaves unanswered the question of how to decide between the claims of rival merchants, while Ralph Davis has made the simple but striking observation that the existence of a protectionist economic *policy* is not visible until the very end of the seventeenth century.[23]

Wool

The wool trade—England's Golden Fleece—was certainly one of the most frequently discussed issues of the seventeenth century. As the major source of England's foreign exchange, wool had always been a constant source of concern for the English. As soon as they were able to manufacture their own woolen cloth the English prohibited the export of wool so as to ensure that they got the maximum benefit from their Golden Fleece.

Adam Smith does not have a separate chapter or even a separate section on the wool trade. He first refers to it in the midst of a discussion on the path of prices in the course of economic growth. Wool, being raw produce, should have risen in price according to theory. Nonetheless, relying on the Reverend Smith, Adam Smith explains this fall in price as the result of interference in the market:

> This degradation both in the real and nominal value of wool, could never have happened in consequence of the natural course of things. It has accordingly been the effect of violence and artifice: First, of the absolute prohibition of exporting wool from England; Secondly, of the permission of importing it from Spain duty free; Thirdly, of the prohibition of exporting it from Ireland to any other country but England.

In a fine analysis of the pricing of joint products, Smith points out that wool provides a greater proportion of the value of sheep in poor countries. It was to be expected that, after the union with England, the price of Scottish wools would fall considerably due to their also being subject to the English prohibitory laws:

> The wool of Scotland fell very considerably in its price in consequence of the union with England, by which it was excluded from the great market of Europe, and confined to the narrow one of Great Britain. The value of the great part of the lands in the southern countries of Scotland, which are chiefly a sheep country, would have been very deeply affected by this event, had not the rise in the price of butcher's-meat fully compensated the fall in the price of wool.

This is all that Smith has to say on this important industry in the first two editions.[24]

In 1781 there was a considerable debate on the export of wool, and in the third edition, published in 1783, Smith returned to this topic in a new chapter entitled "Conclusion of the Mercantile System." Smith begins by acknowledging the political power of the wool manufacturers:

> Our woolen manufacturers have been more successful than any other class of workmen, in persuading the legislature that the prosperity of the nation depended upon the success and extension of their particular business.

However, Smith leaves no doubt as to his feelings on this issue:

> But the cruellest of our revenue laws, I will venture to affirm, are mild and gentle, in comparison of some of those which the clamour of our merchants and manufacturers has extorted from the legislature, for the support of their own absurd and oppressive monopolies. Like the laws of Draco, these laws may be said to be all written in blood.

In the next few pages Smith provides a detailed account of the various restrictions on the growers and transporters of wool: restrictions which were justified by the claim that English wool was superior and a necessary ingredient for good cloth. Without providing any references, Smith claims that "English wool is . . . altogether unfit for it [fine cloth]." On the authority of the *Chronicon* Smith then points out how these restrictions have depressed the price of English wool below that of inferior wool in Amsterdam. The lower price of wool has not, however, significantly reduced the quantity of wool because sheep provide meat and hides as well as wool, and the price of the other two products had risen sufficiently to continue the supply of wool. While the production of wool has not declined, it is to be expected that shepherds would not be as solicitous of the quality of the wool, which would decline. Smith does not find this outcome verified by the facts, so he claims a counterfactual:

> Notwithstanding the degradation of price, English wool is said to have been improved considerably during the course even of the present century. The improvement might perhaps have been greater if the price had been better.

Smith's final words on this topic support a tax on the exportation of wool, an action seemingly at variance with his free-trade principles, and one which has evoked various explanations.[25]

The remarkable feature of Adam Smith's account of the wool trade is its perspective. The first two editions deal with wool only in passing while the third edition stops only to add a vigorous condemnation of the wool manufacturers. How could one guess from such an account that the wool trade was the major export of England for centuries and that more effort had perhaps been expended in supporting this manufacture than any other?

Treaties of Commerce

The chapter in the *Wealth of Nations* in which Adam Smith deals with the Methuen Treaty has a quaint selection of matter. It is entitled "Treaties of Commerce," but only two pages of the whole chapter deal with this general topic. Six pages concentrate on the Methuen Treaty, including an entire transcription of the text of the Treaty. The account itself is somewhat oversimplified since it does not trace the evolution from large surpluses in the early years to moderate surpluses in the 1760s. The final six pages analyze seigniorage in England, a subject so evidently misplaced that Smith found it necessary to apologize for its inclusion.

According to Smith, the figures available on the transfers of gold from Portugal to England were exaggerated because "it would amount to more than two million six hundred thousand pounds a year, which is more than the Brazils are supposed to afford." Smith cites Joseph Baretti as his authority, but Baretti's text is misinterpreted by Smith, as pointed out by Edwin Cannan. The text of Baretti's Letter XVI, is as follows:

> Almost every week a packet sails from Falmouth to Lisbon with only the mail that is sent from London. Mails are not heavy cargo, but when a packet sails back to England, besides the returning mail, it has that hole fill'd with so many bags of Portugal coin, as often amount from thirty to fifty, and even sixty thousand pounds of sterling. A round sum when we look into the almanack, and find that every year has two and fifty weeks.

The expression "almost every week" cannot be equalized to 52 weeks a year, nor can the remark "often amount from thirty to fifty, and even sixty thousand pounds sterling" warrant an average as high or higher than £50 thousand. (Later authors suggest that the Brazilian mines yielded a greater quantity of gold than Baretti reported, especially when the impact of smuggled gold is added to the figures of contemporary sources.)[26]

There is no question that the Methuen Treaty put an end to a series of restrictions on the imports of woolen cloth from England which had been imposed by the Portuguese government. Notwithstanding, the only considerable advantage of the Portuguese trade admitted by Smith, though not "a capital advantage," is the effect of "facilitating all the different round-about foreign trades of consumption which are carried on in Great Britain," produced by the gold transferred from Lisbon. The advantages gained by becoming banker to Portugal are not even noticed.

The most important historical critique of Smith's treatment of the Methuen Treaty was provided by Henry Brougham, who felt that no man "of common understanding" would have accepted such a treaty as Smith described and which Smith found to be "evidently advantageous to Portugal, and disadvantageous to Great Britain." Brougham provides us the background to the Treaty:

> This statement, however, is fundamentally erroneous, inasmuch as it omits to consider the extent and nature of the prohibition repealed in the treaty. In 1644, (the jealous spirit of the French cabinet having a short time before prohibited Brazil goods), Portugal prohibited the entry of all French goods. The hands of the nation were, during the remainder of the seventeenth century, turned to manufacturers, particularly those of wool; and with so much success, that in 1684 the government under Erricira's administration prohibited all importation, either of the raw material or of woollen goods. This occasioned great murmurs, chiefly on account of the diminution sustained by the revenue; and at the same time Britain was endeavouring to supplant the French wines in her home market, by the introduction of the Portugueze. Both governments, therefore, were soon disposed to conclude a bargain, which should again open the Portugueze market to British woollens, and should promote in Britain the use of Portugueze wines. This gave rise to the arrangements which terminated in the Methuen treaty.

Adam Smith quotes the literal terms of the entire Treaty, without giving any indication of the historical background, thereby providing spurious accuracy to his account. After the background given by Brougham, the value of the Treaty becomes evident:

> The paction, then, is short and simple; it is, that Portugal shall repeal the law of 1684, in favour of Britain, and that Britain, in return, shall admit Portugueze wines at two thirds of the duties paid by French wines. The preference is mutual. The prohibition of 1644 against French goods remains in full force: the prohibition of 1684 remains also in full force against French and all other woollens, except British woollens. British woollens alone were admitted; all others excluded. Here, then, is a monopoly of the Portugueze market granted to British goods, in return for a preference given to Portugueze wines over those of France. Wherefore, the advantage granted to British woollens is much more general than that given Portugueze wines. Dr. Smith's objection proceeds entirely from confining his view to the terms of the treaty, which do not expressly say that the laws of 1644 and 1684 are to remain in force, unless so far as the latter is repealed by the treaty.

It may be said that Smith did not wish to mislead his readers and was himself unaware of the historical background, but this scarcely serves to rescue his reputation as an economic historian.[27]

Poor Laws

Adam Smith does not deal directly with the Poor Laws but focuses upon one aspect: the restrictions to the mobility of labor caused by the Law of Settlements. "The difficulty of obtaining settlements," Smith tells us, "obstructs even that of common labour. It may be worth while to give some account of the rise, progress, and present state of this disorder, *the greatest perhaps of any in the police of England*" (emphasis added). These strong words require careful factual justification.

Smith begins by noting the introduction of the Poor Laws upon the abolition of the monasteries and the responsibility for the poor laid upon each parish. This law put every parish on guard against providing for the poor who were not their own. The issue was decided by considering as belonging to the parish only those who had resided there for 40 days. Since parish officers were bribed to provide false settlements, the law was amended to requiring 40 days residence after public notice had been provided in the church. Such a settlement was rarely obtained as no parish wished to take in chargeable poor. In order to permit freer circulation, those who could provide certificates from their own parish were free to be employed in other parishes. However, this only caused it to be against the interest of any parish to give a certificate in the first place, and they were issued only with difficulty.

Smith's entire presentation is dependent upon Richard Burn's, *History of the Poor Laws*. Smith quotes liberally from the *History* and refers to Burn as a "very intelligent Author." At one point he goes beyond Burn in claiming that the parish officers were bribed to provide settlements, but does not provide any independent evidence.[28] He draws much stronger conclusions from his presentation than Burn does: "The very unequal price of labour which we frequently find in England in places at no great distance from one another, is probably owing to the obstruction which the law of settlements gives [to the free movement of labour]." Smith does not back up his claim of widely varying local wages with any specific data. In the next paragraph he assigns the continuation of the law to the inability of the common Englishman, who is otherwise jealous of his rights, to see just how great an infringement this part of the Poor Laws is. Smith concludes: "There is scarce a poor man in England of forty years of age, I will venture to say, who has not in some part of his life felt himself most cruelly oppressed by this ill-contrived law of settlements." Campbell and Skinner, following Sir Frederick Morton Eden, remarked appropriately on this strong assertion that it appears dependent on William Hay, a member of the House of Commons who published his *Remarks on the Poor Laws* in 1735. According to Hay:

> a poor man is no sooner got into a neighbourhood, habitation and employment that he likes, but, upon humour or caprice of the parish, he is sent to another place, where he can find none of these conveniences; not certain long to continue there; for perhaps, after the appeal, he is sent back again, and then hurried to a third place; and sometimes is a great while before he know where he shall be at rest. In the meantime he is at expense in removing his family and goods, or perhaps, not able to carry them with him, is forced to sell them at a disadvantage; he loses his time, and is obliged to neglect his work, which is his only support; so that 'tis no wonder if by this treatment he is very much impoverished; and from being only likely to become chargeable, is actually made so.[29]

Smith's claims were disputed by the Reverend John Howlett, otherwise an admirer, but who doubted very much if Scottish wages were more uniform than English. Howlett claimed that the hard-hearted watched carefully over their money, thereby extracting so much industry from the poor that English paupers earned two to three times as much as Scots did at the same manufacture: "This surely but ill accords with the reasonings of Lord Kames and Dr Adam Smith, who both contend that our system of poor-laws has rendered our labourers worthless and lazy, while those of their own country are industrious and diligent." Howlett goes on to claim that the Laws of Settlement scarcely shackle labor, else how could cities like Manchester grow? It is always demand and supply, Howlett says, that determine the wages of labor, which need not be uniform across the country nor rise with the costs of subsistence. Shortly thereafter, Sir Frederick Eden was to repeat the same points regarding Smith's factual claims in his study on the poor. Smith's account of the Poor Laws is based as much on qualitative inference as on fact.[30]

Corn Trade

The corn trade was certainly one of the most important political issues facing Britain. The bounty on the exportation of corn was one of the most widely controverted issues of the mid-eighteenth century and its suggested replacement by the free importation of corn was to become even more contentious in time. In one way it is very easy to characterize Smith's attitude to facts on this critical policy issue: Smith relied on Charles Smith's *Three Tracts on the Corn Trade* as much as possible and went to Bishop Fleetwood's *Chronicon Preciosum* when the *Tracts* could not be used. Adam Smith does not discuss any corn-trade pamphlets other than the *Three Tracts* nor does he explain why he chooses this pamphlet above the others. Most subsequent commentators have agreed on the dispassionate portrayal of facts by Charles Smith, and Adam Smith's choice of the *Three Tracts* shows good judgement, especially so since the policies approved by Charles Smith are not those advocated by Adam Smith.

The corn bounty is discussed at some length in two different places in the *Wealth of Nations* but the treatment is basically repetitive, so it will suffice to follow that given in Book IV. The central fact, which Adam Smith does not dispute, is that corn has become cheaper during the eighteenth century. Supporters of the bounty insisted that this was proof of its benefit. Smith provides several different arguments to insist that this claim is suspect and even suggests that the low price of corn is a doubtful gain. First, the lower price of corn was not due to the bounty because France, which had no bounty, also enjoyed a similar decline in the price of corn. Smith's strong words are that the decline in price "must have happened in spite of the bounty and cannot possibly have happened in consequence of it." One would think from this claim that there was no theoretical reason to believe that a bounty even *tended* to reduce the price of corn. The theoretical attack on the corn bounty is not the focus of this chapter, but it should be noted that Smith does attempt to make just such an argument in the pages that follow.[31] At one point Smith assesses the tax laid upon the people to support the high prices generated by the bounty to be four shillings a bushel. "Even upon this very moderate supposition," Smith claims that a "very heavy" tax is laid upon the British people to support the bounty. Edwin Cannan comments:

> It is really anything but a moderate supposition. It is not at all likely that the increase of demand caused by the offer of a bounty on exportation would raise the price of a commodity to the extent of four-fifths of the bounty.

Smith goes on to deny at length that the real price of corn is raised at all by the bounty. In support of this proposition Smith claims that "the money price of corn regulates that of all other commodities," a claim modified in the third edition, where "home-made" qualifies "commodities." After a long argument, Smith concludes that "The nature of things has stamped upon corn a real value which cannot be altered by merely altering its money price." If we dismiss the rhetoric about "the nature of things," this is really an empirical proposition. Smith shows no interest in looking for any evidence that would support or refute such an extraordinarily strong proposition. He would not have had to look very far for a model to follow. Arthur Young had considered a similar proposition regarding wages very carefully in *Political Arithmetic* and provided a plenitude of evidence to refute it; indeed, Smith himself appears to have followed Young's lead in the chapter on the "Wages of Labour" in Book I. Sir James Steuart focused on this as the critical point in the Scottish policy debate: "If the Glasgow Merchants *can show from uncontroverted evidence that wages keep pace with the price of oatmeal, rising and falling*, as oatmeal rises or falls, I give up my opposition to their Plan."[32]

Overseas Joint-stock Companies

Attacks on the monopolistic position of many overseas joint-stock companies forms a constant theme of the English pamphlet literature, and the *Wealth of Nations*, as may be expected, takes a strong stand against them:

> The directors of such companies, however, being the managers rather of other people's money than of their own, it cannot well be expected, that they should watch over it with the same anxious vigilance with which the partners in a private copartnery frequently watch over their own. Like the stewards of a rich man, they are apt to consider attention to small matters as not for their master's honour, and very easily give themselves a dispensation from having it. Negligence and profusion, therefore, must always prevail, more or less, in the management of the affairs of such a company. It is upon this account that joint stock companies for foreign trade have seldom been able to maintain the competition against private adventurers. They have, accordingly, very seldom succeeded without an exclusive privilege; and frequently have not succeeded with one. Without an exclusive privilege they have commonly mismanaged the trade. With an exclusive privilege they have both mismanaged and confined it.

The conviction that this description is accurate was apparently buttressed by facts taken from Adam Anderson's *Historical Account . . . of Commerce*. However, Smith does not interpret his facts very carefully in referring to the years between 1681 and 1691 as a period of "great distress" for the East India Company. According to W.R. Scott, the distressed company was providing average dividends of 50 percent per annum for a decade! With the considerable connections of Dundas, Pulteney and, later, Pitt, Smith could have obtained access to the letter books of the company but showed no visible inclination to do so. They would have revealed minute attention to detail and a cry for economy on the part of the directors in London.[33]

Since the root of mismanagement lay in the divided and lowered incentive to efficiency of the management, Smith felt that the profits of the Hudson's Bay Company arose from the fact that it approached a partnership because it had a "very small number of proprietors." When Smith wrote, there were 89 distinct holdings and the number of shareholders appears to have been more numerous in earlier years. Scott's appropriate comment is that Adam Smith "is inclined to ignore its financial successes and to record only the other side—even . . . to assume results to support his pre-conceived opinion."

The first example Smith provided to make his case against monopolistic comments was the Royal African Company. The Company was assumed to have received an effective monopoly by a charter of 1672; to have mismanaged its affairs as a result; and to have failed when it faced private traders after 1688. Walter Galenson has said of this analysis: "Subsequent research has shown that Smith erred in both premises and conclusions." Smith cannot be expected to be aware of "subsequent research," but some of the facts noted by these researchers cannot have been secret in 1776: that the grant of a monopoly was not enough to make it effective; that directors in London tried but could not control the actions of distant agents; that the political power of the West Indian planters was such as to prevent the prosecution of private traders and to prevent collection of the substantial debts owed the Company by the planters.

The political economy of such companies is also neglected by Smith. When he claims that East Indian goods would be cheaper if bought from other European countries, he avoids the emphatic denial of all supporters of the Company since Thomas Mun. Would the Dutch have sold Indian goods as cheaply as the Company did? Assuredly not. Smith's reluctance to grant this point after noting how the Dutch burned half their spice crop to maintain monopoly prices is all the more remarkable.[34]

VI

The *Wealth of Nations* was praised for its factual approach immediately upon publication and a steady chorus of approval has continued to this day. There is no doubt about Smith's ability to bring into significance broad general facts about the growth of civilization. The following link between warfare and opulence is not only interesting in its own right, but it also adds enormously to the book's readability:

> In modern war the great expense of fire-arms gives an evident advantage to the nation which can best afford that expense, and consequently, to an opulent and civilized, over a poor and barbarous nation. In antient times the opulent and civilized found it difficult to defend themselves against the poor and barbarous nations. In modern times the poor and barbarous find it difficult to defend themselves against the opulent and civilized. The invention of fire-arms, an invention which at first sight appears to be so pernicious, is certainly favourable to the permanency and to the extension of civilization.

In addition to this generalized economic history, Smith frequently made claims for more detailed investigations of a more exacting and scholarly nature: for example, when Messance is stated to be a "French author of great knowledge and ingenuity;" when both Bishop Fleetwood and Thomas Ruddiman are criticized for their use of data; or in the glowing acknowledgement to Henry Hope which Smith added in the fourth edition with the claim regarding the Bank of Amsterdam "of which no printed account had ever appeared to me satisfactory, or even intelligible"—these statements are all calculated to suggest a knowledgeable and painstaking scholar.[35]

An examination of Smith's facts and references shows that he sometimes had good judgement in choosing authorities, as in the case of Charles Smith on the corn trade. His reliance upon Adam Anderson's *Origins* for the histories of trading companies misled Smith, according to W.R. Scott. The Reverend Alexander Webster was considered by Smith to be the "most skilful" man in political arithmetic he had known, but James Bonar finds Webster's work to be "full of conjectures, 'computations,' and assumptions," that is, the very defects that brought political arithmetic into disrepute. Smith's wisdom in his choice of sources has thus to be interpreted in a comparative sense: Smith could find out the best available author in a given field, but he did not treat this "best" author with a close, critical eye. Smith characteristically used only one source and used the facts from this source to make his own conjectures. As economic historians have pointed out, the procedure led to mistaken assertions about the behavior of companies. Sometimes his native love of liberty was so strong that he did not look at facts too carefully, as in his claim that slavery was an uneconomic proposition.[36]

Smith's words on some of the policy problems he did treat, such as the Poor Laws, have been characterized as near-propaganda. Bias on such issues must be separated from items which reflect a general philosophical bias, where Smith has a charming weakness for philosophical history.[37] Even though he is, rightly, celebrated as one of the defenders of self-interest, Smith could not resist the picture of feudalism committing euthanasia through trinkets, because it supported the notion of Providence guiding mankind:

> A revolution of the greatest importance to the publick happiness, was in this
> manner brought about by two different orders of people, who had not the least
> intention to serve the publick. To gratify the most childish vanity was the sole
> motive of the great proprietors. The merchants and artificers, much less
> ridiculous, acted merely from a view to their own interest, and in pursuit of
> their own pedlar principle of turning a penny wherever a penny was to be got.
> Neither of them had either knowledge or foresight of that great revolution
> which the folly of the one, and the industry of the other, was gradually bringing
> about.

So far, Smith has mixed success in his attitude to facts. His deficiencies come into sharper focus when we look at his treatment of contemporary policy issues. One of the great surprises here is the number of economic debates he simply avoided discussing in depth. Roughly in order of importance, they are:

1. the question of full employment;
2. the development of underdeveloped regions, such as Ireland or the Scottish Highlands;
3. population in general, and immigration policies in particular;
4. infant industries;
5. enclosures and the efficient size of farms;
6. machinery and its role;
7. the conflict between rich and poor nations.

These omissions only serve to reinforce the points raised earlier by Koebner and Kindleberger that significant quantitative changes seemed to pass Smith by.

In his parting shot at the corn bounty, Smith claims that perfecting the security of property is the real achievement of the Revolution of 1688 and not the corn bounty:

> That system of laws, therefore, which is connected with the establishment of the
> bounty, seems to deserve no part of the praise which has been bestowed upon
> it. The improvement and prosperity of Great Britain, which has been so often
> ascribed to those laws, may very easily be accounted for by other causes. That
> security which the laws in Great Britain give to every man that he shall enjoy
> the fruits of his own labour, is alone sufficient to make any country flourish,
> notwithstanding these and twenty other absurd regulations of commerce; and

this security was perfected by the revolution, much about the same time that the bounty was established.

In view of the myriad of facts that influence the social sciences, it is not unreasonable to call someone a "strong" or an "*a priori*" theorist if some one single factor is claimed to be sufficient to overcome all other potential influences. In this instance Smith's words clearly mark him as an *a priori* theorist. He emphasizes the power of self-interest, when left alone, to be capable, almost by itself, of raising a country to prosperity:

> The natural effort of every individual to better his own condition, when suffered to exert itself with freedom and security, is so powerful a principle, that it is alone, and without any assistance, not only capable of carrying on the society to wealth and prosperity, but of surmounting a hundred impertinent obstructions with which the folly of human laws too often incumbers its operations; though the effect of these obstructions is always more or less either to encroach upon its freedom, or to diminish its security. In Great Britain industry is perfectly secure; and though it is far from being perfectly free, it is as free or freer than in any other part of Europe.[38]

The interpretation of Adam Smith as an *a priori* theorist who used facts solely to corroborate his theories is supported by all the counterfactuals Smith repeatedly uses.[39] It is also suggested by smaller incidents. Smith attributes the freeing of slaves by the Pennsylvania Quakers not to altruism but to the want of profitability, and Smith is confident that corporations were hurting trade in England, a claim that made even admirers ask for the evidence on which this opinion was based.[40]

Smith's desire to uphold the virtues of self-interest and free trade leads him to some simple factual misinterpretations, as noted by W.R. Scott. To enforce his claim that joint-stock companies cannot be successful, Smith considers the wrong ratio indicating the extent to which a joint-stock proprietor will be concerned about the management of the company:

> He regarded the aggregate holding of the management in relation to the total capital of the company as the measure of efficiency, whereas the real standard was the proportion of the original cost of the stock of each individual committee or assistant to his whole wealth. If that proportion were large there were obviously sufficient inducements towards efficiency. Prince Rupert had only £300 original stock in the Hudson's Bay company, but his financial condition was such that this sum was of importance to him, and he appears to have taken a very great interest in the enterprize. In the East India company the qualification of a committee was £1,000 stock, of the governor £4,000, in the Royal African company that of an assistant was £2,000—sums which would

probably be of sufficient importance to most of the adventurers in the
seventeenth century to make them attentive to their duties.

Similarly, we find Smith trying to persuade landowners that they have little
to lose by making the corn trade free; he notes how little is imported under
the existing Corn Laws:

> Even the free importation of foreign control could very little affect the interest
> of the farmers of Great Britain. Corn is a much more bulky commodity than
> butcher's-meat. A pound of wheat at a penny is as near as a pound of butcher's-
> meat at fourpence. The small quantity of foreign corn imported even in times
> of the greatest scarcity, may satisfy our farmers that they can have nothing to
> fear from the freest importation. The average quantity imported one year with
> another, amounts only, according to the very well informed author of the tracts
> upon the corn trade, to twenty-three thousand seven hundred and twenty-eight
> quarters of all sorts of grain, and does not exceed the five hundredth and
> seventy-one part of the annual consumption.

As critics pointed out immediately on the publication of the *Wealth of
Nations*, the existing figures on corn imports were almost irrelevant to what
would happen without the Corn Laws. A slip of lesser significance was
pointed out by David Hume on his first reading of the *Wealth of Nations*.
A seigniorage charge of 8 percent by the French king was implausible,
Hume protested, and Garnier later justified Hume's observation. It would
appear that Smith did not possess much facility for the quantitative
implications of self-interest.[41]

Smith's ability to make acute observations on the behavior of various
classes has been noted earlier. It appears that he had seen corn merchants to
be the most vigorous supporters of the Corn Laws. Smith felt that this was
quite consistent with his theory:

> The corn merchants, the fetchers and carriers of corn between Great Britain and
> foreign countries, would have much less employment, and might suffer
> considerably; but the country gentlemen and farmers could suffer very little. It
> is in the corn merchants accordingly, rather than in the country gentlemen and
> farmers, that I have observed the greatest anxiety for the renewal and
> continuation of the bounty.

A simpler explanation, however, was available to anyone who looked at the
facts about the bounty and the relevant transport costs. Dutch storage costs
were lower than English ones and the bounty was large enough to make it
worthwhile to engage in speculative storage in Holland until English prices
rose. Smith correctly observed how the corn merchants supported the bounty

but did not base his explanation of this interest on a direct examination of the relevant facts. Smith could also be quite oblivious of the noneconomic aspects of an economic measure. In the edition of 1784, he chose to comment at length on the herring bounties, when he had already been Commissioner of Customs for some time, but quite ignored the fact that a major reason for the bounty was the encouragement of seamen.[42]

Sir George Clark has claimed for Adam Smith the position of greatest of economic historians. I am sorry to have provided such a litany of complaints about such an illustrious figure. Having looked at Malthus' use of "facts" in the *Essay on Population* I cannot say that I am entirely surprised.[43] Smith did use an abundance of facts, but he used them to illustrate already established convictions. Perhaps the clearest example is Smith's treatment of a "fact" noted by Sir James Steuart in his *Principles* (1767): the disbanding of soldiers after a war created hardship due to the suddenness of the change, and Steuart (like many contemporaries) felt that the government was obliged to provide assistance to those who had risked their lives for their country. Adam Smith, on the other hand, pointed to the lack of hardship of the disbanded soldiers after the Seven Years War.[44] Smith not only noted that this would support the case for free trade but went a step further and argued that it proved the benefits of abolishing corporations and settlement laws:

> Soldiers and seamen, indeed, when discharged from the king's service, are at liberty to exercise any trade, within any town or place of Great Britain or Ireland. Let the same natural liberty of exercising what species of industry they please be restored to all his majesty's subjects, in the same manner as to soldiers and seamen; that is, break down the exclusive privileges of corporations, and repeal the statute of apprenticeship, both of which are real encroachments upon natural liberty, and add to these the repeal of the law of settlements, so that a poor workman, when thrown out of employment either in one trade or in one place, may see, for it in another trade or in another place, without the fear either of a prosecution or of a removal, and neither the publick nor the individuals will suffer much more from the occasional disbanding some particular classes of manufacturers, than from that of soldiers. Our manufacturers have no doubt great merit with their country, but they cannot have more than those who defend it with their blood, nor deserve to be treated with more delicacy.

What a forcible illustration of the benefits of free trade! Smith's usual source, Richard Burn, does not state the relevant Act, so Smith clearly did some extra work to support his case.[45]

Throughout this chapter, I have tried to separate different levels of facts used in the *Wealth of Nations* and to refer to contemporary usage as the standard of comparison. With the exception of the Reverend Thomas Hepburn's description of the Orkneys, whose factual accuracy I have not checked, in every case the standard of comparison has been Smith's failure to see the theoretical difficulties of his presumed facts or his failure to use facts that were utilized by contemporaries. Some scholars have tried to emphasize the fact that Smith did not write in the age of cliometrics. If this is meant to point out that most of economic literature, including that of today, is full of a similar rhetorical use of facts, it serves the valuable function of reminding us to separate rhetoric from content; but if it is somehow meant to justify Smith's weak use of facts, it only serves to illegitimately lower worthwhile standards. How such an observation bears on the substantive issues discussed in this chapter is thus not at all clear to me, especially since Smith made a definite attempt to present his views as factual.

Given the indiscriminate veneration for Baconian philosophy in Smith's age, any rhetorical strategy not careful about "facts" would face enormous difficulty. Not all facts are equally significant, and I have tried to distinguish the various types used by Smith. The most important class of facts for economic policy did not have a particularly complicated structure in Smith's day, as illustrated by the criticisms of contemporaries, and it is with regard to such "policy facts" that Smith has been found wanting.[46]

Would Adam Smith have been surprised at this portrayal of his own method? Of course he took considerable pains to project the image of someone who kept close to facts. In the appendix to the third edition of the *Wealth of Nations* Smith provided data on the herring fisheries and claimed: "The Reader, I believe, may depend upon the accuracy of both Accounts." T.W. Hutchison quotes Nassau Senior's view that political economy was not "*avide de faits*," and dissents strongly:

> Adam Smith emphatically was "*avide de faits*," and overwhelmingly demonstrated his avidity, and the conception of the subject which this avidity implied, in the *Wealth of Nations*.

It is certainly true that a multitude of factual statements are made in the *Wealth of Nations*; one can see further from Smith's correspondence with Lord Hailes and David Hume that Smith tried hard to obtain historical facts and to form some considered opinion of their accuracy. Thorold Rogers found Adam Smith's views on the late fourteenth and early fifteenth centuries to be inaccurate and commented:

> The ingenious explanation, then, of Adam Smith, that silver was gradually becoming scarcer, . . . is untenable, as Smith himself would have declared had information as to the wages of labour during this period been in his possession.

Such lenient interpretations are entirely justifiable when we consider how scanty was the evidence from those early periods that Smith had to work with.[47] What Smith's admirers constantly imply is that a factual attitude also characterizes Smith's approach to the contemporary economy or to policy issues. Indeed, Thorold Rogers himself does so for Smith's views on the Settlement Laws, but a closer look at contemporary economic changes or at the major policy issues on which Smith spoke does not support this view. By examining closely some of Adam Smith's own words it is possible to get a different picture of his love of accurate facts. After becoming Commissioner of Customs in 1778 he spoke to Sir John Sinclair of his official position as teaching him the value of facts:

> Sir John states that Smith used to admit "that he derived great advantage from the practical information he derived by means of his official situation, and that he would not have otherwise known or believed how essential practical knowledge was to the thorough understanding of political subjects."

Rather a late date to appreciate this point![48] As to Smith's use of conjectural history to supplement his theories, Smith himself was acutely conscious of its limitations. In a letter of 1769 to Lord Hailes, Smith wrote:

> I have read law entirely with a view to form some general notion of the great outlines of the plan according to which justice has been administered in different ages and nations; and I have entered very little into the detail of particulars of which I see your Lordship is very much master. Your Lordship's particular facts will be of great use to correct my general views; but the latter, I fear, will always be too vague and superficial to be of much use to your Lordship.

If only Smith had made public the point that his "general views" were "too vague and superficial" to be of use to historical scholarship![49] Readers would be able to enjoy the *Wealth of Nations* as a superb exposition of moral philosophy but its grand historical impact would be much diminished. On the policy issues that aroused Smith, the intimate relationship between the *Wealth of Nations* and historical facts most resembles that between bulldog and bull; the one was bred to worry the other to death. On issues that are not of immediate concern, the facts still play a subordinate role: they are occasionally allowed to murmur, seldom to speak.

APPENDIX

The following numbers indicate the pages where the editor's notes indicate some discrepancy or error in Adam Smith's references or statements:

Edwin Cannan (New York: Modern Library, 1937)
   pp. 10, 18, 23, 26-7, 45, 61, 77, 119, 122, 133-4, 142, 148, 151, 156, 171, 173,
   178, 182-3, 194, 199, 213, 245, 290, 295, 375, 399, 400, 428, 430, 445, 495, 499,
   503, 513, 518, 537, 545, 547, 550, 554, 608, 615, 655, 663, 676, 685, 688, 702-3,
   763, 770, 842, 881.

R.H. Campbell and A.S. Skinner (Oxford: Oxford University Press, 1976)
   Vol. I: pp. 19, 20, 62, 77, 79, 92, 94, 99, 102, 137, 152, 156, 167, 179, 182, 187,
   192, 195, 198, 203, 204, 213, 216, 218, 222, 250, 263, 267, 302, 304, 313, 315,
   404, 417, 418, 425, 442, 443, 461, 462, 493, 518, 519, 526.
   Vol. II: pp. 547, 551, 587, 598, 727, 730, 740, 742-3, 754, 758, 803, 837, 862,
   867, 948.

I have tried to avoid duplications between the two editions. Since the list is only meant to be illustrative, I make no claims for completeness.

NOTES

In order to avoid excessive length, notes are collected together at the end of each paragraph when possible. The Bicentennial edition of the *Wealth of Nations* is referred to as Smith (1976a). Full details of the works cited are provided in the Reference section at the end of the chapter.

1. Fay (1950); Scott (1912); Hutchison (1988); Viner (1967); Raphael (1985), 73, 92, also see 105.
2. Mirowski (1982); Campbell and Skinner, in Smith (1976a), 51, 59, 60; Judges (1939), 40, voices a mild version of Campbell and Skinner's views.
3. Smith (1976a), 227, 727.
4. Stewart (1793), in Stewart, *Collected Works*, Vol. 10, 33, 34; Wightman (1975), 51; Smith (1976a), 25. D.D. Raphael (1985) notes Smith's speculations on the origins of language as an obvious example of conjectural history and seems inclined to add the four-stages view of history to the same category. As I agree with Raphael on the conjectural nature of the four-stages theory, this view will be given minimal attention.
5. Smith (1976a), 422.
6. Smith (1976a), 729-30 (Bernier), 887-8 (liquor tax); Smith editions: Playfair (1805); Buchanan (1814); McCulloch (1843); Wakefield (1843); Rogers (1880); Cannan (1937); Campbell and Skinner (1976). These appear to be the principal English editors of the *Wealth of Nations*.
7. Smith (1976a), 177.
8. Smith (1976a), 781-2.
9. Stewart (1793), 36.

10. Smith (1976a), 572. Smith's description is substantially accurate; see Alston and Shapiro (1984), 277-85. This paper also contains references to further issues related to inheritance laws.
11. Smith (1976a), 929.
12. Ibid., 639, 640; Bolts (1772). Smith's discussion of the American colonies, an issue he was much involved with, is certainly not replete with figures. Apart from some six pages discussing the enumerated commodities and the later use of tobacco as an example, no data are to be found. When Smith's prediction of an economic distress following the nonimportation Act of 1774 is not borne out, Smith refers to "Five different events, unforeseen and unthought of" as responsible. If Smith's primary authority is the Reverend Josiah Tucker, who was notorious for his demands that Britain set America free, the pattern with the National Debt and the East India Company will have been continued, i.e., the use of a single source and the use of counterfactuals when faced with "unexpected" facts.
13. Kindleberger (1976); Hartwell (1976); Smith (1976a).
14. Koebner (1959), 382. In his *Anecdotes and Characters*, Alexander Carlyle (1973, 185-9) records some casual observations of Birmingham obtained during a stop on a stage-coach journey. Smith too must have travelled along the same route and the general resemblance of their observation is curious.
15. Kindleberger (1976), 4, 6; Hollander (1973), 105. A recent Scottish economic historian (Lenman, 1981, 86) writes of Smith that:

> it was his fate to become a cult-figure for middle-class, liberal industrialists and bankers of the nineteenth and twentieth centuries. They read and misread him in the light of their own circumstances. He knew only his own. Of mechanized industrial production, be it said, he knew virtually nothing. Linen production, or nail-making were both to him essentially handcraft industries. The great engine of economic growth to Smith is therefore not mechanization.

Viner (1965), 96, points out that Smith's attack on the bounties follow the lines established by David Loch (1775) and James Anderson (1777).
16. These points are also considered by Pesciarelli (1989), who comes to a rather different conclusion.
17. Smith (1976a), 66-7.
18. Smith (1976a); Smith (1976b), 215.
19. Rae (1895), 229.
20. Smith (1976a), 418-19; Hilton (1969), 30, 42, 58, casts doubt on the accuracy of Smith's account. In correspondence, Professor Hilton has expressed the opinion that Smith was a seminal thinker but not a historian. Thorold Rogers considers the case to be more ambiguous in that the stock and land lease differed in several respects from metayage (Rogers, 1884, 281).

   Brodrick (1881), 17, had earlier noted the existence of share-leasing in the fourteenth century. Brodrick provides an interesting example of an historian who relies frequently on the *Wealth of Nations* for his facts (39, 49, 58, 63).

   The debate over Henry VII's role is well described in Forbes (1984), 312-13.
21. Anderson (1801), II, 17, 24, 52, 61. There is a brief biographical account of Adam Anderson in Joseph Dorfman's Introduction to the Augustus Kelley reprint.
22. Hepburn ([1757] 1885), 12-29. I have been unable to find any biographical details about the Reverend Hepburn. For Samuel Johnson, see Middendorf (1960) and Selwyn (1979).
23. Wilson (1968); Davis (1966), 307.

24. Smith (1976a), I, 248, 252; John Smith (1747).
25. Smith (1976a), 647-8, 618.
26. Smith (1976a), 546-8; Smith, ed. Cannan (1937). I am indebted to an unpublished essay by Jose Vidal on this topic.
27. Brougham (1803), 541-3.
28. Smith (1976a), 151-8; Burn (1764), 130, 235-6.
29. Smith (1976a), 157; Hay (1735).
30. Howlett (1796), 9; Eden (1928), 52-5. Dugald Stewart is unhappy with the criticisms of Howlett and Eden but he is unable to produce any new facts to support his dissent. Stewart uses the authority of Sir William Young to insist that prosecutions due to the Law of Settlements were frequent (Stewart, 1877, 267-9).
31. Charles Smith (1766); Smith (1976a), 507.
32. Smith, ed. Cannan (1937), 475; Smith (1976a), 515; Young (1774). Quoted by Skinner, in Steuart (1966), liv.
33. Anderson (1801); Smith (1976a), 741.
34. Scott (1912), 450; Galenson (1986), 145-50. Anderson and Tollison (1982) claim to rehabilitate Smith's analysis of the joint-stock company. The theoretical criteria they employ—such as the use of survivorship or the references to principal-agent problems—are questionable but are not of concern here; their claim that Smith's theory was "consistent with the available empirical evidence" is. Anderson and Tollison simply do not meet the direct evidence provided by Scott (1912) and quoted above, e.g., the number of partners in the Hudson's Bay Company. The method they employ is unsatisfactory. Smith, let us suppose, saw banking as a successful joint-stock operation. For Smith to deduce from here that its success was due to the "mechanical" nature of banking is a theoretical deduction, not an empirical observation. Nor was I able to locate the fact of Smith's views being ready by 1774 in the letter that Anderson and Tollison (ibid., 1240) refer to.
35. Raphael (1985); Smith (1976a), 708.
36. Viner (1965), 87. One puzzle here is Smith's failure to condemn the slavery of Scottish colliers in the *Wealth of Nations*, something he had done in his *Lectures*. Anderson's (1989) suggestion that Smith may have been tactful about his mine-owning friends is implausible, because a young professor should have been much more sensitive about giving offense than an established and famous moral philosopher.
37. Wightman (1975), 45. Viner (1965), 88-101, discusses Smith's failure to consider the problems of the Highlands. For more recent discussions of some relevant aspects of Scottish economic history, see Payne (1967). Brougham (1803), 531-2, note G, gives evidence to dispute Smith's claim, 1976a, 587, that slaves are better treated in absolute governments than under republican ones. Also see Anderson (1989). It is curious how Brougham, like so many others, is skeptical of several of Smith's facts as they relate to his own field, but is quite happy to accept Smith's authority for points not under his direct purview (Brougham, 1803, note M).
38. Smith (1976a), 540.
39. Samuel Hollander's position on Adam Smith's relation to facts is not entirely clear. Newton is said to have greatly influenced Smith, but Smith's contention that gravitation was "so familiar a principle" sounds strange. Indeed, the idea of action at a distance implied by gravitation aroused much contemporary dissent. Hollander (1987) also says that "Smith was a great economic historian" (310-12). However, Hollander goes on to argue that Smith used examples to illustrate (and not to deduce) the power of self-interest; that Smith viewed "the direct (inductive) use of data as an impotent procedure;" that Anderson was right in attacking Smith's assumption of the constant real value of corn and

Pownall in attacking Smith's resort to "unforeseen and unthought of events" to save his hypothesis (314-23). This chapter agrees with the latter half of Hollander's position; indeed Hollander himself stresses this view in his defense of David Ricardo.

40. One has to be careful to distinguish between two propositions. First, that, other things being equal, the profitability of slave-owning made slavery desirable. Secondly, that of all factors influencing the decision to uphold slavery, profitability is the most important one. The first proposition is relatively innocuous. The second proposition implies what has been termed the "economistic" outlook, or more recently, "economic imperialism," and is much more controversial. Soderlund (1985) does not quite clarify issues. That religious sect had some influence appears from the considerable difference between the proportions of Anglican and Quaker slaveholders (155); that ethnicity was important is clear from the eschewing of slavery by Germans, despite the absence of any formal discouragements (159). How much remains for economics? Even here, the argument (162-6) that wealthy people supported slavery is apparently contradicted by the later claim (169) that middling Quakers persisted in hiring slaves. Evidence of moral influences on slaveholding is also found earlier (137-43). Eden (1928), 91.

41. Smith (1976a), 461; Scott (1912), 452; *Corn-Bill Hints* (1777).

42. Smith (1976a), 461; Westerfield (1915), 164-6; Viner (1965), 97.

43. As quoted by Hutchison (1976), 509 fn; Rashid (1987).

44. Wilberforce used this example, but in garbled fashion, in his speech to ban the slave-trade: in Hansard (1793).

45. Steuart (1966), I, 122. For the attention highly placed Scotsmen gave to this issue, see *Selections from the Caldwell Papers* (Glasgow, 1883), 166-208; Smith (1976a), 469-70. It would be interesting to know who was right about the transition from war to peace.

46. It is far too often assumed that the extant knowledge and academic standards of Adam Smith's day were so different from our own as to make modern standards quite inapplicable. See Chapter 9 on this point.

47. Hutchison (1988), 357; Knox (1789) disputed Smith's figures on the fisheries; Smith (1976f), 139; Rogers (1884), 276.

48. Rae (1895), 332. Viner (1965), 99, notes how one of the most pressing issues concerning the fisheries was the salt-tax. Since Smith was Commissioner of the Salt Duties as well as Commissioner of Customs he should have been carefully apprised of the situation. Nonetheless, Viner records that "There is no hint in *The Wealth of Nations* . . . that there was anything wrong . . . with respect to the British salt taxes."

49. Smith (1976f), 247.

REFERENCES

Alston, L.J. and M.O. Shapiro (1984) "Inheritance Laws Across Colonies: Causes and Consequences," *Journal of Economic History* (June), 277-85.

Anderson, Adam (1801) *Historical and Chronological Deduction of the Origin of Commerce* (London; reprinted New York: Augustus Kelley, 1967), 4 vols.

Anderson, G.M. (1988) "Mr Smith and the Preachers: The Economics of Religion in the *Wealth of Nations*," *Journal of Political Economy* **96**(3), 1066-88.

_____ (1989) "The Butcher, the Baker, and the Policy-maker: Adam Smith on Public Choice," *History of Political Economy* **21**(4), 641-59.

____, W. Shugart III and R.D. Tollison (1985) "Adam Smith in the Customhouse," *Journal of Political Economy* **93**(3), 740-59.

____ and R.D. Tollison (1982) "Adam Smith's Analysis of Joint-stock Companies," *Journal of Political Economy* **90**(4), 1237-56.

Anderson, James (1777) *Observations on the Means of Exciting a Spirit of National Industry* (Edinburgh).

Appleby, J.O. (1978) *Economic Thought and Ideology in Seventeenth Century England* (Princeton, N.J.: Princeton University Press).

Barnes, D.G. (1965) *A History of the English Corn Laws* (New York: Augustus Kelley, 1965; first published, 1930).

Blackstone, William (1973) *The Sovereignty of the Law: Selections from Blackstone's Commentaries on the Laws of England* (Toronto: Toronto University Press).

Bolts, William (1772) *Considerations on India Affairs . . .* (London).

Bowley, Marian (1973) *Studies in the History of Economic Theory before 1870* (London: Macmillan).

Brodrick, G.C. (1881) *English Land and English Landlords* (London: Cassell, Pelter, Galpin).

Brougham, Henry (1803) *An Inquiry into the Colonial Policy of the European Powers* (Edinburgh: Balfour), 2 vols.

Buchholz, Todd G. (1989) *New Ideas from Dead Economists* (New York: New American Library).

Burn, Richard (1764) *The History of the Poor Laws* (London: Millar; reprinted New York: Augustus Kelley, 1973).

Campbell, R.H. and A.S. Skinner (1982) *Adam Smith* (New York: St Martin's Press).

Cannan, E. (1926) "Adam Smith as an Economist," *Economica* **6**, 123-34.

____ (1930) *A Review of Economic Theory* (London: P.S. King).

____ (1953) *History of the Theories of Production and Distribution*, 3rd edn (London: Staples).

Carlyle, Alexander (1973) *Anecdotes and Characters of the Times*, ed. James Kinsley (London: Oxford University Press).

Chalmers, George (1804) *An Estimate of the Comparative Strength of Great Britain*, new edn (London: Stockdale).

Child, Sir Josiah (1968) *Selected Works, 1688-1697* (Farnborough, Hants.: Gregg Reprints).

Clark, J.M., ed. (1928), *Adam Smith 1776-1926* (Chicago: University of Chicago Press).

Cobbett, William, ed. (1812) *The Parliamentary History of England* (London: Hansard).

Colander, D.C. and A.W. Coats, eds (1989) *The Spread of Economic Ideas* (Cambridge: Cambridge University Press).

Corn-Bill Hints in Answer to the Memorial for the Merchants, Traders, and Manufacturers of the City of Glasgow (Glasgow, 1777).

Cornish, W.R. and G. de N. Clark (1989) *Law and Society in England, 1750-1950* (London: Sweet & Maxwell).

Davis, Ralph (1954) "English Foreign Trade, 1660-1700," *Economic History Review* **VII**(2), 257-72.

____ (1966) "The Rise of Protection in England, 1689-1786," *Economic History Review* **XIX**(2), 306-17.

Defoe, Daniel (1730) *A Plan of the English Commerce*, 2nd edn (London: Rivington); reprinted New York: Augustus Kelley, 1967).

Dicey, A.V. (1914) *Law and Opinion in England* (London: Macmillan).

Eden, F.M. (1928) *The State of the Poor*, ed. A.G.L. Rogers (London: Routledge).

Evensky, Jerry (1987) "The Two Voices of Adam Smith: Moral Philosopher and Social Critic," *History of Political Economy* **19**(3), 447-68.

____ (1989) "The Evolution of Adam Smith's Views on Political Economy," *History of Political Economy* **21**(1), 123-46.

Fay, C.R. (1950) *Great Britain from Adam Smith to the Present Day*, 5th edn (London: Longmans & Green).

____ (1956) *Adam Smith and the Scotland of His Day* (Cambridge: Cambridge University Press).

____ (1960) *The World of Adam Smith* (Cambridge: Heffner).

Fisher, H.E.S. and A.R.J. Jurica (1977) *Documents in the English Economic History* (London: Bell), 2 vols.

Forbes, Duncan (1984) *Hume's Philosophical Politics* (Cambridge: Cambridge University Press).

Galenson, D.W. (1986), *Traders, Planters and Slaves* (Cambridge: Cambridge University Press).

Grampp, W.D. (1986) "The Liberal Elements in English Mercantilism," *Quarterly Journal of Economics* **62**(4), 465-501.

Gray, Sir Alexander (1948) *Adam Smith* (London: G. Philip).

Grice-Hutchison, Marjorie (1978) *Early Economic Thought in Spain, 1177-1740* (London: Allen & Unwin).

Haldane, J.B. (1884) *Adam Smith* (London).

Hartwell, R.M. (1976) "Comment" on Kindleberger (1976), in T. Wilson and A.S. Skinner, eds, *The Market and the State* (Oxford: Clarendon Press), 33-41.

Hasek, C.W. (1925) *The Introduction of Adam Smith's Doctrines into Germany* (New York: Columbia University Press).

Hay, William (1735) *Remarks on Laws Relating to the Poor* (London).

Heckscher, Eli (1955), *Mercantilism*, rev. edn (London: Allen & Unwin), 2 vols.

Hepburn, Thomas (1760) *A Letter to a Gentleman from His Friend in Orkney* (reprinted Edinburgh: William Brown, 1885).

Hilton, R.H. (1969) *The Decline of Serfdom in Medieval England* (London: Macmillan).

Hirst, Francis (1904) *Adam Smith* (New York: Macmillan).

Hollander, Samuel (1973) *The Economics of Adam Smith* (Toronto: University of Toronto Press).

____ (1987) *Classical Economics* (New York: Basil Blackwell).

Howlett, John (1796) *Examination of Mr Pitt's Speech on the Poor Laws* (London).

Hutcheson, Francis (1969) *Collected Works of Francis Hutcheson* (Hildscheim: George Elms).

Hutchison, T.W. (1976) "Adam Smith and the *Wealth of Nations*," *Journal of Law and Economics* **19**(3), 507-27.

——— (1988) *Before Adam Smith* (New York: Basil Blackwell).

Johnson, E.A.J. (1937) *Predecessors of Adam Smith* (New York: Prentice-Hall).

Judges, A.V. (1939) "The Idea of a Mercantile State," *Transactions of the Royal Historical Society*, 4th series, vol. 21, 41-69.

Kindleberger, Charles (1976) "The Historical Background: Adam Smith and the Industrial Revolution," in T. Wilson and A.S. Skinner, eds, *The Market and the State* (Oxford: Clarendon Press), 1-25.

Knox, John (1789) *A View of the British Empire*, 4th edn (London).

Koebner, Richard (1959) "Adam Smith and the Industrial Revolution," *Economic History Review*, 2nd ser., **XI**(3), 381-91.

Lambert, Sheila, ed. (1975) *House of Commons Sessional Papers* (Wilmington, Del.: Scholarly Resources), vol. 19.

Lauderdale, Earl of (1804) *An Inquiry into the Nature and Origin of Public Wealth* (Edinburgh: Constable).

Lenman, Bruce (1981) *Integration, Enlightenment and Industrialisation: Scotland, 1746-1832* (Toronto: University of Toronto Press).

Letwin, William (1964) *The Origins of Scientific Economics* (New York: Doubleday).

Levy, David (1978) "Adam Smith, Natural Law, and Contractual Society," *Journal of the History of Ideas* **39**(4), 665-74.

——— (1987) "Adam Smith's Case for Usury Laws," *History of Political Economy* **19**(3), 387-400.

Lipson, Ephraim (1956) *The Economic History of England*, 6th edn (London: A. & C. Black), 3 vols.

Loch, David (1775) *Essays on the Trade, Commerce and Manufactures of Scotland* (Edinburgh).

Macfie, A.L. (1967) *The Individual in Society* (London: Allen & Unwin).

Magnusson, Lars (1987) "Mercantilism and 'Reform' Mercantilism: The Rise of Economic Discourse in Sweden during the Eighteenth Century," *History of Political Economy* **19**(3), 415-33.

——— (1988) "Corruption and Civic Order: Natural Law and Economic Discourse in Sweden during the Age of Freedom," *Scandinavian Economic History Review* **XXXV**, 78-105.

McNally, David (1988) *Political Economy and the Rise of Capitalism* (Berkeley, Cal.: University of California Press).

Middendorf, J.H. (1960) "Dr Johnson and Mercantilism," *Journal of the History of Ideas* **XXXI**, 66-83.

Mirowski, Philip (1982) "Adam Smith, Empiricism, and the Rate of Profit in Eighteenth Century England," *History of Political Economy* **14**(2), 178-98.

Mizuta, Hiroshi (1967) *Adam Smith's Library* (Cambridge: Cambridge University Press).

Mui, H.C. and L.C. Mui (1984) *The Management of Monopoly* (Vancouver, B.C.: University of British Columbia Press).

Nicholson, J.S. (1909) *A Project of Empire* (London: Macmillan).

O'Brien, Gerald, ed. (1989) *Parliament, Politics and People* (Dublin: Academic Press).

O'Driscoll, G.P. (1979) *Adam Smith and Modern Political Economy* (Ames: Iowa State University Press).

Pagano, Ugo (1985) *Work and Welfare in Economic Theory* (New York: Basil Blackwell).

Payne, P.L. (1967) *Studies in Scottish Business History* (London: Cass).

Perelman, Michael (1984) *Classical Political Economy* (London: Rowman & Allanheld).

____ (1989) "Adam Smith and Dependent Social Relations," *History of Political Economy* **21**(3), 503-21.

Perlman, Morris (1989) "Adam Smith and the Paternity of the Real Bills Doctrine," *History of Political Economy* **21**(1), 77-90.

Pesciarelli, Enzo (1989) "Smith, Bentham, and the Development of Contrasting Ideas on Entrepreneurship," *History of Political Economy* **21**(3), 521-36.

Pocock, J.G.A. (1957) *The Ancient Constitution and the Feudal Law* (Cambridge: Cambridge University Press).

____ (1975) *The Machiavellian Moment* (Princeton, N.J.: Princeton University Press).

Rae, John (1895) *Life of Adam Smith* (London: Macmillan; reprinted New York: Augustus Kelley, 1965).

Raphael, D.D. (1985) *Adam Smith* (Oxford: Oxford University Press).

Rashid, S. (1987) "The *Essay on Population*, the Facts of Super-growth and the Rhetoric of Scientific Persuasion," *Journal of the History of the Behavioral Sciences* **23**, 22-36.

Rogers, J.R.T. (1884) *Six Centuries of Work and Wages* (New York: Putnam).

Scott, W.R. (1900) *Francis Hutcheson* (Cambridge: Cambridge University Press; reprinted New York: Augustus Kelley, 1966).

____ (1912) *The Constitution and Finance of English, Scottish and Irish Joint-stock Companies* (Cambridge: Cambridge University Press).

____ (1937) *Adam Smith as Student and Professor* (Glasgow: Jackson).

Selwyn, Percy (1979) "Johnson's Hebrides: Thoughts on a Dying Social Order," *Development and Change* **X**, 345-61.

Semmel, Bernard (1970) *The Rise of Free Trade Imperialism* (Cambridge: Cambridge University Press).

Skinner, A.S. and T. Wilson (1975) *Essays on Adam Smith* (Oxford: Clarendon Press).

Smith, Adam (1776) *An Inquiry into the Nature and Causes of the Wealth of Nations* (Cardon: Cadell & Strahan).

____ (1805) *An Inquiry . . .*, ed. William Playfair (London: Murray).

____ (1814) *An Inquiry . . .*, ed. David Buchanan (London: Murray).

____ (1843a) *An Inquiry . . .*, ed. E.G. Wakefield (London: Murray).

_____ (1843b) *An Inquiry . . .*, ed. J.R. McCulloch (Edinburgh: A. & C. Black).

_____ (1880) *An Inquiry . . .*, ed. J.E. Thorold Rogers (Oxford: Clarendon Press).

_____ (1937) *An Inquiry . . .*, ed. Edwin Cannan (New York: Modern Library).

_____ (1976a) *An Inquiry . . .*, ed. R.H. Campbell and A.S. Skinner (Oxford: Oxford University Press).

_____ (1976b) *The Theory of Moral Sentiments*, ed. A.L. Macfie and D.D. Raphael (Oxford: Oxford University Press for the Bicentennial).

_____ (1976c) *Essays on Philosophical Subjects*, ed. W.P.D. Wightman (Oxford: Oxford University Press for the Bicentennial).

_____ (1976d) *Lectures on Rhetoric and Belles Lettres*, ed. J.C. Bryce (Oxford: Oxford University Press for the Bicentennial).

_____ (1976e) *Lectures on Jurisprudence*, ed. R.L. Meek, D.D. Raphael and P.G. Stein (Oxford: Oxford University Press for the Bicentennial).

_____ (1976f) *Correspondence of Adam Smith*, ed. E.C. Mossner and J.S. Ross (Oxford: Oxford University Press for the Bicentennial).

Smith, Charles (1766) *Three Tracts on the Corn Trade and the Corn Laws* (London).

Smith, John (1747) *Chronicon Rusticum: Commercials or Memoirs of Wool*, 2 vols. (London: Osborne); reprinted New York: Augustus Kelley, 1969).

Soderlund, Jean (1985) *Quakers and Slavery* (Princeton, N.J.: Princeton University Press).

Speck, W.A. (1983) *Society and Literature in England, 1700-60* (Dublin: Humanities Press).

Steuart, Sir James (1767) *An Inquiry into the Principles of Political Economy* (reprinted, ed. A.S. Skinner, London: Oliver & Boyd, 1966).

Stewart, Dugald (1858-78) *The Collected Works of Dugald Stewart*, ed. Sir W. Hamilton (Edinburgh: Constable), 10 vols.

_____ (1877) *Lectures on Political Economy*, vols 8 and 9 of the *Collected Works* (Edinburgh: Constable).

Sutherland, Lucy (1984) *Politics and Finance in the Eighteenth Century* (London: Hambledon).

Suviranta, Bruno (1923) *The Theory of the Balance of Trade in England* (Helsingfors; reprinted New York: Augustus Kelley, 1967).

Teichgraber, R.F. (1987) "'Less Abused Than I Had Reason to Expect': The Reception of the *Wealth of Nations* in Britain, 1776-1790," *Historical Journal* **30**, 337-66.

Thirsk, Joan and J.P. Cooper, eds (1972) *Seventeenth-century Economic Documents* (Oxford: Clarendon Press).

Tuck, Richard (1979) *Natural-rights Theories* (Cambridge: Cambridge University Press).

Viner, Jacob (1960) "The Intellectual History of Laissez-faire," *Journal of Law and Economics* **3**, 45-69.

_____ (1965) "Introduction," John Rae, *Life of Adam Smith* (New York: Augustus Kelley).

_____ (1967) "Adam Smith," in *International Encyclopaedia of the Social Sciences* (New York: Macmillan).

Walker, D.A., ed. (1989) *Perspectives on the History of Economic Thought* (Aldershot, Hants.: Edward Elgar).

Wallace, Robert (1763) *Characteristics of the Present Political State of Great Britain* (London: Millar; reprinted New York: Augustus Kelley Reprint, 1969).

Westerfield, R.B. (1915) *Middlemen in English Business* (New Haven, Conn.: Yale University Press).

Wightman, W.P.D. (1975) "Adam Smith and the History of Ideas," in *Essays on Adam Smith*, ed. A.S. Skinner and Thomas Wilson (Oxford: Clarendon Press).

Willis, Kirk (1979) "The Role in Parliament of the Economic Ideas of Adam Smith, 1776-1800," *History of Political Economy* **11**(4), 505-44.

Wilson, Charles (1968) "Government Policy and Private Interest in Modern English History," *Historical Studies* **VI**, 85-100.

Wilson, T. and A.S. Skinner, *The Market and the State* (Oxford: Clarendon Press).

Wood, J.C. (1984) *Adam Smith: Critical Assessments*, 4 vols (London: Croom Helm).

Young, Arthur (1774) *Political Arithmetic* (London: Nicoll; reprinted New York: Augustus Kelley, 1967).

5. Public Finance*

I

Book V of the *Wealth of Nations*, which deals with public finance, is by far the most pleasant book of the *Wealth of Nations*. While discussing the expenditures and revenues of the state, Smith has an opportunity to pass judgement on issues of general interest such as education and religion. He does not hesitate to speak his mind on occasion, and whether one agrees or disagrees it is instructive to see an educated mind analyzing the workings of society; in particular, the section on the provision of education and the division of labor are eloquent and instructive.

Even though the book is very long, it is divided into only three chapters. Chapter 1 deals with the proper objects of government expenditure, Chapter 2 deals with the possible sources of government revenue, principally taxation, and the third chapter discusses the public debt. There is very little economic analysis in the first and third chapters so an analytical survey of Book V is perforce largely restricted to the chapter on taxation. Nonetheless, some of his peculiar judgements are worth careful reading, such as his dictum that joint-stock companies cannot succeed in any innovative enterprise because they excessively dilute the responsibility of those at the top:

> The directors of such companies, however, being the managers rather of other people's money than of their own, it cannot well be expected, that they should watch over it with the same anxious vigilance with which the partners in a private copartnery frequently watch over their own. . . . Negligence and profusion, therefore must always prevail, more or less, in the management.[1]

As a consequence, Smith found the companies suitable for joint-stock organization to be very few:

*I am grateful to the participants at the History of Economics Meeting, Boston, 1987, for their comments and especially to R.D.C. Black, Mark Blaug, James Earley, and Michael Perelman.

The only trades which it seems possible for a joint stock company to carry on successfully, without an exclusive privilege, are those, of which all the operations are capable of being reduced to what is called a Routine, or to such a uniformity of method as admits of little or no variation. Of this kind is, first, the banking trade; secondly, the trade of insurance from fire, and from sea risk and capture in time of war; thirdly, the trade of making and maintaining a navigable cut or canal; and, fourthly, the similar trade of bringing water for the supply of a great city.[2]

A curious list, in view of the widespread prevalence of joint-stock companies today. Smith's list reads strangely to an economic historian:

Joint-stock banking, at its inception, was full of surprises, and each institution had different methods. . . . Now, if routine had been the main element in success, it would be difficult to quote any class of business more subject to surprises, and certainly there was very little that was not purely experimental in the first quarter of a century of the history of the Bank of England. Thus if "absence of variation" was the true criterion of success, this institution should not, indeed it might almost be said *could* not, have made its footing good. Methods of insurance, too, were in a constant state of flux; there was no routine, for (except in marine risks) there was no definite knowledge to be taken as a guide.[3]

Smith's biting description of Oxford has often been noted:

In the university of Oxford, the greater part of the publick professors have, for these many years, given up altogether even the pretence of teaching. . . .
 If the teacher happens to be a man of sense, it must be an unpleasant thing to him to be conscious, while he is lecturing his students, that he is either speaking or reading nonsense, or what is very little better than nonsense. . . . The teacher, instead of explaining to his pupils himself, the science in which he proposes to instruct them, may read some book upon it; and if this book is written in a foreign and dead language, by interpreting it to them into their own; or, what would give him still less trouble, by making them interpret it to him, and by now and then making an occasional remark upon it, he may flatter himself that he is giving a lecture. The slightest degree of knowledge and application will enable him to do this without exposing himself to contempt or derision, or saying any thing that is really foolish, absurd, or ridiculous.[4]

His condemnation of the practice of educating young men by sending them on a tour of the Continent under the guardianship of a tutor has so much sarcasm that is worth repeating:

Our young people, it is said, generally return home much improved by their travels. A young man who goes abroad at seventeen or eighteen, and returns home at one and twenty, returns three or four years older than he was when he went abroad; and at that age it is very difficult not to improve a good deal in three or four years. . . . [H]e commonly returns home more conceited, more unprincipled, more dissipated, and more incapable of any serious application either to study or to business, than he could well have become in so short a time, had he lived at home. . . . By sending his son abroad, a father delivers himself, at least for some time, from so disagreeable an object as that of a son unemployed, neglected, and going to ruin before his eyes.[5]

We should not see these views of Smith as either idiosyncratic or unusually perceptive. Other thoughtful contemporaries also came to similar conclusions. For example, the Reverend Richard Watson, professor at Cambridge, and later a bishop, urged the introduction of commercial studies (using such authors as Davenant and Postlethwayt) and pointed out the evils of the "grand tour" as an educational practice:

[W]hose fault is it that young men of fortune stay not more years with us, and reside not amongst us more months in every year? Why must they, as soon as they have huddled through six or eight Terms, be hurried abroad as if it were from an apprehension, that they have learned as much as an English University can teach them? Foreign travel is of great use, when it is undertaken by men who have learned to bring their passions under the control of Reason and Religion; who have had some experience in life, acquired some knowledge of the manufactures, policy, revenues, and resources of their own country; the acquaintance of such men will be sought after by persons of character and learning in every country they pass through, they will be in a condition to receive, because they will possess the ability of communicating knowledge. But the present mode of sending our young men into France and Italy tends only to fill Great Britain with dabblers in Virtu, pretenders in Taste, sociolists in Literature, and Infidels in Religion.[6]

Basing his views on the general efficiency of specialization, Smith opposed the formation of a militia and supported instead a professional army. This aroused the ire of several Scots, such as Adam Ferguson, and Alexander Carlyle tried to hoist Smith with his own petard by turning Smith against himself. Smith's support for a professional army was based on the view that modern warfare is more difficult and more horrid than in ancient times, as well as on the aversion of modern manufacturers and husbandmen to engage in warfare. Carlyle argues that the facts do not support Smith's presumption about the martial capacities of manufacturers and husbandmen. He then goes on to quote Smith's view that "A militia of any kind, which has served several successive campaigns in the field, becomes in every respect a standing army."[7] This observation serves very well Carlyle's purposes in demonstrating that militias can rapidly become serviceable. (Carlyle elides Smith's "several successive campaigns" into a "few" campaigns.) When Smith says a little later that raw troops under fire turn into veterans, Carlyle has good reason to exult:

> He [Smith] mentions the valour of the Russians in Poland, in the year 1756; and that of the English in the year 1739, after a peace of twenty-eight years, when no soldier of our army could ever have seen an enemy. Surprising indeed, that there should be so much virtue in a name, as to make the very same kind of men, artizans, husbandmen, and manufacturers, heroes when called a standing army, and poltroons when called a militia; though in the very same state with respect to exercise and discipline.[8]

Carlyle finds the strength of Smith's case to rest largely in an abuse of language:

> Our author through the whole of his observations on history, seems to me to have inadvertently put the change upon his reader and on himself, whenever it served to support his own opinion. When troops are successful, whatever they were before, he honours them with the name of a standing army: and whenever they are defeated, he degrades them to a militia. The Romans for instance, the most warlike people on earth, lost the battle of Canne, says he, because they were only a militia, and could not resist the standing army of Hannibal. But when Hannibal is defeated on the plains of Zama, it was because this standing army was much reduced: and united with other forces of Carthage, was now become a militia; whereas the Romans under Scipio were a standing army.[9]

It is unique for Smith not to have made a more positive gesture towards a militia in view of the support given the militia by several of his friends as well as Smith's general appreciation of martial qualities, a point emphasized by Carlyle and described below.

The extent to which Adam Smith relies on a general societal framework to infuse values and norms is nowhere more evident than in his recommendation that the state provide public education in order to prevent the monotony and routine of the worker's life deadening his intellectual faculties. The following quote has been frequently repeated but it is such a pleasure to read that I must use it again:

> In the progress of the division of labour, the employment of the greater part of those who live by labour, that is, of the great body of the people, comes to be confined to a few very simple operations, frequently to one or two. But the

understandings of the greater part of men are necessarily formed by their ordinary employments. The man whose whole life is spent in performing a few simple operations, of which the effects too are, perhaps, always the same, or very nearly the same, has no occasion to exert his understanding, or to exercise his invention in finding out expedients for removing difficulties which never occur. He naturally loses, therefore, the habit of such exertion, and generally becomes as stupid and ignorant as it is possible for a human creature to become.[10]

Although it has been less noticed, Smith's sentiments on the necessity of maintaining the warlike spirit of a people are even more remarkable. The fact that he loathes a spirit of cowardice even if it were to arise freely in a people is worth emphasizing:

a coward, a man incapable either of defending or of revenging himself, evidently wants one of the most essential parts of the character of a man. He is as much mutilated and deformed in his mind, as another is in his body, who is either deprived of some of its most essential members, or has lost the use of them. He is evidently the more wretched and miserable of the two; because happiness and misery, which reside altogether in the mind, must necessarily depend more upon the healthful or unhealthful, the mutilated or entire state of the mind, than upon that of the body.[11]

It is primarily to preserve both the martial and intellectual qualities of a people, the loss of the latter making an individual "more contemptible than even a coward," that Smith advocates the provision of elementary education by the state. Such education will have the additional benefits of freeing the people from "the delusions of enthusiasm and superstition," of making them more decent and orderly, and of giving them greater self-respect. Smith would leave us free to choose as we wish after recommending that the government intervene to make sure that some of our most basic preferences are formed "properly."

II

Adam Smith begins his treatment of taxation by stating four maxims, whose truth he takes to be readily apparent, which should guide tax policy:

I.   The subjects of every state ought to contribute. . ., as nearly as possible, in proportion to their respective abilities. [equality]
II. The tax which each individual is bound to pay ought to be certain, and not arbitrary. [uncertainty]

III. Every tax ought to be levied at the time, or in the manner, in which it is most likely to be convenient for the contributor to pay it. [convenience of payment]

IV. Every tax ought to be contrived as both to take out and to keep out of the pockets of the people as little as possible, over and above what it brings into the public treasury of the state. [economy][12]

Smith takes no credit for these maxims, but, with excessive generosity, states that they are all well known: "The evident justice and utility of the foregoing maxims have recommended them more or less to the attention of all nations."[13] He then goes on to examine how far various taxes that have been imposed in different countries do satisfy these criteria. Smith's modesty and clear admission that he is an expositor in the theory of taxation have not prevented his admirers from crediting Smith with pathbreaking originality.[14] It is a welcome change to be able to provide evidence to show that Smith was indeed right in claiming that the maxims of taxation which he elaborated upon were well known. Indeed, the development of the rules of taxation from the guidelines for just laws seems to have been little noticed hitherto.

In 1599, Thomas Milles, a customs officer, states the following general principles at the beginning of his pamphlet on the customs:

> All Common Wealths are established and maintained by Lawes. The life of Law is Reason. Reason in making Lawes aymes at Equitie. Equitie is guided by Certaintie and Indifference, the two Ballances of Justice.[15]

The twin themes of equity and certainty are to be repeated many times in the subsequent literature.

In 1628, Bishop Sibthorpe preached a sermon that has become notorious because of its defense of the royal authority to tax. In the course of this sermon he laid down a guide for the manner in which the king should exercise this right:

> The Dutie therefore of the Law and Interpreters of the same is
> First; to be just, without tyranny . . .
> Secondly; Equall without partialitie . . .
> Thirdly; they must be moderate without extremity . . .
> Fourthly; they must be plain without ambiguitie . . .[16]

By 1664 some bureaucrats had already obtained a significant overview of taxation, as recorded in the Diary of Samuel Pepys:

29th [February]. To Sir Philip Warwick, who showed me many excellent collections of the state of the Revenue in former Kings' and the late times, and the present. He showed me how the very assessments between 1643 and 1659, which were taxes, (besides Excise, Customs, Sequestrations, Decimations, King and Queene's and Church Lands, or any thing else but just the Assessments,) come to above fifteen millions. He showed me a discourse of his concerning the Revenues of this and foreign States. How that of Spayne was great, but divided with his kingdoms, and so come to little. How that of France did, and do much exceed ours before for quantity; and that it is at the will of the Prince to tax what he will upon his people; which is not here. That the Hollanders have the best manner of tax, which is only upon the expence of provisions, by an excise; and do conclude that no other tax is proper for England but a pound-rate, or excise upon the expence of provisions. He showed me every particular sort of payment away of money, since the King's coming in, to this day; and told me, from one to one, how little he hath received of profit from most of them: and I believe him truly. That the 1,200,000*ℓ*. which the Parliament with so much ado did first vote to give the King, and since hath been re-examined by several committees of the present Parliament, is yet above 300,000*ℓ*. short of making up really to the King the 1,200,000*ℓ*. as by particulars he showed me. And in my Lord Treasurer's excellent letter to the King upon this subject, he tells the King how it was the spending more than the revenue that did give the first occasion of his father's ruine, and did since to the rebels; who, he says, just like Henry the Eighth, had great and sudden increase of wealth, but yet by overspending both died poor: and further tells the King how much of this 1,200,000*ℓ*. depends upon the life of the Prince, and so must be renewed by Parliament again to his successor; which is seldom done without parting with some of the prerogatives of the Crowne; or if denied and he persists to take it of the people, it gives occasion to a civill war, which did in the late business of tonnage and poundage prove fatal to the Crowne. He showed me how many ways the Lord Treasurer did take before he moved the King to farme the Customes in the manner he do, and the reasons that moved him to do it. He showed me a very excellent argument to prove, that our importing lesse than we export, do not impoverish the kingdom, according to the received opinion: which, though it be a paradox, and that I do not remember the argument, yet methought there was a great deal in what he said.

An anonymous pamphleteer of the 1690s virtually anticipates all Smith's maxims in his dicta for good taxes.

Could the whole present Want of this Nation be raised by some one way, and that way be more frugal, expedite and certain, than any one, or all, or any select number of Ways now in use no one can deny this assertion that we ought to use that way only, unless such Inconveniences necessarily attend that way, as would appear to equal, if not exceed the benefits of it promised from the forementioned Qualities (viz.), Thrift, Equality, Expedition and Certainty in respect of the sum to be raised.[17]

During the Walpole administration, the criteria for good taxes were often raised during debates on the salt tax in 1732 as well as those on the excise scheme of 1733.[18] The government based its case for the salt duty upon the grounds that both rich and poor contributed as their means permitted,

> Of all the taxes I ever could think of, there is not one more general, nor one less felt, than that of the duty upon Salt. The duty upon Salt is a tax that every man in the nation contributes to according to his circumstances.

The Opposition retorted that a tax which reached those who were barely able to subsist was not their idea of equity:

> It is not always a certain maxim, that those taxes which are most general are least burthensome; upon the contrary, it holds true in all countries, and at all times, that those taxes which are laid upon the luxuries of mankind are the least burthensome.[19]

The financial pamphleteers were "political" economists in that their pamphlets were frequently interspersed with comments on party politics. Sometimes this took the form of comments on the moneyed versus the landed interest, at others on Whigs versus Tories. The pamphlets sold very well and some of the best sellers of the period 1740-67 were concerned with finance. Because of the close link of finance with war, the analysis of several of these pamphlets has been passed over because of their ostensible politics. One might not expect an analysis of the lagged effects of an inflow of gold into a country in a pamphlet such as Malachy Postlethwayt's *Great Britain's True System*.[20] Nonetheless, such is the case.

The financial writers of this period have not been much studied with a view to seeing how they exemplify the growth of economic thought. E.R.A. Seligman's *Incidence of Taxation*, originally published in 1899, took a first step in classifying the pamphlet literature according to their views on incidence. William Kennedy's *English Taxation 1640-1799* is more valuable in that it places the issues in their political context and deals with the growth of ideas. Joseph Schumpeter's monumental *History of Economic Analysis* has several insightful remarks but Schumpeter's knowledge of the primary literature was not extensive and his desire to find a variety of European provisions for Adam Smith's views on public finance gives his work a peculiar perspective. While I have drawn on each of these sources, the selection and arrangement of matter is perhaps new.[21]

The pamphleteers I shall refer to most often are Joseph Massie and Malachy Postlethwayt. Each wrote several works and Postlethwayt in particular was quite prolific. Unfortunately, not much biographical information is available for either of them. This is also true of a more famous figure, Sir Matthew Decker, who has not been rescued from obscurity by Adam Smith's praise. The main pamphlets involved are: Joseph Massie's *Observations upon Mr. Fauquier's Essay on Ways and Means* (London, 1756), Malachy Postlethwayt's *Great Britain's True System* (London: 1756) and Sir Matthew Decker's *Serious Considerations on the High Duties . . .* (London, 1743). In addition, the following anonymous works are of interest: *An Essay upon Publick Credit* (London, 1745) and *Remarks on the Present State of the National Debt* (London, 1764). If I have referred to a pamphlet only once, the quote has been provided from a secondary source, such as Kennedy or Seligman. The selection of financial pamphleteers is not complete by any means. Some very able men, such as Sir John Barnard, have been ignored, as have lesser men such as William Knox and several anonymous pamphleteers.[22]

The first point worth noting about this literature is its firm grounding in a demand-supply explanation of price:

> "It is the plenty, or Scarcity of any Commodity, in Proportion to its Vent and Demand, which must always rule in these Cases, and by which the Trader will make more or less Profit in his Dealings."
>
> "Everyone admits," says the author, "that Quantity and Vent give a Price to any Commodity; it is therefore to be considered in what Cases the Quantity can be commanded or ascertained, in proportion to the Vent, and in what Cases it cannot; for where it can, the Duties will lie on the Consumer; but where it cannot, it will evidently lie on the Producer or Maker as often as the Quantity exceeds the Vent."[23]

With this basis, they went on to provide canons of taxation:

> As the benefit of taxes to the public results only from the clear income, and the evil to individuals extends not only to the gross produce but to every other expense and loss incident and consequential; that tax is most beneficial to the public and least hurtful to the subject which produces a large sum through a cheap collection and which is free from every other eventual charge.
>
> There are three Things necessary to be considered before this or any other proposed Tax is laid; and these are,
>
> I.   Whether it can be paid or not.
> II. What Effect the Payment of it will have upon other Taxes.

III. Whether the Money to be raised by such Tax can be raised in any other Manner that will be less prejudicial to the landed and trading interests of the nation.[24]

Some writers explicitly distinguished between types of tax policy:

All Taxes ought to be laid for one or both of these Purposes. Either it is a Tax of Revenue, the view of which is to supply the Necessities of the Publick, or it is a Tax of Police, intended to operate as a Restraint; for Instance, on the Importation or Consumption of foreign Manufacturers, to the Prejudice of our own, or on some Article of Luxury prejudicial to the Publick.[25]

Others argued that taxes should be laid on the final consumer to minimize distortions in the economy:

"that all Taxes should be laid as near as possible in the last Instance, and upon the immediate Consumer, and in proportion only to what he consumes there being nothing more unjust or absurd, than that a Man should pay a Tax for what he does not consume." He bases his conclusion in favor of taxing the consumer, rather than the producer or importer, largely on the argument that taxes accumulate with each transfer, and "consequently draw with them, through their whole Progress, a Profit on the Tax, as well as upon their first value or prime cost."[26]

Concern over the incidence of taxation had led John Locke to provide a rudimentary general equilibrium account of this issue, which proved highly influential well into the eighteenth century. The authority of John Locke was frequently used during economic debates of the 1730s and 1740s, especially on issues of taxation, and it is worth considering Locke's analytics because his approach was later adopted by both Adam Smith as well as by the Physiocrats. Locke's argument is so deceptively simple that a few words may help the reader. Locke assumes that all workers are earning a bare subsistence and that the rate of profit in all lines must be equal due to competition. If a tax is laid upon wages, the workers must pass it on or die; if laid upon a commodity, the dealers in that good must raise their prices so that their profit rate equals that of other merchants. Hence neither wages nor profits can be made to bear the burden of taxes. It follows that all taxes must be borne by rents, and so a rational tax system would only tax the landed class:

Let us see now who, at long-run, must pay this quarter, and where it will light. It is plain, the merchant and broker neither will nor can; for, if he pays a quarter more for commodities than he did, he will sell them at a price proportionably raised. The poor labourer and handicraftsman cannot: for he just lives from hand to mouth already, and all his food, clothing, and utensils costing a quarter more than they did before, either his wages must rise with the price of things, to make him live, or else, not being able to maintain himself and family by his labour, he comes to the parish; and then the land bears the burthen a heavier way. The merchant (do what you can), will not bear it, the labourer cannot, and therefore the landholder must: and whether he were best to do it, by laying it directly where it will at last settle, or by letting it come to him by the sinking of his rents, which, when they are once fallen, every one knows are not easily raised again, let him consider.[27]

While Locke had already established the analysis of long-run equilibrium, together with a *ceteris paribus* clause, later financial writers emphasized the method of real analysis for clarifying several issues:

It is evident, as we have before observed, throughout this Tract, that the Introduction of Money into Commerce has not any Ways altered the nature of that Commerce. It still consists in an Exchange of Commodities for Commodities; or, in the Absence of those which are wanted, for Money, which is the Representation of them.

Now the case, as above stated, appears in all the simplicity it will admit of; but when we suppose that money, according to the custom and practice of latter ages, is made use of in traffic, and allowed to pass in exchange for commodities, it renders our ideas somewhat more complex and intricate. But every difficulty will immediately vanish, if we only consider them as equivalents.[28]

Adam Smith's treatment of taxation is very much in accord with the accepted wisdom of his contemporaries. He praises the proposed excise scheme of Walpole on the well-worn ground that it would cheapen the costs of labor and lower the costs of collection, and notes that the scheme failed due to party politics. His analytics are based so heavily upon the assumption of a fixed real wage for labor that there is nothing to admire in Smith after having read Locke and Decker. His treatment of other issues varies considerably in quality. Thus, he correctly argues that a tax on a particular species of profit cannot fall on the entrepreneurs in the industry because competition will ensure that all trades earn the same rate of profit. Agriculture, however, is made an exception on the basis of the following curious argument:

But when a tax is imposed upon the profits of stock employed in agriculture, it is not the interest of the farmers to withdraw any part of their stock from that employment. Each farmer occupies a certain quantity of land, for which he pays rent. For the proper cultivation of this land a certain quantity of stock is necessary; and by withdrawing any part of this necessary quantity, the farmer is not likely to be more able to pay either the rent or the tax. In order to pay the tax, it can never be his interest to diminish the quantity of his produce, nor consequently to supply the market more sparingly than before. The tax, therefore, will never enable him to raise the price of his produce, so as to reimburse himself by throwing the final payment upon the consumer. The farmer, however, must have his reasonable profit as well as every other dealer, otherwise he must give up the trade. After the imposition of a tax of this kind, he can get this reasonable profit only by paying less rent to the landlord. The more he is obliged to pay in the way of tax, the less he can afford to pay in the way of rent.[29]

On other occasions, Smith's argument is made correct by the use of a questionable *ceteris paribus*. Consider his treatment of the incidence of a tax on wages:

> A direct tax upon the wages of labour. . . could not properly be said to be even advanced by him; at least if the demand for labour and the average price of provisions remained the same after the tax as before it.[30]

What requires justification in such cases is the proviso that the demand for labor and the price of provisions remains the same. It is probably the presence of such *ad hoc* thoughts that led Francis Horner to praise the analysis of the Physiocrats and to refer to "that amusing, but not very instructive part of the Wealth of Nations, which treats of taxation."[31]

On the whole, Smith's analysis of taxation is plausible rather than penetrating; it provides a modest and sober account of the state of economic thought on taxation in the mid-eighteenth century. William Kennedy's perceptive assessment is worth repeating:

> It has sometimes been supposed that the publication of the *Wealth of Nations* brought to the world a new revelation of the principles of taxation, and that it immediately affected the policy of the Chancellors of the Exchequer. But this is a serious misconception; the only respect in which it bears some relation to the facts is on the subject of trade policy in the Customs. Apart from that, what Adam Smith did was to expand the commercial view of tax questions which we have been following, and to attempt to systematize and rationalize it by bringing it into relation with the distributive theory of the seventeenth century which Walpole expressed. He gave a wider intellectual sanction to a set of opinions already very influential.[32]

III

Providing for the National Debt was one of the important stimulants for discussions of taxation. It divided pamphleteers into two groups: those who believed the burden of the debt to be negligible insofar as the debt remained a domestic debt, and those who argued that the taxes needed to finance the debt were ruining trade. A second concern was the availability of adequate specie to permit all the transactions to be made.

On the first issue, those who supported a continued debt argued that it merely involved payments from the right hand to the left, a viewpoint said to arise from the Prime Minister, Robert Walpole:

> If Sixty Millions of [the Debt] be the Property of the People of Great Britain it seems to me very plain that we are not the richer nor the poorer for that part of the Debt because if the Taxes be collected from the People of Great Britain, the Money arising from those Taxes is paid to the Proprietors of the Public Funds in the Dividends or Interest, which circulating again to purchase the necessaries and Superfluities of Life, enable the farmer to pay his Rent, the Landlord his Taxes, helps to support the Industrious and to consume the Produce of their Labor.[33]

Those who opposed this position, such as Postlethwayt, believed that the increased taxation would raise prices and ruin England's ability to export. The argument that the National Debt was in fact the source of England's public credit was ignored by such writers.

The money obtained as debt could just as easily have been obtained through taxes. The emphasis here is on the circulation of money:

> To make a right Judgment of this Matter, it may be previously necessary to inquire, where all the Money raised by the Parliament to carry on the War, may actually center and circulate; for that Proportion which is spent in the Kingdom, will not impoverish the Nation, so as to disable her from raising some considerable Part, at least, if not the Whole of the Supplies within the Year.[34]

The balance of trade now comes to be discussed as a means of providing enough coin to make the payments of taxes feasible:

> For, if our national debt should keep continually increasing, and our stock of cash should not keep pace with it, . . . we must inevitably stop payment when this happens to be the case. For these fifty or sixty years back, however, our exports have brought in more cash considerably, than what is only just sufficient to answer this purpose.

Therefore our taxes are nothing more, in fact, than a general muster of our circulating cash, whereby a kind of estimate is taken of it, as it were to see whether it is equal or not to the total amount of the annual interest of our national debt. While we are able to collect taxes amongst us to this amount, it is very evident that there can be no necessity to stop payment. And this we have not as yet failed to do.[35]

Since the value of stocks depended upon the general state of confidence and since this in turn depended partially upon the state of the national debt, financial writers were naturally led to discussing banking. It is remarkable how closely some of these discussions anticipated issues of the later bullion debate:

In our present situation, everybody knows that there must be Remittances abroad to pay the Army and to support our Allies; and it is not improbable that so near the Time of opening the Campaign, as this is, the Balance of Drawing and Remitting may be against us; and the Consequence must follow, that Goods, or foreign Specie, must be exported, to answer that Balance, whether you do, or do not discount Bills of Exchange.[36]

The author even goes on to argue for compensatory actions on the part of the Bank of England during such times of stress, much as Henry Thornton was to urge some 50 years later:

I must further observe to you, Sir, that the Business of private Bankers is, to keep in Cash, and Bank Notes, what is sufficient to answer their current Demand, and to employ the remaining Part for their particular Benefit. But the Case of the Bank of England differs widely; because they are sure of having all the Cash deposited with them, that is not absolutely necessary to carry on Trade and Business, and to supply the Necessaries of Life; so that Bank Notes are a kind of real Specie, which are current in all sorts of payment; and therefore so long as there is Property in the Kingdom, they are sure of a more than sufficient Quantity of Cash, to answer any Demand.[37]

In the last chapter of Book V, "Of publick Debts," Smith begins by describing why the debts are typically incurred, what means exist for meeting such obligations and how such debts have grown in Britain. After a brief digression comparing England and France, Smith returns to his historical account and concludes with a slowly built attack on the practice of funding. Smith evidently feels strongly against the practice of funding and criticizes the view (attributable to J.F. Melon and George Berkeley) that the "publick funds are an addition to the national capital" (924). Without showing the phobia against public debts that is visible in David Hume,

Smith nonetheless describes such expenses as a "perversion" and a permanent burden:

> When funding, besides, has made a certain progress, the multiplication of taxes which it brings along with it sometimes impairs as much the ability of private people to accumulate even in time of peace, as the other system would in time of war. The peace revenue of Great Britain amounts at present to more than ten millions a year. If free and unmortgaged, it might be sufficient, with proper management and without contracting a shilling of new debt, to carry on the most vigorous war. The private revenue of the inhabitants of Great Britain is at present as much encumbered in time of peace, their ability to accumulate is as much impaired as it would have been in the time of the most expensive war, had the pernicious system of funding never been adopted.[38]

We are told that the practice of funding "has gradually enfeebled every state which has adopted it" and that one should not expect that grave consequences might not come with any further addition:

> Great Britain seems to support with ease, a burden which, half a century ago, nobody believed her capable of supporting. Let us not, however, upon this account rashly conclude that she is capable of supporting any burden; nor even be too confident that she could support, without great distress, a burden a little greater than what has already been laid upon her.

While Smith's overall feelings about the debts cannot be doubted, it is typical of his procedure that some occasional remarks point in a different direction. At the very beginning of the chapter we are told that "By lending money to government, they [merchants] do not even for a moment diminish their ability to carry on their trade and manufactures. On the contrary, they commonly augment it" (910). This is enough to support the Berkeley-Melon viewpoint. Somewhat later, Smith declares:

> To the honor of our present system of taxation, indeed, it has hitherto given so little embarrassment to industry, that, during the course even of the most expensive wars, the frugality and good conduct of individuals seems to have been able, by saving and accumulation, to repair all the breaches which the waste and extravagance of government had made in the general capital of the society. At the conclusion of the late war, the most expensive that Great Britain ever waged, her agriculture was as flourishing, her manufacturers as numerous and as fully employed, and her commerce as extensive, as they had ever been before.[39]

IV

When we gather together the insights obtained by the financial writers of the mid-eighteenth century we find several items of value. Malachy Postlethwayt, for example, was almost obsessed with the idea of raising supplies by taxation within the year so that future taxes would not burden future trade. How can supplies be raised without imposing some current taxes which will burden current trade? Postlethwayt comes to grips with this issue by nothing other than that his first preference would be a poll-tax, even though it is not politically viable. He appears to have recognized that the only way to get a nondistortionary tax is to have a lump-sum tax, and the poll-tax was the closest approximation he could find. This shows a fair amount of theoretical insight. Joseph Massie, as another example, argued that Portugal deserved special treatment for the following reason: Portuguese consumption of English goods was more elastic with respect to Portuguese revenue than was the consumption of English goods by the French, with respect to French revenue. Joseph Schumpeter has aptly remarked that such a statement is theoretically interesting, regardless of its correctness. There appears to have been a friendly rivalry between the two men. Postlethwayt attacked the residence of landlords in London, and Massie, without naming names, provides a sharp critique of this position.[40]

Taxes are the one economic subject that cannot be usefully discussed if they are not practicable. The unwritten rules for a viable tax scheme are those of sufficiency and feasibility: the taxes must raise the required revenue and they must be implementable. The tax debates of the 1730s and 1740s frequently raised such practical issues as the difficulty of assessment, the costs of collection, as well as the quasi-political argument that some tax schemes, such as the excise, would lead to an "intolerable" multiplication of revenue officials. The public choice school is sometimes traced back to Adam Smith for such views. It will be seen that Smith himself is part of a much older tradition:

> One of the greatest evils of a salt tax, I may say the greatest, because it strikes at our constitution, is the great number of officers which must be employed in collecting that small branch of the revenue.
> All taxes which require a multitude of officers to be employed in collecting them, and which give thereby both occasion and pretence to quarter numbers of useless subjects on the labour and industry of others, become so changeable and oppressive, that they are hardly borne in the most arbitrary governments.[41]

In the unpublished account of funding and taxes drawn up by Charles Townshend and corrected by Adam Smith, there is the claim that Walpole provides "the first symptom of a wise and regular system of finance and which contains the whole principles of that Science, conceived with the utmost clearness and executed with simplicity."

Adam Smith's most important conclusion was that free trade was the optimal policy. Since this left the question of government revenues unanswered, Smith went on to prescribe the use of customs duties for revenue purposes but not for protection. This version of Smith's major policy conclusion sounds very like the movement for free ports that gathered momentum between 1730 and 1760. Joshua Gee first noticed this movement in order to oppose it. Gee does not mention any supporters of the free port idea but his opposition suggests that the idea was growing in strength. A few years later Sir Robert Walpole tried to begin just such a scheme but a factious Opposition prevented him from carrying out the plan.

Perhaps the most interesting, and most neglected, feature of this age is the attempt to introduce something very close to free trade. Walpole's bonded warehouse scheme was quite explicit in this regard, and Walpole himself is reported to have claimed that the scheme would ease other forms of taxation and London would quickly become a "free-port, and by consequence, the market of the world."[42] This policy received increased support in the following decades and the two best-selling pamphlets of the 1740s were concerned with minimizing taxes and making England a free port. Decker's views are somewhat obliquely phrased in a pamphlet purportedly supporting a tax on houses, while William Richardson's views are quite clear even in his own preface:

> The consideration of our numerous monopolies naturally led to an inquiry into the nature of a free-port trade, as well as the strong prejudices against it. . . . Perhaps it may seem strange that no bounty should be proposed as a means to restore trade; but if a free-port will gain us all those trades we are naturally capable of; it will appear to be itself the greatest bounty, and in endevouring to force nature, the experience is certain, but the success doubtful.[43]

In his *Lectures*, Smith maintained continuity with his English predecessors by formulating his ideas in the same language:

> From the above considerations it appears that Britain should by all means be made a free port, that there should be no interruptions of any kind made to foreign trade, that if it were possible to defray the expences of government by any other method, all duties, customs, and excise should be abolished, and that free commerce and liberty of exchange should be allowed with all nations and for all things.[44]

By separating revenue from trade, Smith was able to argue that free trade was optimal and then bring in the conclusion that customs duties could be laid for the sake of revenues. The end result is the same: one way is to support free ports as a policy measure; another is to advocate free trade as optimal and lay customs duties as a concession to practicality.[45] When viewed as a policy measure, even the most radical of Smith's propositions does not involve measures that had not been thoroughly discussed in the half-century prior to the *Wealth of Nations*.

NOTES

1. Adam Smith, *The Wealth of Nations*, ed. R.H. Campbell and A.S. Skinner (Oxford: Clarendon Press, 1976), vol. II, 741 (hereafter referred to as *WN*).
2. Ibid., 756.
3. W.R. Scott, *Joint Stock Companies to 1720* (Cambridge: Cambridge University Press, 1912), 459.
4. *WN*, ibid., 781.
5. *WN*, ibid., 782.
6. Richard Watson, as quoted in the *Universal Magazine* (March 1986), 148-51.
7. Alexander Carlyle, *Letters to his Grace, the Duke of Bucceleugh, on Nation Defence* (London: Murray, 1778), 36.
8. Ibid., 39.
9. Ibid., 42-3.
10. Ibid., 781-2.
11. Ibid., 78. See John Robertson, *The Scottish Enlightenment and the Militia Issue* (Edinburgh: John Donald, 1985).
12. Ibid., 825-6.
13. Ibid., 827.
14. E. Roll, "*The Wealth of Nations* 1776-1976," *Lloyds Bank Review* (1976), reprinted in J.C. Wood, ed., *Adam Smith: Critical Assessments* (London: Croom Helm, 1984), 150; E.G. West, *Adam Smith* (Indianapolis: Liberty Fund, 1976), 206. In view of the intensely applied nature of issues involving public finance, it would be nice to present this review along with some indication of the accompanying economic and political history. Time nor space nor competence permit such an account. For a convenient summary, see Patrick O'Brien, "The Political Economy of British Taxation, 1660-1815," *Economic History Review* (February 1988), XLI(1), 1-32.
15. T. Milles, *The Customer's Apologie* (1599), 1.
16. R. Sibthorpe, *Apostollike Obedience* (1628), E1-E2; *Memoirs of Samuel Pepys*, ed. Richard Lord Braybrooke (London: Warne, 1825), 200-1.
17. Anon., *A Way to Raise what Money shall be Necessary* . . . (no date; but the reference to "our Gracious Deliverer, whom some would style Conqueror," clearly places it in the 1690s).
18. William Cobbett, ed., *The Parliamentary History of England* (London: Hansard, 1812), X, 944.
19. Ibid., 946.

20. M. Postlethwayt, *Great Britain's True System* (1757; reprinted New York: Augustus M. Kelley, 1967), 205-12. In view of Postlethwayt's acknowledged borrowings in 1751 from Richard Cantillon's unpublished *Essai sur la nature du commerce en general*, such an analysis displays a keen eye for recognizing good economic reasoning rather than originality.

21. E.R.A. Seligman, *Incidence of Taxation*, 5th edn (New York: Columbia University Press, 1917; first published 1899); W. Kennedy, *English Taxation, 1640-1799* (London: Bell, 1913); J.A. Schumpeter, *History of Economic Analysis* (London: Allen & Unwin, 1954).

22. The importance of financial issues is also evident in the frequent arguments on the prominence of the "monied interest." For more details on this and related issues, see P.G.M. Dickson, *The Financial Revolution in England* (London: Cambridge University Press, 1968).

23. *The Second Part of an Argument against Excises* (1733); *The Axe (once more) Laid to the Root of the Tree* (1743). As quoted by Seligman, *Incidence of Taxation*, 69 and 71.

24. R. Nugent, *Considerations upon a Reduction of the Land Tax* (London, 1749), 7. Joseph Massie, *Observations upon Mr Fauquier's Essays on Ways and Means* (London, 1756), 5.

25. *A Letter from a Member of Parliament* (1756). As quoted by Seligman, *Incidence of Taxation*, 87-8.

26. *Proposals for Carrying on the War with Vigour* (1757). As quoted by Seligman, *ibid.*, 82.

27. John Locke, *Some Considerations . . .* (1694) in *Works* (London: Thomas Tegg, 1823), 55, 60.

28. Postlethwayt, *Great Britain's True System*, 332; Anon., *Remarks on the Present State of the National Debt* (London, 1764), 6.

29. *WN*, **II**, 856.

30. Ibid., 865.

31. *The Economic Writings of Francis Horner*, ed. F.W. Fetter (London: London School of Economics, 1957), 73.

32. Kennedy, *English Taxation*, 141ff; also see 121-2. A.T. Peacock provides a less critical view in "The Treatment of the Principles of Public Finance in *The Wealth of Nations*," in *Essays on Adam Smith*, ed. A.S. Skinner and T. Wilson (Oxford: Clarendon Press, 1975), 553-67.

33. Anon., *An Essay upon Publick Credit* (London, 1745), 8.

34. Anon., *Remarks*, 4.

35. Ibid., 3 and 2.

36. Anon., *Essay*, 15.

37. Ibid., 19-20.

38. *WN*, 926.

39. Ibid., 929.

40. Postlethwayt, *Great Britain's True System*, Joseph Massie, *The Proposal Commonly Called Sir Matthew Deckers Scheme . . .* (London, 1757).

41. Cobbett, *Parliamentary History*, **X**, 953, 1063.

42. P. Langford, *The Excise Crisis* (Oxford: Clarendon Press, 1975), 32; W.R. Scott, "Adam Smith at Downing Street," *Economic History Review* 6, 81.

43. William Richardson, *Essay . . . Decline of Foreign Trade* (London, 1739).

44. Adam Smith, *Lectures on Jurisprudence* (Oxford: Oxford University Press, 1978), 514.

45. I have read a speech of the Elder Pitt around 1750 (which I cannot locate now!) where Pitt notes unfavorably the change of British tax policy from revenue considerations to protection. However, John Brewer makes a similar remark about Pitt in *The Sinews of Power* (Cambridge, Mass.: Harvard University Press, 1990) but, alas, without accompanying reference.

6. The Policy of *Laissez-faire* during Scarcities*

Except for playful intellectual exercises, or as a first stage of a first approximation in a sustained logical argument, universal principles seem to me to have no useful role in argument, and particular cases or restricted classes of cases to comprise almost everything that is worth arguing about—or dying for.

Jacob Viner

I

How far do principles which are valid in general need to be modified in special circumstances? In particular, are free-market allocations acceptable during seasons of scarcity? It is well known that at least from 1680 onwards a number of English authors argued for the freedom of all internal trades; such freedom was also a basic part of Colbert's policy, and the idea of forming one, unified, national market is certainly basic to Mercantilism. And yet, despite general agreement on the beneficence of such freedom, one species of commodity was continually given special consideration: foodstuffs.[1] Whenever there was fear of a deficient harvest, pamphlets immediately appeared attacking hoarders and speculators for driving up prices. Parliament did not ignore these popular fears and the statute books had laws prohibiting forestalling, regrating and engrossing—as the complex of activities involved in corn speculation were called.[2] From 1750, onwards, the criticism of such laws became frequent and intense, and in 1772, Arthur Young wrote:

---

*The criticisms of Laurence Moss and George Stigler on an earlier version of this chapter showed me the necessity of expanding and rearranging. It is perhaps needless to add that they are not to be implicated in either its general outlook or its errors.

115

> In all cases, whatever is found to be the price of a commodity OUGHT TO BE the price of the commodity; . . . Nothing, therefore, can be more pernicious and at the same time futile than to attempt to regulate that by laws . . . which regulates itself by the vibrations of the market.[3]

Four years later, Adam Smith was to add his powerful voice to the debate. Of all the economic legislation of his time, none came in for stronger criticism from Adam Smith than the laws which were meant to prevent a monopoly of the distribution of the corn.[4] "The popular fear of engrossing and forestalling," Smith said, "may be compared to the popular terrors and suspicions of witchcraft." The tide of public opinion gradually swelled against such government interference, and in 1844 the laws in question were abolished.

If only by omitting a detailed consideration of this problem, all historians of economic thought have heretofore agreed that Smith and the classical economists performed a useful service by attacking legislation which hindered the free movement of corn.[5] The judgement of Smith's contemporaries that the reasoning of the *Wealth of Nations* was conclusive stands unchallenged. In this chapter I take issue with this well-established "Smithian" view of the internal corn trade. It will be argued that the policy of complete *laissez-faire* in the market for foodstuffs, as advocated by the classical economists, can be inadequate in terms of scarcity, and, under certain conditions, may even be detrimental to the general welfare. The next section re-examines Smith's arguments and shows how, on realistic premises, the *effects* of monopoly can be possible without an actual monopoly; as a result, complete non-interference by the state can aggravate a scarcity. Thereafter it will be shown that valid objections to the reasoning of the *Wealth of Nations* had been made by contemporaries but were largely ignored. Finally, some instances of scarcities in India and the remedial measures adopted to relieve them will be discussed.

II

Smith begins by assuring us that the interests of the consumer and the seller are identical: "The interest of the inland dealer, and that of the great body of the people, how opposite soever they may at first sight appear, are, even in years of the greatest scarcity, exactly the same."[6] He goes on to admit that if a monopoly could be formed, it *might* be harmful to the public, but scoffed at such a possibility:

Were it possible, indeed, for one great company of merchants to possess themselves of the whole crop of an extensive country, it might, perhaps, be their interest to deal with it as the Dutch are said to do with the spiceries of the Moluccas, to destroy or throw away a considerable part of it, in order to keep up the price of the rest. But it is scarce possible, even by the violence of law, to establish such an extensive monopoly with regard to corn; and wherever the law leaves the trade free, it is of all commodities the least liable to be engrossed or monopolized by the force of a few large capitals, which buy up the greater part of it.[7]

Indeed, if a famine had been suffered, Smith was sure it was because the government had attempted to regulate that which was properly left free:

Whoever examines the history of the dearths and famines which have afflicted any part of Europe, . . . will find, I believe, that a dearth has never arisen from any combination among the inland dealers in corn, nor from any other cause but a real scarcity. . . and that a famine has never arisen from any other cause but the violence of government attempting by improper means, to remedy the inconveniences of a dearth.[8]

The proper course for the government therefore was to leave the corn trade completely unfettered at all times: "The unlimited, unrestrained freedom of the corn trade, as it is the only effectual preventative of the miseries of a famine, so it is the best palliative of the inconvenience of a dearth."[9]

This strong prescription for governments to heed the maxim of *laissez-faire* is, as is usual with Smith, supported by a detailed argument. This is one of the several points in the *Wealth of Nations* at which the idea of the Invisible Hand guiding human affairs is introduced:

It is the interest of the people that their daily, weekly, and monthly consumption should be proportioned as exactly as possible to the supply of the season. The interest of the inland corn dealers is the same. By supplying them as nearly as he can judge, in this proportion, he is likely to sell all his corn for the highest price, and with the greatest profit; and his knowledge of the state of the crop, and of his daily, weekly, and monthly sales, enable him to judge, with more or less accuracy, how far they really are supplied in this manner. Without intending the interest of the people, he is necessarily led, by a regard to his own interest, to treat them, even in years of scarcity, pretty much in the same manner as the prudent master of a vessel is sometimes obliged to treat his crew.[10]

This is one of the few points in the *Wealth of Nations* where the argument for completely free trade is emphatically made, without any hint of qualification. Let us simplify the problem by ruling out importation,[11] and consider it as follows: at the end of a harvest, the economy possesses an inelastic supply of corn, which is to form its principal foodstuff for the next 12 months. There are thus 12 monthly prices to be considered and Smith's claim is that the observable pattern of prices in the completely unrestrained market reflects only the state of the diminished supply and that this is the pattern of prices which will maximize welfare by best enabling people to bear the scarcity. The opposition urged that, although prices must rise, they could rise much higher than was warranted by the shortage of the crops. Finally, since Smith explicitly refers to other European countries and to India as places where authorities had needlessly meddled, the policy of *laissez-faire* for the internal corn trade is implied to be of universal applicability.

Let us make the assumption about the corn market that Smith considered realistic: there are many farmers and factors, and they do not act in concert. The crux of Smith's argument is that the most profitable price for the merchant is that which will just exhaust the year's supply and is thus a mutually agreeable price between producer and consumer. It is instructive to visualize the workings of such a decentralized process. Every year the farmer sows an amount that should meet the average demand. If he has a normal harvest and hears of the same being true generally, then he will sell his corn to a factor for about the price he had originally anticipated, thereby making normal profits. Suppose, however, the farmer has reason to believe the crop to be generally deficient and therefore, rightly, expects the scarcity to provide higher prices. How high a price is he now to charge his factor? By the atomistic assumption, neither party can gauge accurately how high prices will rise. How far the prices do rise must therefore be, to a large extent, based on expectations formed by reading papers, talking to travellers, or hearing rumors. When Smith states that the dealers will supply consumers "as nearly as he can judge, in [the right] proportion," he fails to specify how the dealer is to acquire knowledge of the state of the market. To the extent that this knowledge is based on inaccurate sources, to that extent must the market fail to function properly. Some 50 years later, Mountifort Longfield was to explicitly assert (what was only implicit in Smith) that the dealers' "information on the subject is generally pretty correct, as their success depends on it."[12] If only we could all be as confident about the accuracy of knowledge our success depends on!

The writings of certain libertarian scholars, especially those of F.A. Hayek, have persuasively argued that the price system is an efficient and accurate mode of conveying information. That this is generally valid cannot be doubted. The question arises whether prices always convey information only about demand and supply, in the usual sense of those terms. It is well known that in some markets, such as that for foreign currencies, for short periods of time, when speculative forces take over, current prices are largely a reflection of expected futures prices, and such expectations need bear no relation to the "objective" state of the market.

Consider now the position for a typical corn dealer who has heard from all sides that the harvest is deficient. As he does not, and cannot, know the exact extent of the shortage, he perceives every increase of the price as a further indication of the severity of the dearth. The knowledge that the harvest is deficient is enough to make him reasonably sure of a further rise in price later in the season as well as of being able to sell all he holds. But in this case the profit-maximizing policy may well be to withhold supply. A small amount withheld by each farmer will sum up to a considerable aggregate and probably lead to a further rise in price and even more withholding. In other words, precisely the effect predicted to occur with a monopoly—high prices and a restricted supply—is seen to be possible with a multiplicity of sellers.

In fact, the situation can be worse precisely because there are many sellers. This is because a monopolist would know the exact extent of the deficiency in supply, and, under Smith's assumption of the most profitable prices being those which just exhaust supply, would raise prices only so far as to make the current output last the entire season. (Not to mention the monopolist's fear of arousing the wrath of the public if they felt prices were exorbitantly high.) With many sellers, however, it will be practically impossible to know the exact extent of the shortage in the harvest. In the expectation of a sharp rise in prices later in the season, it is perfectly possible that the farmers will withhold corn, that is, they "forestall" or "engross," in the language of the eighteenth century. And just because there are many of them it would be easy for the dealers to miscalculate how much prices should be allowed to rise. Smith argued that if dealers did miscalculate and raise prices excessively, they would only hurt themselves, for they would end the season with corn left on their hands and with prices heading downwards because of the prospects of the next harvest. As Smith recognizes, this requires the next harvest to be a good one; there is therefore no reason for speculators to worry about the next harvest in the early months of the season. The extraordinary profits made in years of scarcity is defined by Smith as being necessary to compensate the losses of other years; he asserts that, in the long run, corn dealers only make normal profits because "great fortunes are as seldom made in this as in any other trade,"[13] an argument which assumes that the scarcities which are to provide the bulk of the traders' profits can be anticipated. Adam Smith's case for a free internal corn trade is thus incomplete.

III

Of all the economic policies advocated by Adam Smith, none won such wholehearted approval as the attacks on the laws prohibiting forestalling. How far Smith's authority was enhanced by the public eulogy of the *Wealth of Nations* by Prime Minister William Pitt in 1791 must be a matter of conjecture. Britain experienced scarcities twice at the very end of the eighteenth century—in 1795-6[14] and in 1800-1—and on both occasions Smith's authority was repeatedly appealed to whenever an attempt was made to enforce the laws against forestalling. Indeed, the freedom of the internal corn trade may well be considered the first major applied field in which the principles of the *Wealth of Nations* were tested.

Edmund Burke had strongly reprobated interference as early as 1795 and his pamphlet was now (1800) printed as an authoritative warning against "indiscreet tampering." The able and independent-minded economist, the Reverend John Howlett, acknowledged that he was so far a disciple of Adam Smith in that he believed the fears about forestalling to be as unreal as those about witchcraft. In 1800 the philosopher-poet Samuel Taylor Coleridge wrote at length in the *Morning Post* to explain that high corn prices could not be due to monopoly. By 1802 the Whig *Edinburgh Review*, in the person of the Reverend Sydney Smith, could only have contempt for those who believed monopolies to cause the high price of corn:

> The question of the corn trade has divided society into two parts—those who have any talents for reasoning, and those who have not. We owe an apology to our readers for taking any notice of errors that have been so frequently and so unanswerably exposed.[15]

Not all of Sydney's contemporaries were happy with the reasonings of Adam Smith and the free traders. The municipal authorities of the City of London denounced the speculations of the corn merchants, and in 1800 a dealer called Rusby was indicted for selling corn on the same day and in the same market at a higher price than he had bought. In passing judgment, Lord Kenyon went on to reprobate "modern theories" which had pronounced that such practices were no evil.[16]

What is less well known is that some acute criticisms of the Smithian position were also inspired by the scarcities. Sir William Young, in particular, wrote a penetrating account of the weakness of the *laissez-faire* position.[17] Young did not deny the overall merits of free trade; indeed, he approved of them in general, but felt that corn should be dealt with as a special case. The basis of Young's argument was that corn was an absolute necessity and that therefore one could not boycott a seller for charging an exorbitant price for it, as one could for all other articles "which man, for a certain period, may abstain from the use of." Young introduces a distinction between the farmer and the corn merchant: the farmer not only lacks the capital to hoard large quantities of grain but he is further limited by social pressures in the prices he dare ask: neither constraint acts upon the corn merchant who, in Young's sketch, appears as a rich, purely profit-maximizing speculator.[18]

The farmer may hold back small quantities of grain until later in the season, and this Young considers perfectly proper. It is the accentuation of this hoarding under the influence of the speculator (it is not specified just how) that is the root of the evil. The process feeds on itself, for once the rumors of high prices are bruited, country banks are readier to give credit to farmers, thereby enabling them to hold back even larger quantities of grain. Young explains himself very clearly on these issues, as the following quote demonstrates:

> If, in times of scarcity, the caution and reserve of the farmer is carried yet farther by the jobber and engrosser on speculation; if a further, though small proportion is under such circumstances withdrawn from the market, then that market is no longer served on the level of quantity and price, from estimate founded on natural scarcity, and to a certain degree the scarcity is artificial. If by a further perseverance and credits of the engrosser, the scantiness of supply is extended to a second and third market-day; this petty engross will have created an influence more powerful than any settled combination; with the necessities and eagerness of the consumer, he will have excited the speculation of dealers who never dealt before;—the country banker first musters in the set, at the all of interest, and offers himself a country partner to the farmer. The fact, and the extent of this partnership, and of the advances of the monied man, is loudly and plainly told, in the late extraordinary increase and circulation of country notes. Thus a new and corruptive character of trade and speculation is forced on the farmer, and on all, who may possess an article which in its nature allows to extort price, at the option of him who holds it. Such speculation is far different from that of the manufacturer or cotton merchant; it rests distinctively—not on competition for sale, but on competition for price.[19]

It has been argued so far that, even without a monopoly, for extended periods of time, prices can rise higher than is necessary to clear the market during periods of scarcity. Smith ruled out monopoly because the corn trade was too large ever to be monopolized, but he neglected to consider the possibility that, even with many sellers, in the presence of inadequate knowledge, self-interest can give rise to results similar to that of active collusion. It is *not* being claimed that such prices can persist throughout a season, but only that they can persist for a period of time long enough, say, two months, to justify the clamors of the common people.

Contemporary belief both in the importance of expectations in setting prices and in the existence of withholding crops is not very hard to come by. Warren Hastings, ex-Governor-General of Bengal, expresses himself very clearly on the topic of expectations:

> In truth, the dearness of wheat, the consequent high price of bread . . . are . . . the effect of opinion influencing those who were in possession of the former, to withhold it from sale, unless they could obtain their own terms for it; or altogether, in the hopes of causing a further increase of this price.[20]

While both of Arthur Young's correspondents in Staffordshire account for prices there by some sort of monopoly "samples now uncommonly numerous; showing the corn had been kept back; farmers refused 16*s* expecting that parliamentary discussion would soon make it 20*s*" (Tomlinson); "the stock in hand is considerable . . . but as it will be in fewer hands, no hope of a moderate price" (Pitt).[21] Of the several speeches in Parliament which blamed high prices on speculation, the following quote expresses a viewpoint very close to that espoused earlier:

> I had had occasion, in the course of the last three or four months, to pass through most of the principal counties in England: I had the pleasure to see plentiful crops, and the greatest part well got in, and at small expense. Sir, everybody I met congratulated me in the month of August and part of September, saying, "Now, Sir, we must have bread cheap!" I found in the market, plenty of old wheat brought to what I was pleased to hear was a falling market. Sir, the finest oats were sold the last week in August at Huntingdon at 24*s*, and now I believe they are at 50*s*. A short time afterwards, a report appeared in the public newspapers, purporting to be a report of the board of agriculture. It had a very great effect on the markets; for corn immediately began to rise. Sir, the people upon this became dissatisfied; tumultuous meetings, and mobs seizing the corn, as might be expected, grew into riots. Government very prudently issued a proclamation, which unfortunately, instead of appeasing the people, had a contrary effect, for they considered it as a measure that encouraged and protected the farmers and monopolizers. Sir, upon the back of this came out that letter of the duke of Portland. Sir, until that letter was published, hardly anybody believed in scarcity; but, when it came from the secretary of state, who could doubt it? Sir, these three measures were the cause of corn rising: nothing was to be heard but a cry of scarcity, and that in the most plentiful country. Sir, seeing, as I have, the finest crop growing in various parts of the country, I cannot believe there is a scarcity.[22]

Among political economists, the most interesting, as well as the most detailed, discussion of this problem is by Dugald Stewart, the successor of Adam Smith to the chair of Moral Philosophy at Edinburgh. Although a convinced supporter of Adam Smith on the issue of forestalling, his fairmindedness leads him to concede that prices need not reflect objective conditions in the market. After providing quotations from Arthur Young and Sir James Steuart (the instance from Young is of where the proclamation of a plan to import wheat leads to a sharp *rise* in price), Stewart sums up as follows:

> The foregoing quotation seems abundantly to confirm the truth of the general positions which they were brought to support, that in most countries of Europe the food produced in the country is nearly consumed by the inhabitants, and consequently, that *all great variations in the price of corn are engendered by apprehension, and do not depend on the quantity in the market.* (Emphasis added)[23]

Adam Smith asserts strongly that the internal corn trade is as free from monopoly as it is possible for an industry to be, and it is worth examining briefly the empirical evidence. In the dominant London corn market at Mark Lane, although the freehold property was said to have 80 shareholders, only 14 of these, who were corn factors, effectively controlled the whole and exercised their influence in preventing anyone from obtaining a stand if he were likely to employ himself as a factor.[24] Several knowledgeable men also complained about the increased influence of middlemen at this time. Thomas Erskine expressed a fairly widespread view to Lord Kenyon when he wrote:

> There are now only great landlords (the farmers) and great merchants with great capitals, in lines which were not formerly considered as the occupations of merchants. They sweep the whole country before them, in the purchase of the necessaries of life, and they command the markets.[25]

As to speculators who bought wheat in order to resell at higher prices, "bulls" in modern jargon, the witnesses before the Commons Committee were certain their number and influence was extensive. Everyone knew of such practices although no witness admitted that he or any of his friends was one![26] Given the popular odium against "jobbers"—Rusby's house had been torn down by the mob—it is not surprising that no one was willing to point a finger. Figures are lacking, but it does seem possible that the corn market was considerably influenced by a much smaller number of people than Smith imagined possible.

It is not therefore surprising to find several other thoughtful men adding their voice to that of Sir William Young. The most telling evidence comes from those who were otherwise staunch supporters of Smithian economics. William Wilberforce found occasion to regret the hold that Smith's principles had over the public mind. In late 1800, Wilberforce asked a friend to inquire of neighboring farmers whether the rumors concerning forestalling could be true. While he held to Adam Smith's doctrine "in the main" yet he felt that there was room for abuse.[27] By the spring of 1801, Wilberforce was convinced that forestalling was a real evil and wrote bitterly to Mrs Hannah More of "The callousness, the narrow and foolish wisdom of servilely acquiescing in Adam Smith's general principles, without allowance for a thousand circumstances which take the case out of the province of that very general principle. . . ."[28] Even the prime minister, William Pitt, in his private correspondence showed signs of weakening. He writes of confining legal penalties solely to combinations "or at least to speculations which can be proved to be for the purpose of unduly and artificially raising the price,"[29] thereby admitting that a certain class of speculation was not permissible. Lord Grenville was annoyed at this backsliding from *laissez-faire* and reminded Pitt that "We in truth formed our opinions on the subject together, and I was not more convinced than you were of the soundness of Adam Smith's principles of political economy till Lord Liverpool lured you from our arms into all the mazes of the old system."[30]

A few years later, when William Playfair produced the first edition of the *Wealth of Nations* with an independent commentary,[31] he too, with great deference, objected to Smith's wholesale condemnation of the laws against forestalling; Playfair even adduced an instance of what appeared to be hoarding from personal experience in France. Nonetheless, reverence for Adam Smith had become so great, and the cry for freedom of trade so established a dogma, that the *Edinburgh Review* was able to dismiss Playfair with great contempt.[32]

IV

Ensuring that the market is not monopolized is only a part of the government's duty during a time of scarcity because the competitive market does not worry directly about feeding mouths. If the laborer has insufficient income at current market prices to buy a subsistence bundle, the laws of the market doom him to starvation. And this is where price-guided competitive allocations conflict with a welfare principle that was universally agreed to in Smith's day—*salus populi suprema lex*: the Roman maxim that no law could be above the subsistence of the people.[33] If the free exercise of the laws of property sometimes required that a number of the poor starve, then such a law lost its justification in these circumstances. If small farmers hoarded grain in expectation of a profit, the state could rightfully intervene and impose controls on the small farmer. Similarly, if during a scarcity the rich refused to constrict their stomachs, threw extravagant parties, bought more horses, and so on, then the state also had the right to impose a suptuary law while scarcity persisted.[34]

What the modern theorems about competitive equilibria have demonstrated is that, under certain conditions, chiefly the absence of externalities, in a competitive market consumers achieve the maximum utility that they can get, *subject to* their wealth limitations. There is nothing to suggest that this maximum achievable utility will exceed the utility of the subsistence bundle; if consumers are too poor, they *will* not. Some special assumption, such as irreducibility, is necessary to provide everyone with a positive income at the final equilibrium in the modern general equilibrium models, and even then there is no assurance that this income will suffice to provide subsistence.[35] Hence the competitive market can be ineligible as a welfare-maximizing social mechanism if we adopt the welfare ideal that no individual can be permitted to starve.

The above conclusion is quite independent of socialistic considerations. It is not being argued that individuals have a right to subsist independently of whether or not they choose to work. Many would hold to such a value but it is not germane to the problem. What we *are* arguing is that those who put in a full day's work deserve at least a subsistence bundle, *provided* that such a redistribution of the total available supply is feasible. If there is food enough for only half the population, no matter what, then the above considerations do not apply. But if it can be shown that by restraining the rich consumer and harassing the food supplier it would be possible to give everyone an adequate number of mouthfuls, then equity *requires* that the laws of property be interfered with.

What would be the first-best policy with such a social welfare function? Since subsistence considerations overrule all others, one method that would surely work is that of quantity controls by the government. If directives were sent out to ascertain the exact state of the crops, then it would be possible to ration out the existing supply among all inhabitants if the supply was adequate, and to place orders for imports if it were not. Acquiring the information itself would not be too difficult in a country such as England because it already possessed a well-developed system of local government in the countryside. The clergy and magistrates could be given sufficient power to ascertain, by coercion if need be, the deficiency in supply. Indeed,

Arthur Young managed to get a good deal of information simply by using his position as Secretary of the Board of Agriculture.[36] The second step of actually rationing out the supply, is much more drastic but, unfortunately, it is not really necessary. The real evil, we saw earlier, was the lack of knowledge about the exact state of the crops. Once accurate knowledge on this head were disseminated, experience could be left to guide the farmers and corn dealers to judge how far prices should rise in order to spread out the available deficient crops.

In 1800 Britain only went as far as urging the necessity of a census, in order to be able to deal more effectively with future scarcities; by the Second World War, Britain was using rationing to allocate food.[37]

Asking the government to provide information has, however, its own problems. If accurate information can be a considerable help, the symmetry of the situation requires that inaccurate information leads to equally great distress. If the government announces that the harvest is deficient by one-half when it is only deficient by a fourth, this would perhaps lead to worse problems than the miscalculation by individual farmers. Even the announcement of the true extent of the scarcity could lead to a temporary panic. Dugald Stewart perceived the problem very clearly:

> It is a difficult task for Government to decide, when such a calamity occurs, how to proceed; as the very inquiries which are instituted with a view to remedy the evil, have inevitably, in the first instance, the effect of adding to its magnitude. If no inquiry is made, ministers are accused of negligence; and, after it is undertaken, they are blamed for that enhancement of price which is the natural consequence of a general alarm.[38]

Stewart was perhaps referring to the letter of the Duke of Portland, noted earlier, which stated the deficiency to be at least a fourth, which immediately raised the price of wheat by five shillings a bushel in several places.[39]

The last decade of the eighteenth century was a singularly inopportune time to try out *laissez-faire* with regard to foodstuffs. The upper classes had viewed with utmost concern the possibility of the French Revolution being imitated in England and were certainly not about to play into the hands of the revolutionaries by refusing to intervene in the market because of some abstract theory.[40] One-half of the King's speech of 1800 was taken up with the scarcity of provisions; in very tactful language the King at once asked Parliament to investigate the possibility of "undue combinations" while telling them to be careful not to interfere with the established nature of the trade. What Parliament did do was to prohibit the use of wheat in distilleries and the making of starch as well as to pass a law prohibiting the sale of bread unless it had been baked 24 hours previously, a regulation that had been recommended by the bakers themselves, in order to reduce consumption.[41] It is curious to note that, although everyone in Parliament who spoke of general principles argued for liberty of trade, not one voice was raised against these restrictions on distilleries and bakers; as if these restrictions were not enough, exports of wheat were prohibited and a bounty given on imports. It was a time when men known to prefer free trade repeatedly insisted that they were not so wedded to "bookish systems" as to be unwilling to make exceptions.[42] In order to emphasize the foolishness of the laws prohibiting forestalling, Adam Smith had compared them to the laws about religion. For once, he understated the issue; people can become secular, but they cannot avoid the pangs of hunger.

V

The problem of governmental policy during scarcities should be clearer in the case of a country such as India, but is not. There is, in fact, a large inexplicable element to Indian famines. The most recent in Bengal in 1943, caused at least 1.5 million deaths and was blamed on a sharp reduction in the food supply. A.K. Sen, however, has shown that the official view of the famine, that it was caused by scarcity of rice, has no sound factual basis: the total shortage of food was no more than 5 percent below an average crop.[43] Professor Sen does not offer an explicit hypothesis as to why so many people should have died in the midst of this (relative) abundance, but suggests that radical changes in the mechanism by which the marketable claims of individuals are transferred—"exchange entitlements," as he calls them—may be the true villain:

> An economy in a state of comparative tranquility may develop a famine if there is a sudden shake-up of the system of rewards for exchange of labour, commodities and other possessions, even *without* a "sudden, sharp reduction in the food supply" . . . For example, the 1974 floods in Bangladesh, which destroyed some of the crop, immediately hit agricultural labor hard, by drastically reducing the demand for labour and altering the exchange possibilities open to labourers, through the development of widespread unemployment. This, in fact, ushered in the famine that developed, *preceding* the decline of the output to be harvested.[44]

Stimulating though Professor Sen's theories are, I would like to suggest that alterations in exchange entitlements *alone* cannot account for extreme privation. It is instructive to consider the history of some earlier scarcities in Bengal and Orissa from the viewpoint suggested earlier in this chapter, especially since Sen does not consider the advisability of legislative interference in the market during the Bengal famine of 1943.

The policy of *laissez-faire* was not restricted by Adam Smith to Europe alone. Referring to the catastrophic famine of 1770 in Bengal and Bihar, which carried away a third of the population of the region, Smith said:

> The drought in Bengal, a few years go, might probably have occasioned a very great dearth. Some improper regulations, some injudicious restraints imposed by the servants of the East India Company upon the rice trade, contributed, perhaps, to turn that dearth into a famine.[45]

Smith provides no evidence to justify this assertion and it was a somewhat rash test of his theory, considering that India had a poorer transportation system and a far less developed capitalistic structure than England. Recent research has shown that in the worst-hit area, Bihar, Smith's claim of administrative interference was misplaced. According to Nikhil Sur, the company did all it could to keep the market free:

> Duties on every article of grain were struck off and severe punishments inflicted on persons who were found to be obstructing the import of grain to Bihar province. Moreover, orders were issued to the supervisors to be careful to prevent any set of men from combining together and forming a monopoly.[46]

Eleven years later, when Warren Hastings was Governor-General of Bengal, another famine was rumored. The steps he then took are best described in a memorandum he sent to the leaders of the British administration during the scarcity of 1800-1:

> It was my lot to preside in the government of Bengal in the year 1783, when a scarcity of rice, which is the necessary article of subsistence in that country, as wheat is in this, began to manifest itself. Its influence on the markets was immediate; and every appearance seemed to prognosticate a famine similar to one which had depopulated the provinces of Bengal and Behar about fourteen years ago proceeded from a failure of the preceding harvest, and the consumption of former years. The members who composed the administration chose to put this conclusion to the test. After having applied such measures as were most likely to give a temporary check to the complaint, they appointed a Committee, consisting of some of the senior and most intelligent servants of the Company; whom they invested with ample power to collect accounts of the actual quantities of rice existing in the provinces; to compell every proprietor of it to deliver to their agents an exact account of what he possessed; and in the event of a want of a due supply in the markets, to contribute to it according to

his ability. The threat of confiscation was also proclaimed against any who should attempt to elude the investigation either by secreting their grain, or by delivering false accounts of it: but if I may trust to my memory, only one instance occurred, in which it was found necessary to inflict the penalty. The result of the measure was, that the markets were in a very short space of time abundantly supplied; the price of grain gradually sunk to its level; and from the returns made to the Committee it appeared, that there was a sufficiency to last even to a considerable period beyond the next expected harvest.[47]

Surely here is evidence of an artificial scarcity—founded on little other than opinion—which was dissipated by taking forcible measures to convince people that a little care would suffice to see them through the season.

Yet another major famine struck Bengal and Orissa in 1867. By this time the principles of free trade were firmly entrenched and the only policy measures recommended by the Board of Revenue were to provide public works—otherwise, everything else was to be left alone. The *Calcutta Review* published a severe but balanced critique of the government's policy which provides us with a useful guide to the complexities of famine policy in an underdeveloped economy.[48]

Should a maximum price be fixed, the *Calcutta Review* asked? Definitely not, was the answer: "the mere rumor of an intention on the part of the local authorities to fix a price was enough to make the *modees* shut their shop, and to divert supplies of grain from the district. . . . And it certainly tends to encourage the people to consume more than the supply will warrant."[49] However, the *Review* was not so sure that competition would operate freely everywhere: "Towns may be pointed to in which the whole grain trade is in the hands of one or two *Mahajans*" and in such places "even famine prices are of no avail to tempt outsiders to engage in the trade."[50] Modifications of the general principle were advisable in such situations.

Should the export of grains be prohibited? The *Review* quoted J.S. Mill's argument that free trade maximized world welfare and that such a policy enabled an area to even out its food supplies, over the long run, with another differently situated area. In reply, the *Review* pointed out that several places to which India exported rice simply did not have the capability to supply rice during times of scarcity, while other countries such as Burma, were prompt in prohibiting exports upon rumors of a famine and so mutually beneficial trade was not possible. Nor could it be said that the amounts exported were small: "in the year 1866-67," the *Review* stated, "when people were perishing by thousands of the enormous amount of 4,500,000 mounds was carried away from Bengal alone, a quantity . . . sufficient for the entire annual maintenance of nearly half a million of people."[51] An export prohibition was certainly justified, the *Review* concluded.

Should the government attempt to import grain on its own account? Not if there was any possibility of private speculators being able to do so. The experience of the Irish famine of 1846 had adequately shown that so long as merchants expected government to act directly nothing would be done; only when government explicitly renounced any intention of interference did private importers enter in large numbers. In India, however, special circumstances prevailed, according to the *Calcutta Review*:

> when there is no import trade already in existence, recent experience has shown that even famine prices are not a sufficient attraction to create one, at least to anything like the extent required. If . . . produce runs short, there is in the outlying districts no existing import trade to supply the deficiency, and very little prospects of such a trade springing up.[52]

The government was therefore advised to take measures to ensure both the accuracy of the estimates of scarcity as well as the importation of adequate amounts. It is a measure of the success of the free-trade school that the prohibition on exports and on bounties on imports which were granted without hesitation in 1800 in Britain were quickly dismissed in India in 1867.][53]

The strengths and the weaknesses of the policy of leaving things alone are well exhibited in the contrast between Bengal and Orissa during the famine. The economically well-developed region of Bengal had good transport facilities and the government helped the market by publishing weekly the rates in every district, which:

> induced large shipments from the upper provinces, and the chief seat of the trade became unable to afford accommodation for landing the vast stores of grain brought down the river. Rice poured into the affected districts from all parts,—railways, canals, and roads vigorously doing their duty.[54]

In the more isolated district of Orissa, however, no one gave a thought to importation until it was too late. When the distress was at its height the monsoons made it impossible to provide effective relief. As a result, the suffering in Orissa was far greater than that in Bengal. In view of the ease of importation into Bengal, it would clearly have been foolish to hoard grain, but this was not so in Orissa. The common opinion among informed officials and nonofficials was that speculators had hoarded large amounts. The Commissioner of the district claimed that there was "enough to supply the market for a couple of years"![55] It is tempting to speculate what a Hastings would have done in such a situation.

VI

In conclusion, the main theoretical point of this chapter is that it is possible for a market to exhibit the symptoms of monopoly even with many sellers; furthermore, such a situation is especially likely in the market for foodstuffs. It may be permissible to conjecture whether this early nineteenth-century episode has any relevance today. No other scarcity occurred in England itself in the nineteenth century, and the issue, as well as the laws against forestalling, was quietly forgotten.[56] Nonetheless, the problem arises in slightly altered form in connection with underdeveloped countries. There are perhaps as many solutions to the problem of underdeveloped countries as there are underdeveloped countries, but of relevance to our analysis is a country such as Bangladesh, where a substantial proportion of the population, perhaps one-half, faces chronic starvation. How different is such an example from that of an England facing a scarcity of grain in the 1790s? And if they are similar, then is not state intervention—not state ownership, which is a different question—worth considering for such countries until such time as starvation ceases?

NOTES

1. The other major exception is the usury laws. Adam Smith gave the usury laws qualified approval in the *Wealth of Nations*.
2. The details of the legislation and explanation of the terms may be found in Palgrave's *Dictionary of Political Economy* (London: Macmillan, 1894). The historical aspects of such regulation are dealt with by N.S.B. Gras, *The Evolution of the English Corn Market* (Cambridge, Mass.: Harvard University Press, 1915).
3. Letter to the *London Chronicle*, March 28, 1772. Reprinted in Arthur Young, *Political Arithmetic* (London, 1774), 329-31.
4. Adam Smith, *An Inquiry into the Nature and Causes of the Wealth of Nations*, ed. Edwin Cannan (New York: Modern Library, 1937), 500.
5. For explicit approval, see J.S. Nicholson, *The History of the English Corn Laws* (New York: Scribner, 1904), 18. Jacob Viner's surprising comment on the Smithian argument is that "The later verdict that this was substantially erroneous seems valid to me." Viner does not, however, state any authorities or give any reasons for this opinion (*The Intellectual History of Laissez-faire*, Chicago: University of Chicago Law School, 1961, 66). The next lines would suggest that Viner believed local monopolies to be prevalent.
6. Smith, *Wealth of Nations*, ed. Cannan, 490. Many subsequent classical economists repeat the same argument without any real improvement.
7. Ibid., 491-2.
8. Ibid., 492.
9. Ibid., 493.
10. Ibid., 491.

11. Although importation was possible, it was not from the nearest markets, and the higher costs of transport and risk due to piracy meant that the amounts imported would be inadequate. As a result, one may as well add the amount imported to domestic production, and consider a somewhat less severe scarcity.

12. Mountifort Longfield, *Lectures on Political Economy* (Dublin, 1834), 60. If Longfield had turned to J.R. McCulloch's *Principles of Political Economy* (Edinburgh: Tait, 1830), pt II, ch. III, he would have found a variety of examples of miscalculation by producers. Earlier still, in criticizing Charles King's "demand curve," Dugald Stewart had said, "For some time after the harvest, it seems impossible (in the case of a deficient crop) that any exact relation should obtain between the degree of the deficiency and the augmentation of price; for how should the extent of the evil be guessed at with any accuracy?" (*Collected Works*, vol. 9, Edinburgh: Constable, 1856, 135).

13. Smith, *Wealth of Nations*, ed. Cannan, 494.

14. On the measures taken in 1795-6, see W.M. Stern, "The Bread Crisis in Britain, 1795-96," *Economica* (May 1964), **31**, 168-87.

15. E. Burke, *Thoughts and Details on Scarcity* . . . (London, 1800), 1; J. Howlett, *An Enquiry Concerning the Influence of Tithes* . . . (London, 1801); S.T. Cooleridge, *Essays on His Own Times* (London, 1850), vol. II; "Archdeacon Nares," *Edinburgh Review* (1804), **i**, 128.

16. For details of the trial, see D.G. Barnes, *A History of the English Corn Laws, 1660-1846* (New York: Crofts, 1930), 81-3.

17. Sir William Young, *Corn Trade: An Examination of Certain Commercial Principles* . . . (London, 1800).

18. Ibid., 20-2.

19. Ibid., 28-9.

20. Warren Hastings, "Memorandum on the Scarcity—1800": this document was made available by the Devon Public Record Office. It has been noticed by C.R. Fay in *Huskisson and His Age* (New York: Cambridge University Press, 1951), 228.

21. Arthur Young, *The Question of Scarcity Plainly Stated* (London, 1800), 22. Also see the evidence of Crow, Dumel (25) and Collingwood (28). Only Pilkington of Hartford claims a general acceptance of high prices due solely to seasons.

22. Cobbett, *Parliamentary History*, vol. 35 (London, 1819), 518.

23. Dugald Stewart, *Lectures on Political Economy*, vol. II; printed as Vol. IX of the *Collected Works of Dugald Stewart*, ed. Sir William Hamilton (Edinburgh: Constable 1856, 79). Both Stewart and Young spend much time showing that there was a scarcity, while the real issue was whether prices had not risen too high, given the deficiency. Stewart has a very interesting discussion of this point, where the figures from Charles King's seventeenth-century estimates are shown to have rough correspondence with those of 1800. Stewart appears unwilling to accept King's table (Stewart, ibid., 134-6. Without providing any empirical data, or even conjectures, about the number of parishes which were raising the amount of poor relief according to the price of provisions (or of the numbers involved), Malthus laid the sole blame for the inexplicable rise in prices to this factor (*An Investigation of the Cause of the Present High Price of Provisions*, London: Johnson, 1800). The First Report of the Commons Committee does note the misguided charity of some people in selling flour and bread to the poor at reduced prices, but does not think it at all widespread (Cobbett, *Parliamentary History*, vol. 34, 1433). That intelligent gentry were aware of the evil of such unhelpful actions may be seen from the letter of Thomas Law to Arthur Young in January 1793 (*Autobiography of Arthur Young*, ed. M. Bentham-Edwards (London: Smith, Elder, 1898), 229-31.

24. C.R. Fay, *The Corn Laws and Social England* (Cambridge: Cambridge University Press, 1932), 56-7.

25. W.F. Galpin, *The Grain Supply of England During the Napoleonic Period* (New York: Macmillan, 1925), 24. Lord Hawkesbury (later Lord Liverpool) to Sir Joseph Banks, September 20, 1797 (*The Banks Letters*, ed. W.R. Dawson, London: British Museum, 1958); the Reverend Henry Beeke in a Memorandum on the Corn Trade, 1800: I am grateful to the Devon County Record Office for providing me with a copy of this memorandum.

26. Fay, *Corn Laws and Social England*, 61.

27. *The Correspondence of William Wilberforce*, ed. by his sons (London, 1840), vol. 1, 218.

28. *The Life of William Wilberforce* by his sons (London, 1838), vol. 2, 386.

29. Lord Stanhope, *Life of the Right Honourable William Pitt*, vol. III (London: Murray, 1867), 245.

30. Ibid., 248.

31. Adam Smith, *An Inquiry into the Nature and Causes of the Wealth of Nations*, ed. William Playfair (London, 1805).

32. Francis Horner, "Playfairs edition of the Wealth of Nations," *Edinburgh Review* (January 1806), **vii**, 470-1.

33. When there was a shortage of corn in 1766, the King had overridden an Act of Parliament and prohibited the export of corn. In 1775 Lord Camden, who was generally very much opposed to the Administration on its policy towards the American colonies, justified this royal act by claiming that "the maxim of *salus populi suprema lex* was never more applicable" (Cobbett, *Parliamentary History*, vol. 18, 812).

    Adam Smith makes no mention of the remarkable proclamation of the Chatham-Grafton government on September 10, 1766, which tried to put into execution the laws against forestalling, engrossing and regrating (D.G. Barnes, *A History of the English Corn-Laws*, 1930; reprinted New York: Augustus Kelley, 1968), 39.

34. Although many contemporary pamphlets asking for sumptuary laws are rare, many lamented the general "luxury" of the age.

35. "The hardest part in the specification of the model is to make sure that each consumer can both survive and participate in the market" (T.C. Koopmans, *Three Essays on the State of Economic Science*, New York: McGraw-Hill, 1957, 59).

36. Young, *The Question of Scarcity*, 490-1.

37. M.J. Cullen, *The Statistical Movement in Early Victorian Britain* (New York: Harvester, 1975), 12. Fears of an uncontrolled food market were not left behind when English colonists entered America. See Karen J. Friedmann, "Victualling Colonial Boston," *Agriculture History* (July 1973), **47**(3), 189-205. For the effects of such fears upon government in more recent times, see Tom G. Hall, "Wilson and the Food Crisis: Agricultural Price Control During World War I," *Agricultural History* (January 1973), **47**(1), 25-46.

38. Stewart, *Lectures on Political Economy*, vol. IX, 131.

39. Galpin, *Grain Supply of England*, 16. It is, of course, essential that the government be believed whenever it makes a pronouncement. In Israel, rumors that the price of telephone calls would be raised led to hoarding of telephone tokens. The government's announcements to the contrary did not allay fears and even the efforts by the government to "saturate" the market by issuing a larger amount of new call tokens failed. I am indebted to my colleague, Meir Kohn, for this point.

40. A poster at Bath read: "Peace and Large Bread, or a King without a Head" (Galpin, *Grain Supply of England*, 19).

41. Cobbett, *Parliamentary History*, vol. 34, 1548. It is stated that the prohibition on the sale of freshly baked bread reduced consumption by a sixth.

42. For example, Lord Auckland in Cobbett, *Parliamentary History*, 1495.

43. A.K. Sen, "Starvation and Exchange Entitlements: a General Approach and its Application to the Bengal Famine," *Cambridge Journal of Economics* (March 1977), 1(1), 33-60.

44. Ibid., 34-5. Elaborated upon in *Poverty and Famines* (Oxford: Oxford University Press, 1981).

45. Smith, *Wealth of Nations*, ed. Cannan, 493.

46. Nikhil Sur, "The Bihar Famine of 1770," *Indian Economic and Social History Review* (October 1976), 13(4), 527. Sir W.W. Hunter does state that a maximum price had been imposed in Bengal, but provides no evidence for this assertion (see below, n. 56).

47. Hastings "Memorandum," 1-3. After describing his plan to a friend, Hastings had written on October 20, 1783, that the plan had "the instant effect of opening the Galas in Calcutta where an artificial want had already prevailed" (*Memoirs of Warren Hastings*, ed. G.R. Gleig, London, 1841, 132).

48. "The Operation of the Laissez-faire Principle in Times of Scarcity," *Calcutta Review* (January 1867), 56, 102-17. I have been able to find only two contemporary British periodicals that discuss the famine of 1866-7: the *Contemporary Review*, 4, is largely factual, but *Fraser's* (March 1867), 358-69, argues strongly for the provision of granaries as a long-term remedy, just as Warren Hastings had done in the 1780s. Interestingly, the author of the Fraser article, T.H. Bullock, fully agrees that such scarcities are, to a certain extent, created by the merchants, hence artificial.

49. "Operation of the Laissez-faire Principles," 105. Opposition to the policy of a maximum price is also described by Thomas Law, one of Warren Hastings' commissioners for regulating grain in 1783, in a letter to Arthur Young (*Autobiography of Arthur Young*, 229-31.

50. "Operation of the Laissez-faire Principle," 107.

51. Ibid., 110.

52. Ibid., 113.

53. For the seriousness with which classical economic theory was applied to India, see E. Stokes, *English Utilitarians and India* (Oxford: Clarendon Press, 1959) and S. Ambirajan, "Malthusian Population Theory and Indian Famine Policy in the Nineteenth Century," *Population Studies* (1978), 29(1), 1-14.

54. Sir W.W. Hunter, *Annals of Rural Bengal* (New York: Leypold & Holt, 1868), 44.

55. Ibid., 46 fn.

56. This presentation is surely inadequate because of the neglect of the extensive literature in French, which I have ignored because many of the important primary sources are not available in translation. Of the many accounts in English, I have found that of John W. Rogers Jr, most useful: "Subsistence Crises and Political Economy in Frances at the End of the *Ancien Régime*," *Research in Economic History* (1980), 5, 249-301.

7. Adam Smith's Rise to Superior Fame

When a man has once established his reputation, he is apt to gain more credit than is due to him; and, whatever be his forte, whether wit pleasantry or eloquence, if, by often moving us, he has prepared us to be moved, he may command us at his will.

Joseph Townsend, A Journey Through Spain

I

Why did Adam Smith became so extraordinarily famous? Some people have said that Smith was lucky to have written when "the time was ripe." What does this mean? And could the time have been ripe in both underdeveloped Scotland and highly developed England? To get useful answers the question has to be broken down. Nor is it clear that the *Wealth of Nations* would appeal as much to those who were serious about economics as to those who read it casually, as indeed most readers in the eighteenth century would. Why would the *Wealth of Nations* appeal especially to such casual readers? It is well known that Smith was part of a relatively small group forming the Scottish Enlightenment, that the Scots were disproportionately represented in literary circles and had a reputation of sticking up for each other. One cannot rule out the possibility that these are also facts of relevance in accounting for Smith's rise to fame.

The close-knit character of the Scottish elite helps only partly in explaining Adam Smith's stature in Scotland. We must remember that, for all its lustre, Edinburgh always felt some of the complexes common to provinces. For Adam Smith to be famous in Scotland, it was quite important that Adam Smith be famous in England. And for Smith to be famous in England, it was imperative that some members of the oligarchy espouse Adam Smith's merits. So a study of Adam Smith's rise to fame has to have several layers: what did serious students of economics think, what did interested laymen think and what of those who read for entertainment? And in what ways did reaction in England and Scotland differ?

135

Wesley Mitchell repeatedly claims that Smith rationalized growing individual initiative:

> Individual initiative was becoming a mass phenomenon. It was united with an extraordinary power for spontaneous cooperation . . . [Adam Smith's] theoretical exposition . . . was a set of philosophical reflections upon the advantages of practices which he had seen carried on by contemporaries.

His logic is, however, hard to follow. It is difficult to believe that phenomena such as smuggling or protests against the King, which Mitchell quotes in support of his thesis, have to be explained by a *resurgence* of self-interest. Just the ordinary amount of self-interest will do finely to explain the activities mentioned. Mitchell seizes upon the instances when mobs made Parliament change its course of action as examples of the growing influence of individual initiative. But, as he himself notes, in some of these cases the mob can scarcely be applauded:

> It would be a grave mistake to idealize the public opinion of the eighteenth century. Indeed, the people were often less wise and less tolerant than the much abused majority in Parliament. If the people won a great victory for the liberty of the press and the freedom of representation in the Wilkes affair, if they did well to oppose the long continuation of the American war, if they were right in insisting upon the publication of Parliamentary elections and in condemning the union of the Whigs under Fox and the Tories under North at the great election of 1784, they were wrong in defeating the reform of the excise which Sir Robert Walpole urged in 1733, in forcing the repeal of the bill facilitating the naturalization of Jews in 1755, and again in forcing the repeal of the County Voters Registration Act in 1789. The religious intolerance of the mobs that persecuted impartially the Jews, the Catholics, and the dissenters makes a strong contrast to the liberal spirit of the aristocracy that had come to care little about religious issues. But right or wrong, the people had their way when they were of one mind and excited. The vices and virtues of the political institutions represented the vices and virtues of the people most of the time.

How could Adam Smith possibly rationalize such mixed evidence as this? In fact, as the studies of several scholars have taught us, the one belief definitely held in common by Smith and his predecessors was the power of self-interest. The difference was that Smith made plausible the case that the effects of letting self-interest have free play were generally *desirable*—a point scarcely borne out by Mitchell's examples.[1]

Before turning to those who were pleased by what Adam Smith wrote, it will be helpful to consider briefly whether Smith wrote the *Wealth of Nations* in order to please someone. Two points must be emphasized in order to prevent the misinterpretation that Smith was arguing a "class" theory, in the Marxist sense of economic class. First, Smith appears to have gained his basic economic ideas from the lectures of Francis Hutcheson, and his faith in *laissez-faire* was developed *in nuce* by 1750, well before the industrial strength of Britain was a visible reality. His efforts therefore could scarcely be a case of rationalizing British *industrial* prowess. Secondly, Smith was emphatically *not* pleading a class interest. If Smith can be identified with any one group, then it would be that diverse assemblage of intellectuals who together comprise what is called "The Enlightenment." What class would a "Voltairean intellectual" such as Smith favor? A reading of the *Wealth of Nations* shows that he attacked the landlords, the merchants, the corporations, statesmen—everyone but the worker. So if we are to identify Smith with any one class it should, by exclusion, be the working class! But this is surely not the bias of Smith's class background. The fact that groups as diverse as chambers of commerce and radicals claimed Smith as authority for their views surely emphasizes the complexity of the situation and suggests that any simple explanation of Smith's fame is likely to be false.[2]

The real problem is to explain why Adam Smith was considered *the* economist of the eighteenth century and not just *another* good economist. Economic analysis is of course important, but we must not assume that this is what attracted readers to the *Wealth of Nations*; nor can we forget that the act of reading this book would color readers' perceptions of the scope and history of economics. An outline of the general argument of this chapter may be helpful at this point. A comparison with Sir James Steuart shows that Smith was not yet *the* economist by 1790. Steuart appears to fall into disfavor thereafter but even this does not lead to Adam Smith's superiority. Those who studied economics seriously between 1790 and 1800 found the Physiocrats to be superior. Except for the discussion of domestic monopolies, an issue where Smith's views only reflected those of a significant number of earlier economists, Members of Parliament did not adhere, in any meaningful sense, to the *Wealth of Nations*. We cannot say of the *Wealth of Nations* what has been said with truth of Newton's *Principia*, that:

> There has never been a time when the *Principia* was not seen as an epochal work, and there has never been a time since its publication when Newton was not perceived as one of humanity's leading intellects, much more than merely a genius.

Earning the respect of the studious is a very different thing from gaining popularity with the general reader from the educated classes. Smith's established position as a professor, his connections with the elite, his superior literary style were all bound to give Smith a considerable lead over his competitors. His self-conscious originality and his claim to provide a general theory satisfied the prevalent expectations regarding a work of genius and served to seal expectations of brilliance.[3]

Some politicians greatly helped Adam Smith's cause by publicly praising the *Wealth of Nations* in Parliament. Charles James Fox, during a brief period in office, and William Pitt the Younger, the Prime Minister, both lauded the *Wealth of Nations*. However ignorant Fox and Pitt may have been of the place of the *Wealth of Nations* in the corpus of eighteenth-century economic thought, their praise would have led the educated public to notice the *Wealth of Nations*. It possessed the necessary qualities of style, disinterestedness and grandiloquence to keep alive such interest. Some Christians also perceived the theodicy of the Invisible Hand and assimilated Smithian economics within conservative formulations of the common-law tradition. As a result, we see by 1800 that, with the exception of those who studied economics seriously, Smith had risen to the status of the best modern economist, but as yet he was not in a class by himself.

The Napoleonic Wars occupied public attention between 1800 and 1814. Smithian economics had little to say during these war years. We do not see much serious reference to Smith during the debate on the Paper Pound, but Thomas Spence's attempt to show the irrelevance of the continental blockade served for a while to bring back into focus the basic importance of international trade, the division of labor and Smithian economics. Since the period after 1814, and especially after 1820, is beyond the scope of this chapter, the next paragraph is a combination of fact and conjecture.

All the indications so far suggest that Adam Smith had all the advantages to make his name persist *if* he were once set up as the founder of political economy. Who would want to set up Smith in such a position? A significant clue is found in the fact that his name was most consistently referred to by Whig-Radical Members of Parliament between 1776 and 1800. The Whig-Radicals appear as Smith's most consistent supporters, in and out of Parliament. After 1814, the Whig-Radicals could let loose their anger at years of repression. The Corn Laws provided a perfect occasion for their political and economic goals to find simultaneous vent. In the years between 1790 and 1814 a number of important Europeans, oblivious of the traditions of British political economy, had begun to praise Adam Smith as the founder of political economy. Even during the Napoleonic Wars this praise began to filter into Britain and influence British attitudes. By 1814 those who were old enough to know of Steuart or Quesnay were few and uninfluential in both Britain and Europe. It would appear reasonable to conjecture that, after

1814, the explosive effusion of liberal political feeling led to the crowning of Adam Smith as the first scientific economist.[4]

II

It has long been one of the accepted facts of eighteenth-century intellectual history that Adam Smith's *Inquiry into the Nature and Causes of the Wealth of Nations* rapidly became a popular and influential work upon its publication in 1776. In the 1870s H.T. Buckle wrote confidently that, in terms of its ultimate results, the *Wealth of Nations* was "probably the most important book that has ever been written. . . . Innumerable absurdities, which had been accumulating for ages, were *suddenly swept away*" (emphasis added). Some years later, John Rae, Smith's biographer, felt sure that Lord North had utilized the *Wealth of Nations* as early as 1777 when formulating his tax policy. Even knowledgeable historians of economic thought such as Jacob Hollander wrote as though Adam Smith's ideas immediately became orthodoxy. How long a period did Buckle mean to imply when he spoke of Smith having "suddenly swept away" earlier views? There is much evidence to suggest that although Adam Smith lived another 14 years after the *Wealth of Nations* was published, the victory of Smithian economics did not come during Smith's own lifetime. This contradicts a view still voiced by some scholars. William Petersen, for example, writes: "During his lifetime Smith attained great honor and influence. Within a *few years* of its publication, members of Parliament started citing *The Wealth of Nations* to *settle* their debates" (emphasis added).[5]

In view of the careful, even luxurious, attention that has been bestowed upon all aspects of Adam Smith, it is curious to note that scholars have long been content to consider his rise to fame only in general terms. Jacob Viner, perhaps the best known of Smithian scholars, is by far the most definite in his assessment of Smith's influence: "Not immediately," we are told, "but within a generation, it [the *Wealth of Nations*] became a powerful influence on writers on economic policy." As the statement is limited to *writers* on economic policy, not policy makers, this is a much weaker statement than is visible anywhere else in the literature. No evidence is presented to support this claim, nor is any indication given whether Smith was merely ignored during these early years or whether he was actively attacked. A later scholar, T.W. Hutchinson, provides a more standard account when he describes the effect of the *Wealth of Nations* as "rapid, extensive and profound," but does not commit himself to a specific time period. As the experts have not provided any details on this issue the idea that Smith rapidly gained influence over policy is still widely prevalent.[6]

One possible reason why the question has not been tackled more seriously is the belief, virtually universal till the 1880s and very widely prevalent still, that Adam Smith *founded* the science of political economy. In 1831 the Reverend Richard Whately, Drummond Professor of Political Economy at Oxford, spoke of the subject as having been created "almost within the memory of man"; in 1887 a Maryland newspaper spoke of the *Wealth of Nations* as being "the first and only important work" on political economy; while a very recent author has said that "Adam Smith founded modern economic theory."[7]

Whether or not Smith did rise to fame as rapidly as most accounts indicate is of interest not only to economists but also to historians of science, who have recently spent much effort debating whether science progresses by the accession of incremental truths to a basic structure or by large changes in viewpoint leading to the introduction of a new system. If historians like Buckle are to be believed, Smith not only introduced a totally new view of the subject, a novel paradigm in the terminology of Thomas Kuhn, but also succeeded in winning over his contemporaries almost at once, truly a "revolution" in the history of ideas.

This issue is also of some interest to those economic historians who ascribe importance to free-trade policies as a "cause" of the Industrial Revolution. It was Arnold Toynbee who asserted that "The *Wealth of Nations* and the steam engine destroyed the old world and built a new one." This idea still has its proponents, as may be seen by L.A. Clarkson's refusal to accept the view, supported by most recent economic historians, that the policies of Mercantilism did help British economic growth and by his use of Adam Smith's critique of the colonial system as the basis for his refusal. The editors of the bicentennial edition of the *Wealth of Nations* also seem to support both the interpretations referred to above by referring to the immediate success of the *Wealth of Nations* and arguing that this success was achieved because of its "practical relevance"; in the context, this can only mean the relevance of free-trade policies to British economic prosperity.[8]

The curious point about the long survival of near unanimity regarding Smith's influence is that it has not been backed up by detailed argument. The only evidence John Rae presented to support his assertion that Lord North used the *Wealth of Nations* is the coincidence between some of North's policies and those advocated by Smith. As a historian of English views on taxation has pointed out, however, since the principles justifying North's tax program were widely accepted before 1776, Rae's assertion can only be true "in the narrow sense." Rae's statement that Smith was so popular in Glasgow that busts of him were displayed in many stores has found no supporting evidence at all, while his claim that Smith converted many merchants to free-trade views will be examined later in this chapter.[9] It is also surprising to find Buckle, who has just told us that Smith "suddenly swept away" Mercantilist prejudices, writing that free trade was "vainly struggled against by the most overwhelming majorities of both Houses of Parliament." Referring to the many allusions made to Smith in Parliament, Buckle continues, "Year by year the great truth [free trade] made its way; always advancing, never receding." And yet, if we examine the parliamentary speeches Buckle refers to, we find Smith repeatedly criticized in the last few years of the century for having dismissed outright the possibility of monopolistic effects in the corn and cattle markets.[10]

Not only is the evidence for Smith's popularity harder to find than historians have implied, there is reason to believe that the influence of the "Mercantilists" did not die away after 1776. Thomas Mortimer, for example, was an undistinguished economic analyst who objected to the free mobility of labor; he did not support the entry of nonfreemen into corporation towns because this practice was unjust to someone who had "paid a valuable consideration and submitted to seven years servitude" to get corporate freedom. Nonetheless, when Mortimer republished, with some revisions, his *Elements of Commerce, Politics and Finance* in 1801, a work originally published in 1768, the volume had over 150 subscribers. The surprising thing is that the Marquis of Lansdowne, who credited a conversation on free trade with Adam Smith as having made "the difference between light and darkness through the best part of my life," heads the list of subscribers for a book in which Adam Smith is explicitly attacked.[11]

In 1776 the two most popular writers on economics were the Reverend Josiah Tucker and Arthur Young.[12] Even though neither economist was a full-fledged supporter of free trade, Tucker being a consistent supporter of infant industries and Young of the corn bounty, both writers stressed the importance of commercial freedom. For example, both of them repeatedly criticized the Settlement Laws for restricting the mobility of labor, and domestic monopolies for being contrary to the national welfare.[13]

The advocacy of *freer* trade was thus not a new phenomenon in 1776.[14] Already in 1774 the *Monthly Review* had praised Tucker's *Tract I* as worthy of study by every liberal mind because Tucker had shown that different nations could prosper together. Dugald Stewart was later to praise Tucker for having paved the way for Adam Smith. Nor were Tucker's ideas unknown even in America. John Adams spoke of him as one of the recognized advocates for free trade in 1784; the other was Quesnay.[15] Arthur

Young, on the other hand, had admirers among European royalty and corresponded with George Washington.

In this milieu, finding evidence that Adam Smith was influential in debates on free trade is not the best way of establishing his influence. It will be more instructive to contrast the reception of Smith's ideas with those of an economist whose general outlook was very different from that of Smith, Sir James Steuart. The fondness of Sir James for the idea of a nearly omniscient "statesman," who would guide the economy over troubled waters, was noted and criticized by contemporaries.[16] Nonetheless, Steuart was a serious, perhaps too serious, economist; and his exposition of topics such as money and banking became required reading for all future political economists.

Many literary figures have wondered about the factors leading to fame, and Oliver Goldsmith wrote a letter on just this topic to his "Chinaman." Goldsmith begins by admiring the Chinese for accepting books on merit:

> I have frequently admired the manner of criticising in China, where the learned are assembled in a body to judge of every new publication; to examine the merits of the work without knowing the circumstances of the author, and then to usher it into the world with proper marks of respect or reprobation.[17]

Examining the views of the learned would appear to be an appropriate way to begin. The two most knowledgeable classes would be Members of Parliament and those who wrote for the leading journals. The importance of Parliament in molding public opinion should be obvious; in the absence of an academic status for political economy, the leading journals of the 1770s and 1780s are the most reliable indicators of common opinion. The bulk of this chapter will focus on the different receptions accorded Sir James Steuart and Adam Smith between 1767 and 1790, the year of Smith's demise. There is a considerable difference between ideas acceptable to an important elite and ideas acceptable to the more numerous, but necessarily more diffuse, educated classes. The members of this diffuse group leave fewer clues about how they are influenced, but the task must be attempted.

III

A careful study of the references made to Adam Smith in the Houses of Parliament between 1776 and 1800 leads Kirk Willis to conclude that:

Even twenty-five years after the publication of the *Wealth of Nations*, the Houses of Parliament were largely indifferent to its tenets, suspicious of its truth, and uncertain of its applicability.[18]

While there may be some rhetorical emphasis in this conclusion, it strikes the right note, especially when seen against the background of references in Parliament to other economic writers:

> But Smith remained as yet a minor figure. When economic principles and statistics were offered in Parliament, they were derived from many other sources than the *Wealth of Nations*. The eighteenth-century debates are studded with references to the economic writings of John Locke, David Hume, Gregory King, Charles Davenant, Sir Josiah Child, Sir William Petty, Dean Josiah Tucker, and Arthur Young. Moreover, the number of citations of Smith is minute compared to those of these other writers. For instance, while there are slightly over forty references to Smith in the eighteenth-century debates, there are literally hundreds of citations of Arthur Young's great works. Indeed, Smith runs a poor ninth or tenth in comparison with other economic authorities.[19]

The first instance when Smith's ideas are supposed to have been applied are the taxes laid on menservants and on property sold by auction in 1777, followed by an excise on malt and an inhabited house duty in 1778. Since the principles behind such taxes were commonplace, it is likely that Lord North was simply using Smith as a convenient reference and does not justify Stephen Dowell's claim that North had become "a disciple of Adam Smith." In 1778 Alexander Wedderburn, a former student, asked for Smith's opinion on the troubles in the American colonies, but it is not clear whether this manuscript circulated beyond a few members of the administration. One year later, Smith's opinion was again privately solicited by Henry Dundas, an important Scottish politician and friend, and the Earl of Carlisle, a society acquaintance, on proposals for freer trade with Ireland. These incidents undoubtedly indicate influence in one sense, but it is important to realize that such influence arose primarily from personal, academic and social connections and not necessarily from a consideration of Adam Smith's superiority as a social philosopher. In other words, the publication of the *Wealth of Nations* was probably irrelevant to Smith's consultative role.

The first explicit reference to the *Wealth of Nations* was made on November 11, 1783 by Charles James Fox in the unlikely context of a debate on the "address of Thanks to the King Speech":

> There was a maxim laid down, in an excellent book upon the Wealth of Nations, which had been ridiculed for its simplicity, but which was indisputable as to its truth. In that book it was stated, that the only way to become rich, was

to manage matters so, as to make ones income exceed ones expenses. This maxim applied equally to an individual and to a nation. The proper line of conduct, therefore, was by a well-directed economy to retrench every current expense, and to make as large a saving, during the peace, as possible.[20]

The trite nature of the reference has been noticed by many as has the irony of Fox's making this remark without knowledge of, or interest in, political economy. Willis divides those who referred to Adam Smith during the next quarter-century into three groups: (a) personal friends and society acquaintances; (b) those who studied economics with some seriousness; and (c) radicals and Foxite Whigs. This division is of some significance, as will be seen later. The attraction of Smith for students of economic policy concerns us here and it is significant to note that, with the exception of the debates on *domestic* monopolies in 1796-7, the economic principles of the *Wealth of Nations* are not discussed and Smith is either referred to as a source for facts or his opinion is stated without explication of his principles. The use of Smith in debates on domestic monopolies is revealing. The position taken by Smith, that monopolies in the corn trade were nonexistent, reflected a view espoused by many before 1776 and is certainly not original. The fact that such an issue provided extensive referrals to Smith, rather than his more original views on international trade, shows how the "textbook" qualities of the *Wealth of Nations* are beginning to dominate.

If we survey the major economic policy measures after Lord North there is little reason to suppose that the influence of the *Wealth of Nations* was being felt. The Younger Pitt, who was later to do so much to popularize the *Wealth of Nations*, enjoyed his first major parliamentary success with the India Act of 1784. It owed nothing to Smith, and Pitt seems to have ignored all the criticisms of the monopolistic practices of the East India Company made by Smith. Pitt's next initiative was the liberalization of trade with Ireland. However, he was guided by the Reverend Josiah Tucker and not by Adam Smith. Bernard Semmel has convincingly demonstrated that Pitt not only used the arguments but also "sometimes the very phrases" of Tucker's writings. Despite the considerable use made of Tucker both in 1784 and in the debates on the American colonies some ten years earlier, Tucker was *persona non grata* in elite circles and his views were quoted without his name.

The consolidation of customs and excises took place next. Despite Willis' claim that this reform "owed much both to Adam Smith and to Pitt's love of the intricacies of government and passion for comprehensiveness," this bill again falls entirely into line with the common wisdom of Smith's day. That a multiplicity of laws led to contradictions and made execution of the laws difficult was a long-standing theme in English legislation. As in the case of Lord North's taxes, Smith's presence is more ornamental than instrumental.[21]

In 1786 the historic Commercial Treaty with France was negotiated. A letter to the *Gentleman's Magazine* (March 1787) suggested that the proposed liberalization of trade with Ireland and the commercial treaty with France were due to the influence of the *Wealth of Nations*, but historians have been unable to find concrete evidence to support such a claim. The Irish trade measures were debated on the respective merits of the principles of the Reverend Josiah Tucker and David Hume, while the inner bureaucratic work was done by William Knox, Sir Lucius O'Brien and Sir Richard Heron, men whose correspondence reveals no evidence of Smithian thinking. The French Commercial Treaty on the other hand was negotiated by William Eden, a man who had opposed freer Irish trade and who, after describing the *Wealth of Nations* as an important contribution to political science, went on to speak of theorems on trade which look correct on paper but are not to be trusted in practice. Two detailed studies have been made of this treaty and neither of them claim that the treaties were based and argued on other than pragmatic considerations. Smith was referred to only once in Parliament, by Robert Thornton, a minor supporter of government— the first such reference, by the way—but that was in support of a position already reached and not one that taught new principles. In looking over the opinion of the manufacturers on this treaty in the British Museum (Add. Mss 34462), I was struck by the fact that none of the manufacturers made any reference to considerations beyond their own; those who felt they could produce more efficiently than the French wanted no duties at all, while those who did not feel thus emphasized the need for protection. John Ehrman suggests that it was really ideas like those of Sir James Steuart that continued as the basis for policy:

> A position really closer to that of Government [than that of Adam Smith] was the earlier one of Sir James Steuart, whose prime object (unlike Smith's) remained a favourable balance, but who saw this as a balance not of "trade" but of "wealth," to be provided by a favourable exchange of services and commodities whose value derived from a combination of "matter" and work.

R.F. Teichgraber has argued that the line of influence may even be traced in a direction opposite to that usually assumed:

> Smith may not have been the leading economic authority for parliaments of his time, but it seems that only with the success of the Anglo-French negotiations did he become an authority at all.[22]

IV

Adam Smith's refusal to make any reference to the work of Sir James Steuart in his *Wealth of Nations* is widely held to have been responsible for the general neglect of Steuart in the nineteenth century. Early commentators on this issue, such as J.B. Say, felt that the neglect was entirely justified, and this opinion was echoed for most of the nineteenth century. More recent studies of Sir James have shown that the view that Steuart's work in economics was below consideration is untenable. Nonetheless, it is still widely agreed that Steuart did not achieve more fame in his own day largely because of Smith's neglect of him. A.S. Skinner says that Smith dealt Steuart "a great blow," while A.J. Youngson is even more explicit: "By cutting Steuart out of the *Wealth of Nations* Adam Smith cut him out from serious consideration by almost all subsequent writers." Such impressions only gain ground from Steuart's own opinion that, if he were to write a life of his dog, "it would be a work as voluminous as my *Political Oeconomy* and perhaps as little relished by the public."[23] Two propositions are implicit in the views stated above: (a) that Steuart's book was little read before the publication of the *Wealth of Nations* and perhaps not at all thereafter; and (b) that the *Wealth of Nations* achieved a dominating position so rapidly and so successfully that Smith's neglect of Steuart would in fact lead to a general neglect of the latter. An examination of contemporary periodicals and books suggests that both the above propositions are more than a little misleading.

Ever since the appearance of S.R. Sen's book on Steuart, it has been recognized that the *Political Economy*, while no best-seller, certainly did not gather dust on the shelves, as had been thought for a long while. A.S. Skinner has recently shown that both George Scott and David Hume were "exceedingly pleased" with the manuscript and that Hume's later criticisms appear to be limited to the "form and style" of Steuart's volumes. The book sold slowly but steadily despite its tortuous style and difficulty of subject matter. More importantly, Steuart received good reviews from the two major periodicals, the *Monthly Review* and the *Critical Review*. The praise of the *Critical Review* is more discriminating than that of the *Monthly Review* and worth noting. It begins by praising Steuart for applying philosophy to civil policy and for laying down no system, instead leaving readers to form their own conclusions. After a long discussion of various issues in the *Political Economy*, stretching over three issues of the *Critical Review*, the review concludes by stating that "upon the whole, we must consider this work as a code for future statesmen and ministers in Great Britain, and as opening sources of political knowledge not hitherto investigated."[24] It is known that the review of Steuart in the *Monthly Review* was written at the request of Steuart's friend, George Scott. No such evidence exists with regard to the *Critical Review,* and this makes its high praise all the more valuable.

In the years that followed, Steuart's ideas reached the public principally through the numerous references made to him by Arthur Young. As Young was the most prolific author on economic subjects in the period 1767-76, this must count for a little. Only two or three general works on economics were produced in this period; and the author of one of them, Thomas Mortimer, refers to Steuart as an "excellent modern author." Nor did the reviews forget Steuart, for the *Monthly Review* referred twice to him in the next two years as providing correct views on taxation and the national debt.[25] What should have pleased Steuart most, however, was that he was considered the principal reference on economics for the new *Encyclopaedia Britannica*[26] in 1771, a proper compliment for his efforts from his fellow Scotsmen. That Steuart was deeply disappointed by the reception of his volumes is undoubted, but it seems to reflect more accurately the extent of his ambition than the manner in which the public treated him.

If Steuart's book cannot be said to have been neglected before the *Wealth of Nations* was published, it can actually be said to have acquired a higher status for a while after 1776. Smith's total neglect of Steuart in the *Wealth of Nations* has given rise to considerable comment. As we have seen, several authors have even stated that Steuart owes his obscurity to Smith's omission. Andrew Skinner has pointed to the Glasgow merchants' *Memorial* of May 1777 as the first public instance of Smith's early success. In opposition to this established view Clyde Dankert has remarked that if Steuart's framework were otherwise relevant, then Smith's neglect alone could not explain the want of readers for the *Political Economy*. Since many of Steuart's views were formed during his sojourn in the relatively underdeveloped countries of Europe, and since Scotland itself was underdeveloped with respect to England, if Smith really had won over the Glasgow merchants as completely as Steuart thought he had, it would be quite significant.[27]

The first point to be noted is that protests against the protection of agriculture were nothing new: From 1745 onwards a steady stream of pamphlets attacked the bounty on corn; and because oatmeal was common food in Scotland, the same considerations would apply there. The protest itself is therefore well accounted for on the score of self-interest, but this motive does not explain the language of the merchants' *Memorial* or their confidence in asserting that free importation is generally beneficial.

The debate over the importation price of oatmeal gave rise to at least four pamphlets;[28] of these three favor the higher importation price while the fourth argues for completely free import and export of corn. The curious fact, however, is that the pamphlet in favor of free corn trade makes no reference at all to Adam Smith. Of those which favor protection to agriculture, one refers to Smith only implicitly, and the other refers to him not at all, taking for its authorities Sir James Steuart, Arthur Young, and Mirabeau. The most interesting pamphlet for our purposes is the one that explicitly attacks Smith's ideas.[29]

After calling the *Wealth of Nations* an excellent publication, the author of *Corn-Bill Hints* goes on to say that "general principles of ingenious philosophic men" in economics are like "grand specifics in medicine": they are valuable, but require "skillful hands in applying them to particular cases." He goes on to note Smith's erroneous assertions about the small amount imported and his mistaken assumption that agricultural labor was mobile; he asks why free trade cannot be violated for the sake of national independence with regard to subsistence, as it can for national defense? On the whole, it may be said that while Smith was greatly respected in Scotland, he did not immediately become the oracle of economic wisdom that popular opinion has sometimes considered him.

It is time to go back a year, to 1776, to see how the *Wealth of Nations* was received upon publication; the natural gauges of this reception are the leading periodicals. The most influential of the contemporary journals was undoubtedly the *Monthly Review*, whose circulation the Reverend John Howlett estimated as twenty times greater than any other contemporary journal. The *Wealth of Nations* was warmly received by the *Monthly Review* in a lengthy summary, extending through four issues. The review bestows high praise, but the concluding paragraph makes it clear it was the beauty of the overall system that was being commended and not necessarily all the individual arguments:

> In order to give our Readers a connected view of the valuable materials contained in this work, we have been under the necessity of protracting our general survey of it to such a length, as leaves us no room for strictures on particular parts. We shall therefore only add, that after a careful examination of our Author's general principles, they appear to us to have been formed with the most mature deliberation, and on the most solid grounds.[30]

The hesitation over parts of Smith's ideas became more apparent when the *Monthly Review* came to review Governor Pownal's critique of the *Wealth of Nations*. After praising the originality of Smith's book and the merits of Pownal's attack in general terms, the *Monthly Review* deigns to enter into a discussion of individual points, "leaving it to the able and ingenious Author of the valuable work which has given birth to them to defend his own system, and to the Public to judge the merits of the dispute."[31] Although the general quality of reviews of this period does not reach the high excellence of the early nineteenth century, it is worth noting that the *Monthly Review* considered "Dr Smith's fundamental doctrine" to be "that commerce should be left at perfect liberty without the interference of law."

A year later, in a detailed review of James Anderson's *Observations on . . . National Industry*, the *Monthly Review* considered Anderson's principles to be "universal" and discussed them without reference to those of Adam Smith. It does mention Smith in the course of the article, but this is because Anderson had directly attacked Smith's treatment of the corn bounty. It expresses a very high opinion of Adam Smith's abilities but, significantly, suggests that he had some explaining to do: "we think it is incumbent on this ingenious author [Smith] to reconcile the seeming contradictions and inaccuracies of reasoning here pointed out, or to give up the argument entirely."[32]

What is quite surprising is that Smith is but once referred to in the articles on economics in the next ten years, and that one piece is the notice of the *Additions and Corrections* to the second edition of the *Wealth of Nations*. Smith was praised very highly once again, by the same reviewer who had summarized his book in 1776.[33] Since the *Monthly Review* was edited by dissenters and was generally on the side of political and commercial liberty, they might have been expected to be the first to apply Smithian ideas to economic problems; but this does not seem to have been the case.

Indeed, when Smith is next mentioned by name it is to be criticized. In reviewing the pamphlet *New and Old Principles of Trade Compared* (1787), the *Monthly Review* notes that the "new" principles are those which argue for universal free trade and that the author of the pamphlet is a partisan for the new ideas. The *Monthly Review* expressed its own doubts at length:

> Though it should even be proved in a satisfactory manner (which would be no easy task) that every political regulation that has been adopted, had proved hurtful, and not beneficial to trade, we should only, even in that case, be authorised to infer, that it is a matter of great difficulty to discover what regulations would tend to encourage trade,—without presuming to say that none could be found which would be beneficial.[34]

The journal urges cautious judgements which limit themselves to specific conclusions from well-proved concrete factors, and warns against "boldly drawing general conclusions from a few facts." This last procedure it attributes to "the ingenious Dr Adam Smith, who has frequently fallen into the same error, and by the weight of his authority has drawn after him a great number of inferiour imitators. Among these, we must rank the author of the treatise now before us."[35] The most widely read of contemporary periodicals was therefore not a convert to the new ideas of *laissez-faire*; on the other hand, the very language of the *Monthly Review* indicates that free trade had won several, perhaps influential, converts.

If we turn from the *Monthly Review* to its chief rival, the *Critical Review*, the picture is similar. The *Wealth of Nations* is given a lengthy review and not a simple summary in the fashion of the *Monthly Review*. Occasionally the reviewer is directly critical—for example, Smith's view that the propensity to barter is an innate principle of human nature. What strikes the reviewer most is Smith's advocacy of free trade and his pedagogical excellence. This is brought out in the concluding remarks:

> The abstract reasoning which Dr Smith occasionally advances, he never fails to illustrate and confirm by such apposite and familiar examples as place all the propositions he deduces in the most striking and incontestible light: and if, to obtain this end, he has frequently entered into details which may be thought to favour too much of minuteness, it ought to be remembered, that the useful speculation of philosophy can only become universally advantageous, by being rendered perfectly intelligible to readers of every capacity. The rational theory which he has developed of national prosperity will remain equally permanent and just in every age and country.[36]

The *Critical Review* took no note of Pownal's critique; but when it came to review Anderson, it too agreed with Anderson and against Smith.[37] Both the *Monthly Review* and the *Critical Review* thus place themselves in the peculiar position of bestowing very high praise on an author while refusing to defend one of the most important practical applications of his ideas.

Curiously, the *Critical Review* does not notice the *Additions* to the *Wealth of Nations* in 1784. That it was unconvinced by the new ideas is apparent in its support for Lord Sheffield's plan for restricted trade with the United States in 1784; reviewing a pamphlet with more liberal views, the *Critical Review* commented, "we cannot help suspecting the local attachments of a writer, who urges the propriety of liberal policy, in opposition to what seems to be the true interest of Great Britain in a matter of the highest importance." Nor does the *Critical Review* refer to Adam Smith's defense of the Navigation Laws when it found itself puzzled by Dean Tucker's attack on this popular statute.[38]

Further evidence of the imperviousness of the *Critical Review* to the ideas of the *Wealth of Nations* is visible in its review of William Paley's *Moral and Political Philosophy*. Very high praise is bestowed on Paley's economic views, which are quite distant from those of Smith, because Paley judges all economic policies not by their effect on national income but by their tendency to augment population.[39] While recognizing that Paley's theses are not new, the *Critical Review* nonetheless warmly recommends this portion of the book "on account of its intrinsic merit."

Equally revealing is the *Critical Review*'s attitude to the pamphlet *New and Old Principles of Trade Compared*, which we met earlier in connection with the *Monthly Review*. Free-trade principles are admitted to be true in theory yet disastrous in practice. It is odd that Smith is never mentioned by name, thereby suggesting that he was perhaps one of several, though perhaps the most widely read, advocate for the new ideas:

> Could all the nations of the earth be persuaded to adopt this liberal system, it would dry up the source of many sanguinary wars, and would greatly promote the general comfort and happiness of mankind. But in practice, should the government of this country, for example, admit of the free exportation of wool and the free importation of manufactured silk during one year, by way of experiment, we should see, at the end of it, thousands of our manufacturers starving in the streets.[40]

On the whole, it seems reasonable to assert that neither of the two major periodicals of the latter half of the eighteenth century held Adam Smith to be a reliable guide on economic policy at the time of his death in 1790.

It may be expected that Scottish periodicals would pay greater attention than English ones to their illustrious professor. There are two to be considered: the *Scots Magazine*, which began in 1738 and lasted well into the nineteenth century; and the *Edinburgh Weekly Magazine*, a short-lived but interesting local production between 1768 and 1788. Neither journal, however, shows any special interest in Smith. The *Scots Magazine* does notice the publication of the *Wealth of Nations* but follows its usual practice of borrowing a review, this time from the *Monthly Review*, and does not bother to provide any independent comments. There are no further references to Smith in the years that follow until we come to 1787, when Smith is mentioned in connection with the proposed French Commercial Treaty and in 1788 when Smith's view as to the fecundity of Highland women was quoted by a correspondent.[41]

The *Edinburgh Weekly Magazine* is a little more promising. The appearance of the *Wealth of Nations* was greeted with a fulsome panegyric:

> When Science, say the poets, descended from heaven, the dignity of her steps on earth surpassed description; the homage, first paid her by Genius, was in the spirit of true devotion. The scientific may sometimes be sophists, but the wise are always sufficiently possessed of themselves to know they are men. In the

first rank of the superior order of philanthropists must we class the author of the present inquiry; a work of equal ingenuity, industry and utility.[42]

How much of Smith's message the *Magazine* absorbed is doubtful, for in the next issue it is much concerned by Sir Charles Whitworth's tables showing that the balance of trade with several countries was against Britain.[43] Smith's contribution is vigorously praised in the *Magazine*'s review of *The Utility of Employing Machines*, probably written by James Anderson. Earlier numbers quoted Smith on why trade was flourishing, and later ones on the slow growth of manufactures in any country, which was presented as a reason why Britain should not worry about American economic growth.[44]

It does not appear that either of the two Scottish periodicals is especially careful to back the claims of free trade. In fact, the ideas of David Loch, a relatively ordinary writer on economics, who was waging a "buy Scottish" campaign at this time, received much more attention than those of Smith. S.G. Checkland has perceptively noted that the Scots were more concerned with economic development than with an abstract economic theory that bore little relation to their own economic experience, having grown to economic maturity in the shelter of the protected colonial trade.[45]

Adam Smith was not always seen as irrelevant to Scottish problems. In the lectures he delivered at Glasgow Smith took a much more positive attitude toward government intervention. He was even a member of various societies that tried to encourage industry in Scotland. The extensive free-trade position adopted in the *Wealth of Nations* may have surprised such contemporaries as Adam Ferguson and John Millar. In the years after the *Wealth of Nations* was published it was not Adam Smith but the rather "Mercantilist" John Knox or the interventionist James Anderson who were more widely read. None of the typically Scottish problems, such as the development of the Highlands or the fisheries, attracted Smith's concern and the Scottish public treated Smith as something of an outsider in turn. In this connection we may note that even Lord Kames, Smith's first literary patron, did not share Smith's free-trade ideas.[46] It is therefore understandable that Sir James Steuart would be of at least as much interest to them as Adam Smith, a point highlighted by Steuart's position as prime economic authority for the *Encyclopaedia Britannica* as late as 1796. The issue is raised most forcefully, however, by Steuart's obituarist, who makes a thinly disguised reference to Adam Smith as plagiarist:

It is needless to praise those works: the public will do ample justice to the last and greatest of them, when it has thrown from its literary maw the high-seasoned cookeries of the plagiarists who have obtruded Sir James's facts, principles, and reasonings on the world, without acknowledging from whence they were derived.[47]

It has been the main aim of this section to suggest that the traditional view of the victory of Smithian ideas is unacceptable for the period ending in 1790. Sir James Steuart was not ignored, and the complex of ideas he represented remained of considerable importance. Scholars have been too quick to look for signs of Smith's early influence. A casual reading of the contemporary literature can easily foster such a belief. Thus, William Eden praises the *Wealth of Nations* in his *Four Letters* to the Earl of Carlisle. This praise does not indicate agreement with Smith's views, however, because as soon as the question of free trade with Ireland comes up, Eden speaks of theorems of trade that are true on paper but not so in practice. More interesting is the extract from the dedication of the Reverend David Williams' *Lectures* presented by the *Gentleman's Magazine*. Williams requests the Prince of Wales to

> command, from the dreary shores of Caledonia, the philosophic statesman of Britain—give the profound "Historian of the Wealth of Nations" the daily direction of half an hour of your time; contemplate with him, the venerable but disordered machine, which you may be called to set in motion . . . and you will enable Englishmen to indulge their native generosity, by rejoicing in the obvious progress of liberty through the world.

On the face of it, the extract would suggest that Smith was the primary authority on economics. Actually, in the text itself Steuart is called "the most profound and original of all writers on political subjects," who has dug out invaluable ore from the bowels of the earth, some of which Smith formed into metal. Contrary to first appearances, therefore, Williams was really a follower of Steuart and recommended Smith only because Steuart was dead. In academic circles, essays written by fellows of Oxford in 1787 and of Trinity College Dublin in 1794 place Smith and Steuart on a par, without superiority to either.[48]

There is no evidence to show a clear preference for Smith over Steuart until 1790. This is quite remarkable in view of Adam Smith's established advantages as a well-known professor and literary stylist. After 1790 the French Revolution was to color all events. In his *Political Economy* Sir James Steuart departed from his heavy, formal style to wax eloquent over the Spartans. This could only arouse suspicion at the best of times and during the fearful years of the French Revolution it must have repelled the great majority of readers.

After this review of the contemporary evidence regarding the attention paid to Adam Smith in his own lifetime it should not come as a real surprise to find that Smith's death did not set the Scottish intellectual world a'mourning. His admirers resented this fact; and Sir Samuel Romilly wrote on August 20 to a French lady, a month after Smith's death, that "I have been surprised and, I own, a little indignant to observe how little impression his death has made here. Scarce any notice has been taken of it, while for above a year together after the death of Dr. Johnson nothing was to be heard of but panegyrics of him." The age of "Smithian economics" was yet in its infancy.[49]

V

Even though there is no definite evidence to establish Smith's superiority over Steuart in popular estimation before 1790, there is no doubt that the situation had altered drastically in favor of Adam Smith by 1815. In 1793 Jeremiah Joyce produced a summary of the *Wealth of Nations*, thereby indicating that it was used in classrooms; and in 1811 Daniel Boileau was to refer to the "standard text" of Smith. In 1806, the *Critical Review* reversed its earlier attitude and spoke of Steuart's views as "quackery," while the High Church *British Critic* considered meddling with the *Wealth of Nations* as "profane."[50] As for those who doubted the wisdom of leaving the internal corn trade alone, the Reverend Sydney Smith expressed his contempt by stating that "the question of the corn-trade has divided society into two parts—those who have any talents for reasoning, and those who have not." Why did Adam Smith achieve overwhelming pre-eminence? Recent scholarship has established that the analytical abilities of Smith and Steuart were not so very disparate as to occasion the almost complete neglect of Steuart throughout the nineteenth century, and so the explanation has to be sought elsewhere than the analytical merits of the two works.

It is curious to note that, even when Steuart fell from popularity, Smith's analytics were not accorded first place by his fellow Scots. The Scots literati were always a close-knit group as befits a provincial elite:

> The Scots literati tended to operate on two different, but not contradictory levels. Their material they deliberately tried to make as universal as possible, but in the manoeuvres which presented them with the crucial opportunities to seize Fame and Fortune they took it for granted they would be supported by a Phalanx of fellow-Scots.[51]

Nonetheless, when Dugald Stewart began lecturing on economic topics he gave clear preference to the French Physiocrats over Adam Smith:

> if, on the one hand, the language of the Economists be more precise and definite, and the result of a more accurate metaphysical analysis than that of Mr Smith . . . the doctrines inculcated in the *Wealth of Nations* are, on the other hand, of greater practical utility.[52]

The most distinguished economist to emerge from Stewart's classroom was Francis Horner (James Mill is the only rival to this position and his presence as a regular student seems uncertain). In polite restrained language Horner accused Smith of having borrowed from the Physiocrats:

> We intend to show, that, in the celebrated treatise of Dr Smith, though that author denies the ultimate incidence of taxes upon land, the principles which he has established involve this conclusion. That Smith did not precisely distinguish the real import of the economical system, is now confessed, we believe, even by those who agree with him in rejecting it. We are further satisfied that he derived a much larger portion of his reasonings from them, than he himself perhaps recollected; that his principles on the formation and distribution of national riches approaches more nearly to those of Quesnai, than he was himself aware; and that, to have recognised an entire coincidence, it was only necessary for him to have followed out his analysis a few steps farther.[53]

Henry Brougham, Stewart's other distinguished student, also adopted Physiocratic principles in his book on colonial policy. When we remember that the Malthus of the early edition of the *Essay on Population* was also definitely Physiocratic, there is little doubt that *among those who studied economic writers seriously* Sir James Steuart was of equal importance with Adam Smith till 1790 while the Physiocrats were considered superior down to 1800. Popularity, however, does not come by impressing the serious reader but the casual one.

In commenting upon Smith's fame, the literature has frequently noted Adam Smith's "good fortune," but the factors giving rise to such fortune have not been detailed. Oliver Goldsmith considered this question in one of his essays. In England, Goldsmith finds merit to have but secondary importance. As wealth is of most importance in a free, commercial society so the wealthy have the greatest influence in deciding literary merit:

> In England there are no such tribunals erected; but if a man thinks proper to be a judge of genius, few will be at the pains to contradict his pretensions. . . .
>
> As almost every member of society has by this means a vote in literary transactions, it is no way surprising to find the rich leading the way here as in

other common concerns of life, to see them either bribing the numerous herd of voters by their interest, or brow-beating them by their authority.

A great man says, at his table, that such a book *is no bad thing*. Immediately the praise is carried off by five flatterers to be dispersed at twelve different coffee-houses, from whence it circulates, still improving as it proceeds, through forty-five houses, where cheaper liquors are sold; from thence it is carried away by the honest tradesman to his own fire-side, where the applause is eagerly caught up by his wife and children who have been long taught to regard his judgment as the standard of perfection. Thus when we have traced a wide extended literary reputation up to its original source, we shall find it derived from some great man, who has, perhaps, received all his education and English from a tutor of Berne, or a dancing-master of Picardy.[54]

In examining this question we must move carefully once again, because the initial supporters of Smith were political radicals and it was only later that the conservatives understood the virtues of Smith's economics.

Since Smith's close connection with the elite, and especially the intellectual elite, may be of importance, let us note some of the people who came to study under Smith following publication of the *Theory of Moral Sentiments*. John Millar, who later wrote *A Historical View of the English Government* . . . was one of Smith's students; the Earl of Buchan, who was quite infatuated with Smith and Millar, was another; Henry Erskine—Lord Chancellor Erskine—attended; James Boswell came in 1759; Lord Shelburne, not yet Prime Minister, sent his younger brother, Thomas Fitzmaurice, to study under Smith; while from the far shores of Geneva, Tronchin, Voltaire's physician, sent his son to Glasgow with instructions "to study under Dr Smith."

It is useful to begin by looking at some general features of literary fame before turning to specific aspects of English and Scottish society to see the charms of the *Wealth of Nations* for the oligarchy and its followers. The different receptions received by David Hume and Rapin suggest the relevance of style and presentation:

Rapin's many volumes are composed largely of re-productions of parliamentary speeches, interspersed with comments by the historian. By comparison, Hume's *History* is both economical and eloquent. He deliberately placed any lengthy digressions into footnotes, and his own gift for the carefully balanced sentences and subtle ironies that graced the finest neoclassical prose makes his *History* infinitely more attractive than the heavy sentences of Tindal's translation of a foreign work.[55]

Elegant expositions of simple and general rules were what the educated classes wanted. This eminently reasonable demand persisted well into the nineteenth century. When Sir Henry Maine authoritatively summarized the progress of society from "status to contract" he won over his audience:

> The force and style of this passage explain in part why *Ancient Law* made such a tremendous impact on publication. The authoritative ease and fluency with which Maine formulated his ideas carried great conviction. He presented his findings as axiomatic propositions, which had only to be stated to be immediately accepted. One of the features of *Ancient Law* was the absence of references to sources. Unlike the traditional antiquarian treatise, it was not loaded with footnotes.[56]

Who can deny the charm of authoritative simplicity, unburdened by the details of scholarship? In Adam Smith's time, the much lower level of specialization made such demands extend even to such seemingly unphilosophical topics as military thought. Azar Gat characterizes Guibert's *Essai général de tactique* as containing brilliant military propositions but finds the extent of Guibert's fame explained by other factors:

> [It] was Guibert's belief—characteristic of the period—that his work offered a definitive system of tactics, finally creating a science of war, and it was the comprehensive expression that he gave to the ideas of the Enlightenment, that made his book a success with the *philosophes* and the talk of the salons.

The self-conscious originality and scientific posture are noteworthy:

> Guibert wrote the *Essai* with a pronounced and conscious intention to create an immortal masterpiece; this is apparent in every line of his work. . . . The ambitious young man acknowledges no predecessors. As usual, all competitors are brushed aside with a thoroughness only to be equalled by Jomini. . . . Military science, Guibert asserts, must adopt the methods that brought success in other sciences. The works of Newton, Leibnitz, and D'Alembert are the models to be followed.

Who can blame Guibert for giving the educated classes what they wanted to hear:

> Guibert's contemporaries were accustomed to the publication of masterpieces that laid the foundation of one sphere or another of human life and thought. The *Essai général de tactique* was accepted as one of these works.[57]

The marked literary superiority of Smith can safely be presumed to have gained him readers who wished to have an acquaintance with political economy but were not interested in digging deep. There existed a ready market for interesting tracts on economics. Sir Matthew Decker's *Serious Considerations* went through seven editions, Berkeley's *Querist* through six, Tucker's *Essay* through four; and even Postlethwayt's ponderous and unreadable *Universal Dictionary of Trade and Commerce* went through four editions between 1752 and 1774. This interest was evenly spread throughout the British Isles. Whether the original place of publication was London, Dublin, or Edinburgh, good works soon tended to be reprinted in all three capitals. In the 1750s, without any encouragement from Hume or Smith, the brothers Foulis reprinted several of the classics of English economics, such as the works of Sir Josiah Child, Thomas Mun, and Joshua Gee, while Davenant's collected works were reprinted by Sir Charles Whitworth in 1774. The importance of a knowledge of trade was well recognized, and in the margin of a manuscript on trade with Russia was written "no man sho'd be elligible to sit in the H[ouse] of C[ommons] that has not a competent knowledge in geography and the trade and manufacturers of Great Britain."[58]

In this atmosphere, any work that was well written, easy to read, and comprehensive in the branches of political economy could reasonably expect an extensive circulation. When David Hume and William Strahan, the publisher of the *Wealth of Nations*, compared the sales of Smith's book with Edward Gibbon's *Decline and Fall of the Roman Empire*, they were actually paying a compliment to Smith's style by suggesting that the readability of an analytical work could even be compared with that of a historical one. Although Smith is occasionally obscure, he provided the language with many eloquent and memorable passages.[59]

A further problem that haunted writers on political economy was that of establishing their own objectivity. Even the philosopher John Locke found it necessary to protest his disinterestedness before stating his views on money and the rate of interest. William Letwin has examined this issue carefully and asserted that even though Smith did not need the help, his established position as a professor of moral philosophy helped him gain credibility in the eyes of his readers.[60] Steuart, on the other hand, was a known Jacobite who had obtained pardon only with difficulty. Furthermore, the readiness with which Steuart invoked a "statesman" to solve economic problems could not have been reassuring to his readers.

In addition to "internal" factors such as style and objectivity, "external" factors also played a role in popularizing free-trade ideas in general and Adam Smith in particular. Too many material interests are involved for ideas to be accepted which conflict with the interests of powerful, particular groups. We have already seen how the ideas of Smith and Steuart ran neck and neck despite all the advantages Smith possessed. In advocating free internal trade Smith was advocating nothing new but only telling the English what they were already practicing. The advocacy of free international trade, however, struck a new chord and came at a very opportune time from the self-interested viewpoint of English manufacturing interests. As Britain's industrial superiority manifested itself in unmistakable terms by 1800, so too, we may expect, did free trade appear as the best policy to British manufacturers. The merchants' petition of 1820 is one of the landmarks in the history of free trade. The extent to which liberal trade policies and British interests coincided has been carefully examined by Bernard Semmel in his important book, *The Rise of Free Trade Imperialism*.[61]

VI

The public admiration of politicians and the praise of partisan admirers played a part in serving to keep Smith prominently in the public eye. These are, of course, normal components of "fame"; but the close attention paid to Smith's intellectual qualities have made it easy for us to forget this point. There is a curious remark in Adam Smith's obituary regarding the fame of the *Wealth of Nations*. We are told that "it was not at first so popular as it afterwards became"[62] and that the book's general popularity began with a reference to it made in Parliament by the leading Whig spokesman, Charles James Fox, to the effect that Smith had shown that nations grow rich only as individuals do, by spending less than they earn. The obituarist goes on to comment that though the remark was trite it served to encourage the sales of the *Wealth of Nations*.

"It has been seriously suggested," wrote John Rae in his biography of Adam Smith, "that the fortunes of the book in this country was made by Fox quoting it one day in the House of Commons." Rae thought the suggestion peculiar and countered by noting that in November 1783 two editions had been sold and a third was on its way. The obituarist did not claim that the book or Adam Smith would have remained unknown but only that Fox gave the first great boost to the sales of the *Wealth of Nations*. The respect of a leading politician is one of those external events that can help an author. On what grounds can we dismiss the claim of the obituarist?[63]

We do not know how many copies of the first edition of the *Wealth of Nations* were printed, but the second edition had only 500 copies. Since the first edition sold out within a year, one would expect the publisher to have had optimistic expectations, so most probably 500 copies of the first edition would also have been printed.[64]

Adam Smith was by no means indifferent to the sales of the *Wealth of Nations*. He wrote eagerly to Strahan:

> Neither you nor Mr Cadell have wrote me anything concerning the new Edition of my Book. It is Published? Does it sell well? does it sell ill? does it sell at all?[65]

There is no evidence that the *Wealth of Nations* was continuing to sell well in the second edition. Indeed, there is evidence to the contrary, but scholars have been so convinced of the transparent merits of the *Wealth of Nations* that they have treated the evidence as sallies of humor on Smith's part. In letters to Cadell and Strahan, written on successive days, Smith asks for some copies of the *Wealth of Nations* to be sent as gifts, and remarks, in almost identical terms, to both Cadell and Strahan: "I am afraid I am not only your best, but almost your only customer for this second edition" (Oct. 25 and 26, 1780).[66]

The letter to Andreas Holt, one of the recipients of the presentation copies, has the marks of a careful intellectual biography. Smith refers to the period of gestation of the *Wealth of Nations*, his activities during those years, the role of the Duke of Buccleuch, the publication and reception of the *Wealth of Nations*, the animosity aroused by the obituary on Hume, Smith's acceptance of the Commissionership of Customs, and so on. Regarding the immediate reception of the *Wealth of Nations* Smith writes: "I have however, upon the whole, been much less abused than I had reason to expect."[67] Since Smith's most detailed attack on the "Mercantile System"—meaning thereby the large privileged overseas companies—did not appear until the third edition of 1783, there appears to be some wishful thinking on Smith's part. One would be hard pressed to find any instance of "abuse" of the *Wealth of Nations*. The typical reaction was that the book had much that was both good and bad, as in Arthur Young's critique[68] that it was the ablest extant work, yet full of errors.

Since the available evidence does nothing to cast doubt on the hypothesis that the *Wealth of Nations* was not selling quickly between 1778 and 1780, it is worth taking the obituarist more seriously and examining Smith's connection with Charles James Fox. The Radical-Whig disposition of Adam Smith is not doubted by any scholar (except Walther Eckstein, and he is satisfactorily refuted by D.D. Raphael in the Introduction to the *Theory of Moral Sentiments*), so the connection seems quite natural. Smith wrote very favorably of the Fox-North coalition which came to power in March 1783:

> It would give me the greatest pleasure to believe that the present Administration rests on a solid Basis. It comprehends the worthiest and ablest men in the nation, the heads of the two great Aristocracies.[69]

We have no evidence to show that Smith was in direct contact with Fox during the months of power. That Fox should single out Smith's work for a banal observation is nonetheless significant. This is the same Fox who was vigorously to oppose the Commercial Treaty with France three years later, who openly avowed his ignorance of political economy, and who pooh-poohed Lauderdale's admiration for Adam Smith.[70]

Regardless of Fox's actual motivation in referring to Smith in Parliament, did the reference have any influence? We have a clear indication in the postscript of a letter to Strahan on November 20, 1783, some four weeks after Fox's speech:

> Cadel, to whom I beg to be remembered, is anxious on account of something which fell the other day from Mr. Fox that we should set about the new edition immediately.[71]

The importance of this letter was noted by Homer Vanderblue, who owned the letter, but it has been ignored by later scholars. In the latest, bicentennial edition of Adam Smith's *Correspondence*, Fox is inexplicably changed to Rose. Why the words of William Rose would cause Cadell to rush to print a new edition is not at all clear.[72] Even with Cadell's urging, the third edition did not appear till a year later, in November 1784. One thousand copies were printed. Within two years a fourth edition of 1,250 copies appeared and the fifth (1789) and sixth editions (1791) saw even larger printings of 1,500 and 2,000 copies respectively. The *Wealth of Nations* was steadily growing in repute and popularity. It is perhaps impossible to disentangle all the factors leading to its eventual dominance but the possibility that Fox's reference in Parliament helped cannot be entirely ignored.

Some 50 years later, Lord Brougham received a letter from an unknown correspondent urging him to refer in Parliament to the work on political economy just published by the Reverend Thomas Chalmers, and it concludes by reminding Brougham how much Smith's book had benefited by the eulogy bestowed upon it by the Prime Minister, William Pitt, in 1791.[73] The eulogy of Pitt alluded to is such as few subsequent economists, including Lord Keynes, have enjoyed:

> There was a further cause for the increase of national wealth—the constant accumulation of capital, wherever it is not obstructed by some public calamity or by some mistaken and mischievous policy. Simple and obvious as this principle is, and felt and observed as it must have been in a greater or less degree even from the earliest periods, I doubt whether it has ever been fully developed and sufficiently explained but in an author of our own time, now

unfortunately no more (I mean the author of the celebrated treatise on the Wealth of Nations) whose extensive knowledge of detail and depth of philosophical research will, I believe, furnish the best solution of every question connected with the history of commerce, and with the system of political economy.

If ever public praise could establish a scholar's authority, Pitt's speech must have done so. The aspect of the *Wealth of Nations* singled out for praise by Pitt—that liberty and property suffice to provide economic growth—had been a part of British economic thought for over a century, and Pitt's words are more indicative of Pitt's own lack of knowledge than of Smith's originality.[74]

That Pitt was simply not well-read in economics becomes apparent when Pitt declined to follow Smith's views on the balance of trade in 1797:

> There were many different theories of the balance of trade; but he would not subscribe to any of them, upon however high authority they might stand, without consulting his own judgment. Much as he respected the opinions of that great writer, whose works the hon. gentleman had quoted, he could not help dissenting from several maxims which he had advanced. He thought that great author, though always ingenious, sometimes injudicious.[75]

Slightly earlier, William Wilberforce, one of the men who made an early reference to Smith in Parliament, expressed doubts about the applicability of Smith's ideas during times of scarcity.[76] Nonetheless, these second thoughts did not spread very far and an important reason for this fact was the partisan backing Smith received from several prominent young intellectuals. Francis Horner refused to publish an annotated edition of the *Wealth of Nations* because he was "reluctant to expose Smith's errors before his work has operated its full effect."[77] Some years later, when Lord Lauderdale published a critique of Adam Smith, it was savagely criticized in the *Edinburgh Review* by Henry Brougham.[78] Smith gained from the extravagant praise of the famous, even when it was based on callow thoughts.

The attraction of the approach adopted in the *Wealth of Nations* is its close link with natural-rights arguments and political radicalism. The fact that Smith had placed human labor as the primary agent for creating wealth no doubt helped this link. Smith's sympathy for laborers and farm workers and his hostility towards masters and landlords has long been noted. Combined with the general emphasis on liberty (one recalls the radical stress on liberty given by his old teacher, Hutcheson), the ideas would appear as a powerful dissolvent of traditional ideas, especially in Europe, a fact appreciated by such commentators as Charles Ganilh and Adolphe Blanqui:

> Wealth, produced by labour—restores man to his primitive dignity, through the sentiment of his independence, through his obedience to laws common to all, and his sharing in the benefits of society in proportion to his services. (Charles Ganilh)

> there were no longer any sterile occupations, since every body was capable of giving things an exchange value, by means of labor. What an encouragement to men ill-favored by fortune and to those who did not expect the boon of an inheritance! (Adolphe Blanqui)[79]

The link between natural-rights economics and political radicalism would have been evident to contemporaries and it perhaps explains the fact that the first parliamentary reference to the *Wealth of Nations* was made by someone ignorant of economics: Charles James Fox, the leader of the Radical Whigs.

Subsequently, we find some early favorable references to Smith in William Godwin and Tom Paine, while one of Smith's earliest admiring editors, Jeremiah Joyce, also provides evidence of being a political radical by his sharp criticism of that instrument of tyranny, the National Debt. Another admirer of Adam Smith, Thomas Archard, wrote a pamphlet defending the suppression of the French nobility. Lord Lauderdale, later a sharp critic, was a radical in his youth, when he is said to have "worshipped" Smith.

The difference between the philosophical view supporting free trade as an extension of individual liberty and free trade as an economic proposition is well brought out in the writings of Thomas Paine. The guiding light of Paine's politics strongly emphasized liberty:

> Government is no farther necessary than to supply the few cases to which society and civilisation are not conveniently competent; and instances are not wanting to show, that everything which government can usefully add thereto, has been performed by the common consent of society, without government.
>
> The more perfect civilisation is, the less occasion has it for government, because the more does it regulate its own affairs, and govern itself; but so contrary is the practice of old governments to the reason of the case, that the expences of them increase in the proportion they ought to diminish. It is but few general laws that civilised life requires, and those of such common usefulness, that whether they are enforced by the same forms of government or not, the effect will be nearly the same.[80]

The argument was extended to using trade as an example of successful private management:

> In those associations which men promiscuously form for the purpose of trade, or of any concern in which government is totally out of the question, and in which they act merely on the principles of society, we see how naturally the various parties unite; and this shews, by comparison, that governments, so far from being always the cause or means of order, are often the destruction of it.[81]

We would of course expect Paine to be appreciative of Smith's *Wealth of Nations*, and this is indeed the case in the only explicit reference Pain appears to have made:

> In these chartered monopolies, a man coming from another part of the country is hunted from them as if he were a foreign enemy. An Englishman is not free of his own country; every one of those places presents a barrier in his way, and tells him he is not a freeman—that he has no rights. Within these monopolies are other monopolies . . .
>
> Are these things examples to hold out to a country regenerating itself from slavery, like France? Certainly they are not, and certain am I, that when the people of England come to reflect upon them they will, like France, annihilate those badges of ancient oppression, those traces of a conquered nation. Had Mr. Burke possessed talents similar to the author of "On the Wealth of Nations," he would have comprehended all parts which enter into, and, by assemblage, form a constitution.[82]

However, if we look for any affinity between Paine and Smith extending beyond the desire for an economical government (which also appears in Paine's comments on the Physiocrats) we shall be disappointed. Paine consistently gives an importance to gold and silver quite incompatible with Smith's diatribe on Mercantilism. This is already apparent in Part I of the *Rights of Man* (376-8); it is continued in Paine's treatment of the balance of trade, which is not Mercantilist but not Smithian either, and Paine is again quite far from Smith in his views on the benefits of the National Debt:

> As to the national debt, however heavy the interest may be in taxes, yet, as it serves to keep alive a capital useful to commerce, it balances by its effects a considerable part of its own weight; and as the quantity of gold and silver is, by some means or other, short of its proper proportion, being not more than twenty millions, whereas it should be sixty, (foreign intrigue, foreign wars, foreign dominions, will in a great measure account for the deficiency), it would, besides the injustice, be bad policy to extinguish a capital that serves to supply that defect.[83]

That Paine was really quite distant from Smith comes out quite clearly in his attack on the adverse balance with the East Indies:

> The opening of South America would produce an immense field of commerce, and a ready money market for manufactures, which the eastern world does not. The East is already a country full of manufactures, the importation of which is not only an injury to the manufactures of England, but a drain upon its specie. The balance against England by this trade is regularly upwards of half a million annually sent out in the East-India ships in silver; and this is the reason, together with German intrigue, and German subsidies, that there is so little silver in England.[84]

An examination of Paine's earlier writings shows virtually no development of his economic thought. The same ideas are to be found in his writings of the 1770s as in the *Rights of Man*. If the popularity of Paine is indicative of the thinking of a significant minority in Britain, then it would appear that the *Wealth of Nations* would be much admired for its support of liberty even though Smith's specifically economic ideas may have been neither absorbed nor understood. The point is further strengthened by Lord Cockburn's comment that Smith's death was ignored by all except the political youth of Scotland:

> The middle-aged seemed to me to know little about the founder of the science [political economy] except that he had recently been a Commissioner of Customs and had written a sensible book. The youth—by which I mean the Liberal young of Edinburgh—lived upon him.[85]

In 1793 the Marquis of Lansdowne even went so far as to claim that the ideas of the French Revolution were not new but had in fact been propounded earlier by such respectable British authors as Adam Smith and Dean Tucker. Dugald Stewart stated that people who once associated with Adam Smith felt embarrassed about any association with "liberal" principles in the wake of the French Revolution. Nor should this entirely surprise us. That Adam Smith had a partiality for radicalism is evidenced by his admiration for both Rousseau and Voltaire:

> Voltaire set himself to correct the vices and follies of mankind by laughing at them, and sometimes by treating them with severity, but Rousseau conducts the reader to reason and truth by the attractions of sentiment and the force of conviction. His "Social Compact" will one day avenge all the persecutions he suffered.

James Beattie criticized David Hume's skepticism in his *Essay on Truth* and later wrote to Lady Wortley Montagu that, even though he had known Smith well once, after the publication of the *Essay on Truth*—"*nous avons changez tout cela.*"[86]

The early supporters of Free Trade in English economic thought in the 1680s and 1690s were almost certainly motivated by political considerations—in that free trade with France, the traditional enemy, was a part of the Tory agenda. Ashley's influential view that Smith's contribution lay in making a Tory doctrine, free trade, acceptable to Whigs is liable to misinterpretation unless it is recognized that the underlying reasons for the same policy had changed considerably. With the rise of Sir Robert Walpole, the Whigs began to cautiously adopt the same "Tory" attitudes towards trade with France. Philosophically speaking, the attitudes of the natural-rights school were far more consonant with the writers of *Cato's Letters* or the Commonwealthmen surrounding Lord Molesworth. The attitudes that encouraged the philosophy of *laissez-faire* had considerable roots in liberal religious and political thought, as noted by Jacob Viner and M.L. Myers. It is no accident that both John Locke and, a half century later, Bishop Law embody the same complex of political and theological notions.[87] When Francis Horner refused to make public his criticisms of the *Wealth of Nations* because the good effects of that book were yet to be spread further he may well, as a staunchly liberal Whig, have had the politico-economic impact in mind. The attitude is more explicit in John Stuart Mill's stated reason for adhering to *laissez-faire* in 1833:

> In the meantime that principle, like other negative ones, has work to do yet, work mainly of a destroying kind, and I am glad to think it has strength enough to finish that after which it must soon expire; peace be with its ashes when it does expire, for I doubt much if it will reach the resurrection.[88]

Insofar as the movement towards a philosophic basis for free trade had socio-political origins, Smith supports the thesis of Leo Rogin that "new systems first emerge in the guise of arguments in the context of social reform."[89]

VII

For the Continent, points of minor relevance to Britain assume great importance. C.R. Fay pointed to the emphasis on liberty as part of Smith's exhilarating message, while Edwin Cannan claimed that justification of the businessman was one of the significant aspects of the *Wealth of Nations*. In those countries that were highly monarchical, Smith's message would appeal only to a few radical spirits—they would be unsettling for the Establishment. The French Revolution would upset all established ideas and establishments and a different configuration could be expected to prevail thereafter. The distaste for centralization and despotism engendered by Napoleon would be combined with a desire to mobilize effectively domestic resources in all the conquered territories such as Germany and Italy and would make Smith's views inherently welcome, when we combine these features with the privileged position of England as the center of economic liberalism.[90]

The existence of a deep-seated interest in improving their economies, and agricultural productivity in particular, is visible in the extensive correspondence of Arthur Young and Sir John Sinclair with European nobility. In 1796 Professor C.J. Kraus noted how this concern had spread:

> But tell me, how does it come that so many counts are turning to the study of Cameralia [i.e., political economy], which so far as I know has never happened before? . . . Is law losing its former position of honor? Have the Cameralia risen in power and glory?[91]

That Adam Smith achieved a superior status by the 1820s has been noted by scholars but the difficulties in separating out Smithian from other influences are considerable. Referring largely to France, Melchior Palyi was impressed with the importance of the Physiocrats as precursors:

> As a matter of fact, the physiocrats helped to pave the road for the success of the *Wealth of Nations* while they lost the capacity to obstruct that success to any important degree. To some extent, at least, Adam Smith profited immensely by the general spread of their ideas, since what *he* offered was or worked itself out as the direct continuation and refinement of the physiocratic doctrine.[92]

The importance of the Physiocrats in Germany was explicitly denied by C.W. Hasek in 1924 but the detailed research of Keith Tribe has established the fact that Smith was seen largely as a follower of the Physiocrats.[93]

The publication of the *Wealth of Nations* was received with critical praise in Germany. J.G.H. Feder noted Smith's affinity with the Physiocrats, his (unacknowledged) criticisms of Sir James Steuart, and makes shrewd comments on the limitations of unrestricted competition:

> The inferior goods and deceptions which result from too great competition, since customers can be obtained only through low prices and easy credit; the ruin of many who under such freedom choose attractive but unprofitable trades; and the result that many an able man, especially if he is likewise honest, is

forced under through excessive competition, appear to be evils that outweigh any gains of such complete freedom.[94]

Till nearly 1800, we find only limited instances of Smithian ideas. Some devoted followers of Smith's ideas are to be found but the general neglect is also visible. George Sartorius felt obliged to reply to the publisher's complaints of slow sales in a review: "Smith will not long remain on the shelves, for reason will assert itself in the end."[95]

The French Revolution served as a forcible dissolvent of all traditional ideas and the fact that Smith's ideas slowly gained momentum after 1795 cannot simply be coincidental. The despotic system of Prussia and the centralized one of France meant that the only viable direction of change was towards greater liberalism and Smith's views struck with messianic force in this context. The statistician A.F. Lueder was so charmed with the ideas of freedom gained from the French Revolution and from Adam Smith that he even regretted having spent most of his life studying statistics, which only served to lay obstacles in the way of freedom.[96]

In France, J.B. Say, Ganilh and Blanqui all show the impact of democratic freedom as being of paramount importance in giving precedence to Smith. Palyi notes how it is the sudden preeminence that needs explaining:

> The change from the position of a hardly quoted respectable author to that of a great thinker of wide influence was indeed an enormous one and must have occurred rather suddenly some time during the early Napoleonic years. In 1808, at any rate, even a purely technical pamphlet of a high official of the Kingdom of Italy, G. Tamassia's *Del fine delle Statistiche* (Milano, 1808, pp. 6f.) could not do better than start out with a long citation from Adam Smith on the duties of sovereigns as the foundation on which the author bases his own *lezione*.[97]

When we turn to the reforms in Prussia associated with Stein and Hardenburg, the evidence for Smith's influence is murky. Hasek is mindful of the difficulty of disentangling Smith from others:

> specific influences are difficult to trace. The revolution in France, Physiocratic views, the great war, as well as Smithian doctrines all left their impress on the statesmen of this period.[98]

Stein entered the bureaucracy under Heinitz, who was influenced by the Physiocrats. He criticized some of Smith's views on free trade and on guilds, and his writings show an inability to distinguish Smith's ideas from those of Ganilh, Lauderdale or Sismondi.[99] The views of Stein, as well as those of his lieutenant Vincke, appear to be based more on pragmatism and a general admiration for English liberal institutions. Hardenberg, on the other hand, appears to have been quite uninfluenced by Smith and owed all his liberal ideas to the impact of the French Revolution. We must be cautious about ascribing any turn towards free trade as being due to Smith. It is well known that much of the so-called Mercantilist literature harped on the benefits of "freedom," and the acceptance of liberal ideas can be just as easily "explained" as pragmatic adaptations of earlier ideas. Of the two items in the Stein-Hardenberg reforms that are supposed to be due to Smith's influence—numbers 34 and 50—number 34 is entirely compatible with earlier ideas, and only number 50 shows distinctive signs of Adam Smith in both language and substance. Since Stein did not draft the reforms and since there is doubt whether he read the final version, we are entitled to deduce that someone in the bureaucracy was under Smith's influence, but we are not sure who. The link between the agrarian interests of East Prussia, which would naturally turn towards free trade, and the acceptance of Smith's ideas cannot be ignored.[100]

Sartorius spoke of his duty to spread the truths of Adam Smith and Garve credited Smith with providing new views on all aspects of social life. Garve spent his leisure hours translating the *Wealth of Nations*, yet the same Garve venerated the ideas of Frederick II:

> It is really fortunate for an author in the Prussian states that in respect to many points in state economy he is able, in any general investigation of what should be done, to agree with those rules which form the basis of the actions, or at least of the views, of his prince.

Sartorius himself doubted Smith's notions on value, on the measure of value and on the unlimited application of free trade. C.J. Kraus thought the *Wealth of Nations* the most beneficial work since the New Testament:

> For truly Scheffner is right in saying that the world has seen no more important book than that of Adam Smith; certainly since the times of the New Testament no writing has had more beneficial results than this will have, when it has become better known and has penetrated further into the minds of all who have to do with matters of state economy.

Yet even this devoted follower of Smith, who followed him so faithfully as to introduce a digression on silver in the midst of his chapter on rent, was willing to support protective duties for some goods.

Whether or not Smith intended it to be so, the fact that he was seen to espouse labor as the true source of value had an enormous psychological impact upon continental readers accustomed to political absolutism. In addition to the quotes of Blanqui and Ganilh provided earlier, we find Kraus writing in Prussia that "The unit or measure of exchange value [labor], which Smith discovered is as important for state economy as the unit discovered by Galileo in physics for velocity." When we turn to economics proper, the considerable difficulty of finding ideas or actions peculiarly attributable to Smith—as opposed to what may be expected from pragmatic policy needs, or from a desire to emulate the English, or from direct economic interests or even as residues of Physiocratic thought—makes plausible the suggestion that Adam Smith's unique stature owes as much to his Whig-Radical position on politics as to the arguments supporting economic freedom.[101]

VIII

The fact that a majority of influential men did not support the basic ideas of the *Wealth of Nations* until the mid-1790s should cast doubt on any attempt to find causal links between Adam Smith and the Industrial Revolution, as Toynbee had done. Indeed, since all authorities agree that several leading industries had clearly begun their "revolution" by 1780, even if Adam Smith's views had been directly accepted it would still be perplexing to show how a book published in 1776 could have significantly caused the widespread economic changes visible some four years later. It has been asserted earlier in this essay that a general move towards freeing trade from restrictions was well under way by the 1750s. This widespread support for freely functioning markets, which was quite independent of Adam Smith, may well have had something to do with stimulating the Industrial Revolution. But there is surely a significant difference between the assertion that the *Wealth of Nations* had considerable impact on the course of the Industrial Revolution and the assertion that *some* of the ideas *common* to Smith and his distinguished predecessors had such an impact.[102] Dugald Stewart expressed the difference neatly when he agreed with Smith's free-trade policies, even while noting his unhappiness with Smith's reasoning:

> But although in my *practical* conclusions on the more important questions, I am disposed to agree with Mr. Smith, I shall have frequent occasion to differ from him widely in stating the first principles of the science, as well as in my opinion of the logical propriety of various technical phrases and technical distinctions which he has sanctioned with his authority.[103]

In summing up his study of the popularity of the *Wealth of Nations* between 1776 and 1790, R.F. Teichgraber begins by stating:

It remains hard to tell whether the *Wealth of Nations* during Adam Smith's lifetime was ever seen as more than one of several equally respectable works championing liberal economic policy or whether it ever exercised any fundamental influence on the way in which contemporaries thought and acted. So the notion that the *Wealth of Nations* had an immediate impact on its time certainly ought to be put to rest.[104]

The French Revolution contributed to the acceptance of Adam Smith in at least two ways. On the one hand, it made the propagation of Physiocratic ideas, with their support of political absolutism, not only distasteful, but also obnoxious to those in the establishment. Honest Whig that he was, Dugald Stewart found this a most unjustified reproach and complained later of the political bigotry that had tried to silence his appreciation of Physiocratic economics.[105] Secondly, the French Revolution made defenders of the establishment seek out ideas that supported the existing order more actively. The Invisible Hand proved to be of great importance here. Especially after Burke's denunciation of grand *a priori* theories, the English looked for theories that supported their own pragmatic individualism. The widely admired notions of Judge William Blackstone provided an appropriate starting point:

> As therefore the creator is a being, not only of infinite *power*, and *wisdom*, but also of infinite *goodness*, he has been pleased so to contrive the constitution and frame of humanity, that we should want no other prompter to inquire after and pursue the rule of right, but only our own self-love, that universal principle of action. For he has so intimately connected, so inseparably interwoven the laws of eternal justice with the happiness of each individual, that the latter cannot be attained but by observing the former; and, if the former be punctually obeyed, it cannot but induce the latter.[106]

It is important to emphasize that the concept of a global harmony in the British system was widely accepted well before Adam Smith wrote the *Wealth of Nations*. When conservatives looked for a defense of property rights, the doctrine of an Invisible Hand leading to beneficial results for society became readily acceptable. In 1797 the Reverend John Howlett, a good economist and liberal clergyman, could confidently pronounce that "The grand and leading error in our reasonings upon this subject seems to be, that we ascribe too much to human contrivance; too little to providential superintendence."[107] The most effective popularizer of political economy in the mid-nineteenth century, the Reverend Richard Whately, took the Invisible Hand argument as a proof of the existence of God and thought Adam Smith superior to the Reverend William Paley as a Natural Theologian![108] It is critically important to distinguish such conservative support for Adam Smith from that provided by the Whig-Radicals. With the Radicals, it was the belief in freedom in general—freedom in politics, economics and religion—that motivated them: the good consequences that followed were of secondary importance; for the conservatives, on the other hand, the beneficence of the established system of property rights was fundamental and this required no more freedom than those already glorified by Blackstone. Smith provided a convenient and readily accepted codification of conclusions already accepted. For the Radicals, it was the premise of greater freedom with the implied promise of an egalitarian future that was most important. The Radicals were active in their following, the conservatives were passive.

The merits of Josiah Tucker, Arthur Young, and Sir James Steuart as economic analysts are comparable to those of Adam Smith on many issues, and Smith is distinguished largely by the range of his economic output. Tucker and Young may well have been more popular among the common sort, but this was precisely their problem. They lacked the gentility and refinement to be adopted by an age acutely conscious of such virtues. Young was too closely identified with agriculture to serve as a suitable authority on economic policy in general. Tucker was eligible and was even briefly tutor to George III when he was still the Prince of Wales. But Tucker's detestation of war led him to be an outcast during the glorious years of the Seven Years War. He even maintained a perverse sense of independence and resolutely refused offers of patronage. This alone would suffice to sink him. Sir James Steuart had no hope of popularity with the educated elite. An exile who was out of touch with British modes of thought, he did not fail to attract serious readers, but there were not many of these. For this limited class of readers, the Physiocrats were even more attractive than Adam Smith during 1790-1800. The French Revolution, however, effectively settled any possibility of meaningful debate between Smith and the Physiocrats. When the storm was over, Dugald Stewart wrote ruefully of his attempts to praise Physiocratic economics in the 1790s.[109]

Adam Smith wrote well, thereby gaining all in the educated classes as a potential audience; his rhetoric supported the British bias for free trade and made the *Wealth of Nations* an elegant statement of common prejudices; Smith's cosmopolitanism led Bentham to call the *Wealth of Nations* a treatise on "universal benevolence" and those of a liberal radical bent provided Smith with a steady phalanx of unwavering support. Perhaps Smith's greatest triumph lay in being perceived as an establishment thinker. Some of the factors that conduced to this end had little or nothing to do with Smith's conscious actions. British industrial supremacy meant that a powerful lobby not only saw no reason to object to free trade but even viewed it as a means of furthering its self-interest. As an academic and moral philosopher Smith carried an aura of dispassionate integrity; but the most important point was to gain the initial ascendancy. The decisive step here was probably the appeal of the *Wealth of Nations* to Whig-Radical thinkers. Next in importance was Smith's own assiduous cultivation of patronage. However radical his personal views may have been, he "played the game." From the earliest help given by the Duke of Argyll to the cultivation of Charles Townshend, to his position as unofficial adviser on fiscal matters and finally becoming Commissioner of Customs, Smith took pains to keep himself, honorably to be sure, but definitely as a cooperative and deferential intellectual.[110]

It has been argued earlier that the *Wealth of Nations* was not written to please any group, but this does not mean that Adam Smith's station in life may not have influenced potential readers, especially by leading him to be seen as an insider. Smith's position as a privileged insider was vital in deciding his writing strategy. He could afford to ignore Steuart, Tucker, and Young, whereas those writing after 1776 could not do the same to Smith. However unwordly and absent-minded Smith was about worldly affairs, he was careful and calculating about literary fame. Campbell and Skinner express the point pithily: "In all the changes in political administration [from 1776 onwards] Smith had direct personal links with the administration."[111]

In conclusion, it may be useful to ask what light the rise of Adam Smith sheds on a problem that economists have often puzzled over in recent years: the applicability to economics of Thomas Kuhn's view that the history of science consists of a succession of radical changes in viewpoint. The *Wealth of Nations* certainly envisioned the economy differently from its predecessors. Instead of being a complicated and unstable machine,[112] the economy was now seen to be basically stable and self-operating. Two problems that had troubled pre-Smithian thinkers were considered to be of minor importance by those who accepted the Smithian vision. These were the difficulty of achieving full employment[113] and the reconciliation of private and public interest. These are very important issues and there seems good reason to speak of a shift in economists' perceptions of the significant problems calling for solutions. In this sense, the approach of Kuhn is helpful in reminding us that the "progress" that political economy achieved in the period 1776-90 did not consist of an accumulation of many incremental additions to the body of economic truths but lay rather in a decidedly new way of looking at familiar facts.

Kuhn has also emphasized the fact that rival points of view tend to be "incommensurable," in that rival paradigms frequently use the same words but give them different meanings. The older meaning of "wealth" carried with it connotations of power, hence Adam Smith's restriction of "wealth" to mean solely economic wealth, or opulence, was a significant restriction in one sense. It was a liberating usage in another sense because it validated the carrying out of economic deductions unhampered by political considerations. Clarity was achieved at the cost of divorcing economics from politics.[114]

It is important to add the fact that such "progress" in economics is dependent upon factors that are not normally considered part of "science." The first of these appears to be literary style. Joseph Schumpeter noted that Smith

> never moved above the heads of even the dullest readers. He led them on gently, encouraging them by trivialities and homely observations, making them feel comfortable all along. While the professional of his time found enough to command his intellectual respect, the educated reader was able to assure himself that, yes, this was so, he too had always thought so.[115]

Economics had not yet become a professional field with its own recondite jargon, and it would be a mistake to underestimate the importance of the qualities indicated by Schumpeter in attracting and winning over readers.

Moreover Kuhn's framework does not adequately emphasize that new paradigms are often established with a decided element of partisanship.[116] That Charles Lyell, the founder of modern geology, and Charles Darwin, the originator of the theory of evolution, were unfair to their predecessors has been often remarked upon in recent years.[117] Adam Smith's presentation of Mercantilism has been called by Eli Heckscher, an admirer of Smith, "free-trade propaganda";[118] as noted earlier, in the years following 1800 the bias of some economists played a part in raising Smith in popular esteem; by 1830 political economy was so identified with free trade that when John Rae published some very intelligent criticisms of Smith, even kindly critics smiled at him: "Fallacies of the Wealth of Nations! As if the work which has opened a new era in political science . . . could be treated as a book of fallacies."[119]

As Adam Smith's superior writing style, the praise of the oligarchy, as well as the compatibility of Smith's message with British prejudices made the *Wealth of Nations* ever more widely read, its internal features served to suggest the view that Smith was the great founder of the science. The paucity of references to other economists, the many derogatory remarks on those who were referred to, the total omission of Sir James Steuart, the Reverend Josiah Tucker, and Arthur Young, the misrepresentation of the Physiocrats, the caricature of the Mercantilists and the self-conscious proclamation of new and generous doctrines—by all these means were readers led to believe that the search for other, earlier economists was a waste of time. As the *Wealth of Nations* became a popular text, it slowly became the first and only book on political economy. In a subject so immediately relevant as political economy, and one so riddled with political, philosophical and material interests, the sociology of knowledge would appear to be of as great importance as the scientific merits of opposing viewpoints.

NOTES

1. W. Mitchell, *Types of Economic Theory* (New York: Augustus Kelley, 1967), vol. I, 74, 76, 93. These influential notes have circulated in manuscript form since the 1920s.
2. E. Ginzberg, *The House of Adam Smith* (New York: Columbia University Press, 1930). C.R. Fay, *Adam Smith and the Scotland of His Day* (Cambridge: Cambridge University Press, 1956).
3. Kirk Willis, "The Role in Parliament of the Economic Ideas of Adam Smith," *History of Political Economy* (1979), **11**, 505-44; Salim Rashid, "Adam Smith's Rise to Fame: a Re-examination of the Evidence," *Eighteenth Century* (1982), **XXIII**, 64-85; R.F. Teichgraber III, "'Less Abused Than I Had Reason to Expect': the Reception of *The Wealth of Nations* in Britain, 1776-90," *Historical Journal* (1987), **30**(2) 337-66. These appear to be the only recent studies of the immediate popularity of the *Wealth of Nations*. Teichgraber writes: "We still know astonishingly little about the process by which Smith's book was canonized" (365). Richard Westfall, "Newton and the Scientific Revolution," in *Newton's Dream*, ed. M.S. Sayer (Montreal: McGill-Queens University Press, 1988), 4-18.
4. The rapid (and permanent) fall of Malthus from favor with the Whigs is evidenced by his complete exclusion from the *Edinburgh Review* after his support for the Corn Laws in 1814. Earlier, Malthus was not only highly praised, but also used as something of an authority on economic questions by the *Edinburgh Review*. Frank O'Gorman's views about the Whig party after the American wars can perhaps also be applied to the period after 1814: "The [French Wars] may have kept the [Whigs] out of office and consigned them to years of frustratingly impotent opposition, but in the end it rescued their reputations" (*The Emergence of The British Two-Party System, 1760-1832*, London: Edward Arnold, 1982, 11).
5. H.T. Buckle, *History of Civilisation in England* (New York: Appleton, 1920), 154. Buckle's praise gains authority by being erroneously ascribed to Edmund Burke by Soule. See also G. Soule, *Ideas of the Great Economists* (New York: Mentor, 1951); J. Rae, *Life of Adam Smith* (1895; reprinted New York: Augustus Kelley, 1965); J. Hollander, "The Founder of a School," in *Adam Smith 1776-1926* (Chicago: University of Chicago Press, 1928), 22-52. This impression is only heightened by the language of historians who speak of Adam Smith as having "revealed" the wealth to be gained by industry and commerce: for example, F. Manuel, *The Age of Reason* (Ithaca, N.Y.: Cornell University Press, 1951), 43. W. Petersen, *Malthus* (Cambridge, Mass.: Harvard University Press, 1979), 10.
6. Jacob Viner, in *International Encyclopedia of the Social Sciences* (New York: Macmillan, 1968), s.v. "Adam Smith"; T.W. Hutchinson, *On Revolutions and Progress in Economic Knowledge* (Cambridge: Cambridge University Press, 1978), 23. This book has much material and many references relevant to the topic of this chapter.

7. R. Whately, *Introductory Lectures on the Political Economy* (London: Murray, 1831), 3. For the Maryland newspaper, see the cutting kept in the Vanderblue collection of Smithiana, Kress Library, Harvard Business School. See also Petersen, *Malthus*, 8. The journalistic literature has many references to Adam Smith as the founder of political economy, e.g. I. Preebles, *The Lion in the North* (London: International Publishing Service, 1971).

8. L.A. Clarkson, *The Pre-industrial Economy in England 1500-1750* (London: Batsford, 1971), 208; Adam Smith, *The Wealth of Nations* ed. R.H. Campbell and A.S. Skinner (Oxford: Clarendon Press, 1976), 42-5 (hereafter referred to as *WN*).

9. John Rae, *Adam Smith* (London, 1896); W. Kennedy, *English Taxation, 1640-1799* (London: Bell, 1913), 142; W.R. Scott, *Adam Smith as a Student and Professor* (Glasgow: Jackson, 1937), 105-7.

10. Buckle, *History of Civilisation in England*, 155; Cobbett, *Parliamentary History* (1800), **33**, 824-5; *The Correspondence of William Wilberforce*, ed. R.I. Wilberforce and S. Wilberforce (London: Murray, 1840), vol. 1, 218.

11. T. Mortimer, *The Elements of Commerce, Politics and Finance* (London: Longman, Rees, 1801; first published 1768), vi-xii. Admittedly, a list of subscribers is "soft" evidence. Rae, *Adam Smith*, 153.

12. On Tucker and Young, see W.E. Clark, *Josiah Tucker, Economist* (New York: Columbia, 1903); R.L. Schuyler, *Josiah Tucker* (New York: Columbia, 1931); *Arthur Young and His Times*, ed. G.E. Mingay (London: Macmillan, 1975); E.P. Hunt, *Arthur Young on Industry and Economics* (Philadelphia: The Author, 1926).

13. J. Viner, *Studies in the Theory of International Trade* (New York: Augustus Kelley, 1937), 92, finds only five authors prior to Adam Smith who were full-fledged supporters of free trade. If we consider instead those who supported *freer* trade, the list can be at least doubled.

14. *London Magazine*, January 1773, 26-7.

15. *Monthly Review* (1774), **50**, 131; *The Collected Works of Dugald Stewart*, ed. S.R.W. Hamilton (Edinburgh: Constable, 1856), vol. 10, 136; B. Semmel, "The Hume-Tucker Debate and Pitt's Free-Trade Proposals," *Economic Journal* (1965), **75**, 759-70; J. Fiske, *The Critical Years* (Cambridge: Riverside, 1898).

16. A. Skinner, ed., *Principles of Political Oeconomy* (Chicago: University of Chicago Press, 1966), vol. 1, xlvii. Steuart later wrote, "I frankly acknowledge that I have, perhaps, on some occasions, been more apt to consider myself in the light of a political matron, than that of a jovial and free-born Englishman" (quoted ibid., vol. 1, 11).

17. Oliver Goldsmith, *Essays and Belles Lettres* (London: Dent & Dutton, 1934), 158.

18. Willis, "The Role in Parliament of the Economic Ideas of Adam Smith," op. cit., 544.

19. Willis, op. cit., 510.

20. Cobbett, *Parliamentary History*, Vol. 23, 1152.

21. Smith's correspondence also suggests that he had little to do with North's reforms. See letter 197 from John MacPherson (Nov. 1778) and letter 208 to Andreas Holt (Oct. 1780) in *The Correspondence of Adam Smith* (Oxford: Oxford University Press, 1977).

22. John Ehrman, *The British Government and Commercial Negotiations with Europe 1783-1793* (Cambridge: Cambridge University Press, 1962), 180. This book contains further references to the literature. Teichgraber, "'Less Abused',"op. cit., 362.

23. J.B. Say, *A Treatise on Political Economy*, ed. C.C. Biddle (Philadelphia: Lippincott, 1834); A. Skinner, ed., *Political Oeconomy*, vol. 1, lii; A.J. Youngson, review of Skinner's edition of Steuart's *Political Oeconomy*; *Scottish Historical Review*, vol. 46-47 (1967-68), 170-71.

24. S.R. Sen, *The Economics of Sir James Steuart* (Cambridge, Mass.: Harvard University Press, 1957); Skinner, ed., *Political Oeconomy*, vol. 1, xlv-xlvi; *Critical Review* (1768), **24**, 32.

25. A. Young, *Political Arithmetic* (London, 1774); Mortimer, *The Elements of Commerce*, 40. The importance of Arthur Young during this period can be seen by examining, e.g., *The Kress Library of Business and Economics Catalogue* No. 1 (Cambridge, Mass:: Harvard University Press, 1940). See also *Monthly Review* **38** (1768), 78 and **40** (1769), 43.

26. *Encyclopaedia Britannica*, 2 vols (Edinburgh, 1770).

27. Skinner, ed., *Political Oeconomy*, vol. 1, liii. Viner considers the treatment of the highland economy conspicuous by its absence in *The Wealth of Nations*; see Jacob Viner, *Guide to John Rae's Life of Adam Smith* (New York: Augustus Kelley, 1965), 101.

28. *Considerations on Our Corn-Laws* (Aberdeen, 1777); *Corn-Bill Hints in Answer to the Memorial for the Merchants, Traders, and Manufacturers of the City of Glasgow* (Glasgow, 1777); *Essay on the Corn-Laws* (Edinburgh, 1777); *Thoughts Respecting the Proposed New Corn-Bill* (Edinburgh, 1777).

29. *Corn-Bill Hints*, esp. 16-20. This pamphlet is noticed by Skinner in his biographical sketch.

30. Review of the *Wealth of Nations*, *Monthly Review* (1776), **55**, 92.

31. *Monthly Review* (1777), **56**, 117-20.

32. *Monthly Review* (1778), **59**, 365.

33. According to C.C. Nangle's identification, the reviewer is William Enfield, one of the staff members of the Dissenter's Academy at Warrington. See Nangle's *The Monthly Review, First Series, 1749-1789: Indexes on Contributors and Articles* (Oxford: Oxford University Press, 1934).

34. *Monthly Review* (1778), **59**, 417-18.

35. Ibid.

36. Review of the *Wealth of Nations*, *Critical Review* (1775), **40**, 433.

37. *Critical Review* (1777), **44**, 434.

38. *Critical Review* (1784), **57**, 148, and (1785), **59**, 367, respectively.

39. Review of William Paley, *Moral and Political Philosophy*, *Critical Review* (1789), **67**, 509.

40. Ibid.

41. *Scots Magazine* (1787), **48**, 521, and (1788), **51**, 322.

42. *Edinburgh Weekly Magazine* (1776), **32**, 83.

43. Ibid.

44. *Edinburgh Weekly Magazine* (1776), **35**, 135; (1777), **39**, 250; (1780), **50**.

45. S.G. Checkland, "Adam Smith and the Biographer," *Economica* (1967), **34**, 71-9.

46. See Kames's *Sketches of Man* (Edinburgh, 1774).

47. Obituary of Sir James Steuart, *Edinburgh Weekly Magazine* (1780), **50**, 261-2. It is significant that exactly the same review is printed, without comment, by the *Scots Magazine*.

48. *Four Letters to the Earl of Carlisle from William Eden, Esq.* (Edinburgh, 1779), 46 and 70; *Gentleman's Magazine* (1789), **59**, 928; David Williams, *Lectures on Political Principles* (London, 1789), 247; W. Benwell, "In What Arts have the Moderns excelled the Ancients" (1787), reprinted in *Oxford Prize Essays* (Oxford: Oxford University Press, 1836).

49. Quoted by Rae, *Adam Smith*, 435; Lord Cockburn, *Memorials of My Own Time*, quoted ibid., 436.

50. J. Joyce, *A Completed Analysis, or Abridgement of Dr. Adam Smith's Inquiry into the Nature and Causes of the Wealth of Nations*, 3rd edn (London: Whittaker, 1821; 1st edn, 1793); D. Boileau, *Introduction to Political Economy* (London: Cadell & Davies, 1811); *Critical Review* (1806), 7; *British Critic* (1812), **15**, 121. Instructive contrasts between Smith and Steuart are also drawn in the *Annual Review* (1805) and the *Literary Journal* (1806).

51. B. Lenman, *Integration, Enlightenment and Industrialisation* (Toronto: University of Toronto Press, 1981), 39.

52. Dugald Stewart, *Lectures on Political Economy*, vol. I, 268 and 302-6.

53. Francis Horner, Review of Canard's *Principles*, *Edinburgh Review* (January 1803); reprinted in F.W. Fetter, *The Economic Writings of Francis Horner* (London: London School of Economics, 1957), 73.

54. Goldsmith, *The Citizen of the World*, Letter 57, in *Essays and Belles-Lettres*, 158-9.

55. D. Wexler, *David Hume and the History of England* (Philadelphia: American Philosophical Society, 1979), 17.

56. P. Stein, *Legal Evolution* (Cambridge: Cambridge University Press, 1980), 97.

57. A. Gat, *The Origins of Military Thought* (Oxford: Clarendon Press, 1989), 45-9.

58. Sir Lewis Namier, *England in the Age of the American Revolution*, 2nd edn (New York: St Martin's Press, 1961), 34. For further evidence on this issue, see the entire section, 29-35.

59. *Letters of David Hume to William Strahan*, ed. G. Birkbeck Hill (Oxford: Oxford University Press, 1888), 315. Adam Smith's literary abilities have often been praised; see, for example, L.L. Price, "Adam Smith and Recent Economics," in *Economic Science and Practice* (London: Murray, 1900).

60. "If my notions are wrong, my intention I am sure, is right" (John Locke, *Some Considerations of the Consequences of the Lowering of Interest*, in *Works*, London, 1823, vol. 5, 4); William Letwin, *The Origins of Scientific Economics: English Economic Thought, 1660-1776* (London: Methuen, 1963), 221-2.

61. See W. Smart, *Economic Annals of the Nineteenth Century* (London: Macmillan, 1910), ch. 34; B. Semmel, *The Rise of Free Trade Imperialism* (Cambridge: Cambridge University Press, 1970).

62. The obituary is reprinted in Fay, *Adam Smith and the Scotland of His Day*, 33.

63. Rae, *Adam Smith*, 61.

64. R.H. Campbell and A.S. Skinner, eds, "Text and Apparatus," in *WN*, 61-2.

65. *The Correspondence of Adam Smith*, ed. E.C. Mossner and I.S. Ross (Oxford: Oxford University Press, 1977), 229.

66. Ibid., 248.

67. Ibid., 251.

68. M. Perelman, *Classical Political Economy* (London: Rowman & Allenheld, 1984).

69. Smith, *Correspondence*, 269.

70. Rae, *Adam Smith*, 289.

71. Smith, *Correspondence*, 270.

72. Homer B. Vanderblue, *Adam Smith and the "Wealth of Nations"* (Boston, Mass.: Privately Printed, 1936).

73. Brougham Papers, University College Library, London. Catalogued under Thomas Chalmers.

74. *Mr. Pitt's Parliamentary Speeches*, ed. W. Hathaway (London: Longman, Hurst, Rees & Orme, 1808), vol. 1, 358.

75. Cobbett, *Parliamentary History* (1797), 562-3.

76. Cobbett, *Parliamentary History* (1800), **33**, 563.

77. *Memoirs and Correspondence of Francis Horner*, ed. Leonard Horner (London: Murray, 1842), vol. 1, 23.

78. Lord Lauderdale, *An Inquiry into the Nature and Origin of Public Wealth* (Edinburgh: Constable, 1804); H. Brougham, "Lord Lauderdale's Inquiry into the Nature and Origin of Public Wealth," *Edinburgh Review* (July 1804), **IV**(8), 343-76; S. Smith, "Archdeacon Nares," *Edinburgh Review* (1802), **6**, 130. In this connection, it may be noted that Lauderdale is reported as having once said regarding Adam Smith on political economy: "he [Smith] is everything" (see Rae, *Adam Smith*, 289).

79. Much of the evidence on this point has been gathered in Ginzberg, *The House of Adam Smith*; Charles Ganilh, *An Inquiry into the Various Systems of Political Economy* (New York; Augustus Kelley, 1966; originally published 1812), 46; Adolphe Blanqui, *History of Political Economy in Europe* (New York, 1880), 386.

80. *The Writings of Thomas Paine*, ed. M.D. Conway (New York: AMS Press, 1967), vol. II, 407, 408.

81. Ibid., 409.

82. Ibid., 314.

83. Ibid., 478.

84. Ibid., 511.

85. *The Writings of Thomas Paine*, vol. II, 407-9 (388, 457, 501), 314, 478, 511-2. Rae, *Adam Smith*, 436.

86. Rae, *Adam Smith*, 292 and 372. Smith is said to have spoken of both Rousseau and Voltaire "with a kind of religious respect." Beattie's letter is in the Huntington Library, California. For Smith's continuing serviceability to radical causes, see W. Stafford, *Socialism, Racialism and Nostalgia* (Cambridge: Cambridge University Press, 1987), and N.W. Thompson, *The People's Science* (Cambridge: Cambridge University Press, 1984). Michael Perelman has gathered together a fair amount of evidence showing how resentful Smith was at having to be beholden to his social superiors: "Adam Smith and Dependent Social Relations," *History of Political Economy* (Fall 1989), **21**, 503-20. He has also noted Smith's radicalism was more *petit bourgeois* than working class.

87. W.J. Ashley, "The Tory Origin of Free Trade Policy," *Quarterly Journal of Economics* (July 1897), **11**, 335-71. Ashley's views are repeated by E.R.A. Seligman in his Introduction to *The Wealth of Nations* (New York: Dutton, 1910). P. Langford, *The Excise Crisis* (Oxford: Clarendon Press, 1975); C. Robbins, *The Eighteenth Century Common Wealth Man* (Cambridge, Mass.: Harvard University Press, 1959); M.L. Myers, *The Soul of Modern Economic Man* (Chicago: University of Chicago Press, 1983); J. Clarke, *English Society 1660-1832* (Cambridge: Cambridge University Press, 1985); Jacob Viner, *Religious Thought and Economic Society* (Durham, N.C.: Duke University Press, 1978).

88. As quoted by D.H. MacGregor, *Economic Thought and Policy* (Oxford: Oxford University Press, 1949), 70.

89. L. Rogin, *The Meaning and Validity of Economic Theory* (New York: Harper, 1956), xiii. This point of view has also been upheld by many scholars in dealing with social philosophies, e.g., M. Cowling, "The Use of Political Philosophy in Mill, Green and Bentham," *Historical Studies* (1965), **5**, 141-52.

It is also of interest to note how some well-known industrialists, such as William Strutt, were strong radicals. Margaret C. Jacob, "Scientific Culture in the Early English Enlightenment: Mechanisms, Industry and Gentlemanly Facts," in A.C. Kors and P. Korshin, eds, *Anticipations of the Enlightenment in England, France and Germany* (Philadelphia: University of Pennsylvania Press, 1987), 134-64.

90. C.R. Fay, *Great Britain from Adam Smith to the Present Day* (London: Longmans, Green, 1928), 8; E. Cannan, "Adam Smith as an Economist," *Economica* (1926), **6**, 123-34.

91. C.W. Hasek, *The Introduction of Adam Smith's Doctrines into Germany* (New York: Columbia University Press, 1925), 116-17.

92. Melchior Palyi, "The Introduction of Adam Smith on the Continent," in *Adam Smith 1776-1926* (Chicago: University of Chicago Press, 1928), 199.

93. Hasek, *Adam Smith's Doctrines*, 6; K. Tribe, *Governing the Economy: The Reformation of German Economic Discourse, 1750-1840* (Cambridge: Cambridge University Press, 1988).

94. Hasek, *Adam Smith's Doctrines*, 64.

95. Ibid., 66.

96. Ibid., 83.

97. Palyi, "Introduction of Adam Smith," 190.

98. Hasek, *Adam Smith's Doctrines*, 126. Also see 95-6.

99. Ibid., 101, 103.

100. Ibid., 111-12, 104, 107 and 132.

101. Ibid., 71, 75, 87.

102. Stewart, *Lectures*, vol. I, 9.

103. This is not to deny that, although Smith's arguments often resembled earlier ones, the *Wealth of Nations* may still have reinforced and accelerated prior trends.

104. Teichgraber, "'Less Abused'," 364.

105. Salim Rashid, "Economists and the Age of Chivalry," *Eighteenth Century Studies* (1986), **20**, 56-61.

106. William Blackstone, *The Sovereignty of the Law*, ed. Gareth Jones (Toronto: University of Toronto Press, 1973), 29.

107. Reverend John Howeltt, *Dispersal of Apprehensions* (London, 1787), 21.

108. Salim Rashid,"Richard Whately and Christian Political Economy at Oxford and Dublin," *Journal of the History of Ideas* (1977), **XXXVIII**, 149-155.

109. Rashid, "Economists and Chivalry," 60.

110. This is evident in almost every letter Smith writes to his social superiors (*The Correspondence of Adam Smith*).

111. R.H. Campbell and A.S. Skinner, *Adam Smith* (New York: St Martin's Press, 1982), 208.

112. See J. Mills, *Essays, Morals, Political and Literary* (London, 1773).

113. This difficulty has also been emphasized by T.W. Hutchison, *Before Adam Smith* (Oxford: Blackwell, 1988), ch. 1.

114. In "The Interpretation of the 'Balance of Trade': A 'Wordy' Debate," (*Research in the History of Economic Thought and Methodology* (1994), **12**, 93-111) I have shown the persistence of a political connotation to "wealth" throughout the seventeenth century and into the mid-eighteenth century; while in "The Political Balance of Trade . . .??" (*Research in the History of Economic Thought and Methodology* (1993), **11**, 73-92) it is argued that the period when the balance of trade was given almost hysterical importance, 1660-1700, was a time when the French balance of trade was really the issue.

115. J. Schumpeter, *History of Economic Analysis* (London: Allen & Unwin, 1954), 185.

116. Such statements are, of course, meant to be relative to a physicist; Kuhn probably seems to emphasize the sociological aspect too much. For a recent discussion of the different methodological approaches, see Joel Jalladeau, "Research Program versus Paradigm in the Development of Economics," *Journal of Economic Issues* (1978), **23**, 583-608. D.P. O'Brien treats Adam Smith's popularity from a different viewpoint in "The Longevity of Adam Smith's Vision: Paradigms, Research Programs and Falsifiability in the History of Economic Thought," *Scottish Journal of Political Economy* (1976), **23**, 133-52.

117. See C.D. Darlington, *Darwin's Place in History* (Oxford: Blackwell, 1959), 60-2.

118. E. Heckscher, *Mercantilism* (London: Allen & Unwin, 1955), vol. 2, 332.

119. Quoted by R.W. James in *John Rae, Political Economist* (Toronto: University of Toronto Press, 1965), vol. 1, 163.

8. Adam Smith's Interpretation of the History of Economics and its Influence in the Eighteenth and Nineteenth Centuries

It is not a sin in a historian to introduce a personal bias that can be recognized and discounted. The sin in historical composition is the organization of the story in such a way that bias cannot be recognized.

Herbert Butterfield, The Whig Interpretation of History

I

It is not to be expected that the history of a subject will excite any interest until the subject becomes aware of its own distinctness. It is therefore not surprising that Adam Smith's *Wealth of Nations* not only provided economics with its first generally readable treatise, which laid the analytical foundations for the future, but also that it defined the past of the subject. As such it was the base from which future historians of economic thought operated and Smith's viewpoint was to be dominant for the next hundred years. Eli Heckscher, certainly no hostile critic, called Smith's presentation "free-trade propaganda"[1] and it is interesting to examine what element of truth there is in this assertion and what influence such a view may have had. As the reference to Heckscher indicates, Adam Smith's treatment of Mercantilism has been frequently referred to by scholars interested in that subject; however, a direct study of Book IV of the *Wealth of Nations*, considered as a chapter in the history of ideas, appears to be missing. R.S. Howey has recently written that "Smith has not received credit for his historiographic contribution . . . Two centenaries have failed to give him his historiographic due."[2] I aim in this chapter to examine Smith's historiographic merits, without necessarily sharing Howey's laudatory view.

In the case of Adam Smith, there is no doubt that a substantial part of Smith's fame was based upon the belief that he was saying something radically new. (This claim will be documented in the second half of this chapter.) The curious fact is that Smith himself is the authority for the views of his predecessors.[3] It would be a little hard to expect Smith to paint his predecessors in their best colors since his own merits depend upon their appearing in dark hues. A closer look at Smith's view of the history of economics is in order.[4]

In Book IV of the *Wealth of Nations* Smith dealt successively with the "Mercantile System," coined to denote largely the ideas of his British predecessors, and the "Agricultural System," or the works of the French Physiocrats. The bias of the theorist is already visible: what of those who wrote good sense on specific topics, such as banking or taxation, but did not formulate an overall system? British economics had been propagated and refined by debate on practical issue—when occasion rose, pamphlets were written for or against a particular economic measure and the attempt to assess the literature prior to 1776 through the spectacles of a "system" is particularly misleading. Furthermore, Smith makes no mention of the economic principles and issues debated in Parliament; for example, he could have stated how in the 1730s Prime Minister Walpole was converted from the belief that taxes should be proportional to income to the view that luxuries are the proper articles of taxation, necessitating a progressive tax.[5]

Before turning to the details of Smith's presentation, it is useful to point out that perhaps its most important general defect *vis-à-vis* the past is his failure to point out that concern for unemployment was a primary concern throughout this period and especially so after 1720.[6] How the poor could be employed was a particularly pressing problem for the English, who, because of the Poor Law, had to maintain the poor in good times and bad; to make them earn their bread was quite preferable to maintaining them in idleness. By contrast, the problem of unemployment is rather casually treated in the *Wealth of Nations*.

II

Adam Smith begins his presentation of the mercantile system by pointing to the popular notion "that wealth consists in money, or in gold and silver." He then goes on to assert: "In consequence of these popular notions, all the different nations of Europe have studied . . . every possible means of accumulating gold and silver in their respective countries."[7] Having found the root of the mercantile system to be its identification of real wealth with gold and silver, Smith can proceed to criticize at length the absurdity of this identification, as well as its consequences. The only authors referred to in Smith's discussion of the mercantile system are Thomas Mun and John

Locke, and I shall argue below that Smith does less than justice to both of them. Let it be noted here, however, that at the end of almost 20 pages criticizing Mercantilist thought Smith seems to make a concession:

> Some of the best English writers upon commerce set out with observing, that the wealth of a country consists, not in its gold and silver only, but in its lands, houses and consumable goods of all different kinds. In the course of their reasonings, however, the lands, houses, and consumable goods seem to slip out of their memory, and the strain of their argument frequently supposes that all wealth consists in gold and silver, and that to multiply those metals is the great object of national industry and commerce.[8]

After we have been provided with a lengthy analysis of the errors involved in identifying real wealth with gold and silver we are now told that we should not expect to find the earlier writers actually making such an identification. Instead, we should look at the "strain of their argument" and deduce the simplistic error through this sieve. Smith appears willing to concede that (a) the Mercantilists did not identify the precious metals with real wealth; and (b) one way to make sense of the Mercantilist policies is to *impute* to them such a belief (which they may have already denied). It is important to assess whether this is a fair procedure.

As a student of the Classics, Adam Smith must have been familiar with Cicero's eloquent speech on the desirability of sympathetic interpretation:

> What statute, what senatorial decree, what magisterial edict, what treaty or agreement, or (to speak once more of our private concerns) what testament, what rules of law or undertakings of formal pacts and agreements cannot be invalidated and nullified if we choose to sacrifice the meaning to the words without taking into account the plan, the purpose and the intention of the writer? Why, the familiar speech of every day will not have a consistent meaning if we set verbal traps for one another.[9]

Smith's own teacher, Francis Hutcheson, had reiterated the same point with regard to philosophical disputation:

> If words taken in their simple and unfigured sense import something contradictory and absurd, but not when interpreted as figurative; they are to be deemed figurative.[10]

In his lectures, Smith himself did not hesitate to pay attention to the original meanings of words as well as their evolution over time.[11] And yet the mercantile system deserved neither a sympathetic reading nor a study of historical changes. If Smith had not added the last qualification about "some of the best English authors," one could have said that Smith was guilty of reading his sources superficially. However, once one recognizes that intellectuals of the calibre of Sir William Petty and John Locke were aware of the nature of real wealth, is it fair to continue to portray them as erecting economic policy on false first principles? Could there not have been some reason why the Mercantilists focused their attention upon money? As a matter of fact, Smith tries to answer several of these more serious reasons of the Mercantilists—such as the needs of a transactions medium and the avoidance of domestic employment—in the course of Book IV, without ever removing his characterization of the mercantile system as defined by a puerile confusion between the precious metals and real wealth. The great majority of readers of the *Wealth of Nations* read it as literature; intricate economic arguments would pass them by, but everyone could smile about an age which thought that the accumulation of metals could serve a useful purpose. As we shall see in the next section, even the best economists accepted Smith's caricature of the mercantile system.

In examining Smith's presentation of the ideas of the "Mercantilists," I begin with some general observations. First, Smith shows little historical understanding of the evolution of British economic thought. By quoting only Locke and Mun, he gives the impression that there was a uniform set of ideas propagated between 1629, when Mun wrote, and his own day. He makes no effort to distinguish between different shades of Mercantilist thought, and the increased emphasis given to full employment in later years escapes Smith altogether. In this connection, it is only appropriate to repeat that the problem of achieving full employment is never seriously treated in the *Wealth of Nations*. We are told either that displaced workers can find some other employment or that society can never hire more workers than its capital permits; hence one should attempt to increase capital, not employment. The difference from his predecessors must be carefully noted. Secondly, Smith fails to refer to the predominantly practical interest of the previous writers. If Smith had pointed out that Mun's pamphlet was originally circulated at a time of monetary crisis, when Mun's own East India Company was under attack for exporting bullion, and that he wrote to oppose a policy of direct state control of the foreign exchange, readers would have a different picture of Mun's contribution to English economic thought. A more accurate portrayal of the circumstances which gave rise to pamphlets such as Mun's would lead us to believe that money was somehow connected essentially with the functioning of the economy and was not simply a veil which hid real economic relations. We might also be led to suspect that it was money as a medium of exchange and as a form of liquid investible surplus that aroused the Mercantilists rather than the simplistic idea that Smith fathered upon them.[12]

If we turn to the various authors specifically cited in the *Wealth of Nations* there is little to allay any suspicions of unfairness on the part of Smith. Some authors are presented with high praise. The author of the *Memoirs of Wool*, the Reverend John Smith, is a "very accurate and intelligent author," while the author of the *Three Tracts on the Corn Trade*, Charles Smith, is an "ingenious and well-informed author." A closer look, however, shows that Smith used these gentlemen only to extract facts. As soon as we look at economists who also were known to provide general views of economics, Smith's generosity is halted.[13]

The list of authors cited by Adam Smith is very long indeed. By restricting the list to earlier British economists we still obtain many famous names: Mun, Locke, Lowndes, Child, Davenant, Cantillon, Decker and Dobbs are certainly respectable names. The omission of both Petty and Mandeville is curious, in view of the emphasis they both gave to the division of labor.[14] It is too easy an answer to claim that Mandeville was avoided because of his notorious reputation—but then how can we explain the flurry of Smith's appreciative comments upon David Hume?

It is sad to note that when Smith does refer to the predecessors listed above it is either to quote a fact or to contradict them. Neither does he take particular care with his references. Lowndes, Davenant, and Dobbs are all misquoted, and Cantillon is quoted only to be contradicted. In view of the penetrating economic analysis of Cantillon's *Essai*, one is led to wonder about Smith's wisdom in this case.

Cantillon's *Essai*, with its attempt to develop a comprehensive system based on a few principles, is however of a very different nature than staple Mercantilist literature. Sir Josiah Child, eminent merchant and director of the East India Company, is much more congenial to the English frame of mind. All Smith does is to refer to Child's view on regulated companies. Now Child was perhaps the first author to argue that the balance of shipping was a better indication of the success of British trade than the balance of trade. This would remove him from the "Mercantilist" as pictured by Smith. Not only are Child's arguments against the modes of computing the balance of trade almost the same as those utilized by Smith, but Child also supported the removal of government restrictions on merchants:

> All our laws that oblige our people to the making of strong, substantial (and, as we call it, loyal) cloth, of a certain length, breadth, and weight, if they were duly put in execution, would in my opinion, do more hurt than good, because the humors and fashions of the world change, and at some times, in some places (as now in most) slight, cheap, light cloth will sell more plentifully and better,

than that which is heavier, stronger, and truer wrought; and if we intend to have the trade of the world, we must imitate the Dutch, who make the worst as well as the best of all manufactures, that we may be in a capacity of serving all markets, and all humors.[15]

A look at the list of "vulgar errors" pointed out by Child in his preface will show clearly the large extent to which Smith's later conclusions were anticipated by Child.

Finally, Smith's treatment of John Locke must be considered. As Locke was one of the most widely quoted authors on trade (as on politics), we would expect Smith to exercise particular care in his portrayal of him. Nonetheless, Smith attempts to foist upon Locke the belief that gold and silver are especially desirable because of their durability. This brings forth the following comment from Edwin Cannan: "There is very little foundation for any part of this paragraph." A careful reading of Locke will show why he thought money to be necessary for nations threatened by hostile neighbors:

> Money is also necessary to us, in a certain proportion to the plenty of it amongst our neighbors. For, if any of our neighbors have it in a much greater abundance than we, we are many ways obnoxious to them [sic]. 1. They can maintain a greater force. 2. They can tempt away our people, by greater wages, to serve them by land or sea, or in any labor. 3. They can command the markets, and thereby break our trade, and make us poor. 4. They can on any occasion engross naval and warlike stories, and thereby endanger us.[16]

Plenty of money is a weapon in the eyes of Locke—not just a passive instrument of commerce. The fact that Locke wrote his pamphlet to support recoinage at the old par and that these were also the times when the English were involved in fighting the French, a war whose credit needs brought the Bank of England into existence, gives much force to Locke's argument. A consideration of ideas (carefully quoted) in relation to circumstances was not, however, Smith's forte.

A survey of Adam Smith's presentation of the mercantile system would appear to justify Eli Heckscher's characterization of these chapters as "free-trade propaganda." By imputing a Midas-like belief to his predecessors, by failing to consider their ideas in relation to the political and economic circumstances of the age, and by a cursory treatment of the problem of unemployment, Smith significantly altered subsequent perceptions of the contributions of the British economists during 1600-1776. There are three distinct ways in which Smith blackened the ideas of his British predecessors. First, he failed to note that "wealth" denoted both riches *and* power to the

Mercantilists, hence much of the sting of his attack was directed only at words.[17] Secondly, the singleminded attention focused upon the balance of trade occurred only between 1660 and 1700 and was motivated largely by political rivalry and fear of French domination. Smith had earlier shown an awareness of this and it was subsequently pointed out to him by William Robertson—but readers of the *Wealth of Nations* were not to know.[18] Finally, the long tradition of pragmatic distrust of government intervention, supported and strengthened by the common law tradition and by the legal decisions of judges, makes no appearance in the *Wealth of Nations*. If, in addition, we also consider the failure to recognize the theoretical merits of writers such as Cantillon or the valuable practical policies of merchants like Child, then it is hard to resist the conclusion that Smith wrote with a determination to highlight his own originality and merits.[19]

We cannot begin to discuss Smith's presentation of the Physiocrats without providing a small tribute to the outstanding quality of French economic thought in the century preceding the *Wealth of Nations*. How the clarity of Nicole's analysis of self-interest—followed by the application of this analysis to the economy, all motivated by compassion for the poor of France—could have been missed for over 200 years is a mystery. Lionel Rothkrug provided the first glimpse of this buried treasure in his *Opposition to Louis XIV* (1965).[20] Murray Rothbard was one of the few scholars who appreciated the significance of Rothkrug's book and this was one factor which permanently colored his appreciation of Adam Smith. Since the publication of T.W. Hutchison's magisterial, *Before Adam Smith*, it will no longer be possible for English-speaking economists to pass over the French with indifference.[21] Careful, pointed quotes, presented in context, make it obvious that the Jansenists have first claim to be the first modern analysts of self-interest in economics. When we add the ideas of such followers as Pluche, the French have a good claim to being considered the founders of modern economics. (Indeed, such distinguished Nobel laureates as Maurice Allais have urged this.)

Smith's presentation of the Physiocrats is somewhat happier—even though his arguments refuting the "Agricultural System" are not quite correct, the portrayal is fairer than his picture of the Mercantilists. In terms of the history of economic thought Smith might have pointed out that the doctrine that all taxes fell on land was in fact an English one,[22] having been asserted by Locke and repeatedly referred to thereafter, for example, during the debates on Walpole's excise scheme. The important point for the future of economics, however, is that a school of economists, the Physiocrats, who had received scant attention in Britain until Smith wrote, were now brought into the limelight. Apart from Arthur Young,[23] who spent much time refuting Physiocratic views on tax incidence, there is virtually no other reference to the Physiocrats in the economic literature between 1755 and 1776.[24] The pamphlets by French authors, especially Mirabeau, are reviewed in the popular journals, but with no recognition of the existence of a well-defined school of thought in France. When the *Monthly Review* reviewed the *Eloge de Quesnay* it spoke of the Physiocrats in a matter-of-fact way—it was just another of the good doctor's services to mankind.[25] And when the *Monthly Review* reviewed the *Wealth of Nations*, the one chapter in that volume it did *not* refer to was Smith's discussion of the Physiocrats.[26] The omission was either because they were already too well known or because they were considered unimportant. As there is scarcely any evidence to suggest that they were well known, and as, even in this case, they would at least gain a mention, it seems that the Physiocrats were both relatively unknown and considered unimportant prior to the publication of the *Wealth of Nations*.

The subsequent importance of the Physiocrats in British political economy is explained by two factors. First, the Scots kept in close contact with pre-Revolutionary France, and Dugald Stewart, in particular, admired the Physiocrats. Since Stewart provided the only lectures on political economy at any university prior to 1807, and since many famous Englishmen flocked to Edinburgh in 1799-1800 to hear Stewart, this gave the Physiocrats very favorable coverage. Secondly, when the *Wealth of Nations* did begin to be considered the dominant authority on economics, roughly from 1790 onwards, all authors of whom Smith had spoken well acquired a lustre. As a result, English authors who favored the agricultural interest often referred to the Physiocrats for their doctrine that land was the source of real wealth.

Although Dugald Stewart admired Adam Smith, he admired the Physiocrats even more and he was not at all happy at the way Physiocracy had been described in the *Wealth of Nations*. Stewart insisted that a careful presentation of Quesnay's system was needed "in order to correct those misapprehensions of its nature which have prevailed to a considerable degree, *in consequence of the account of it given by Mr. Smith.*"[27] In Book IV of the *Wealth of Nations* Smith criticized the Physiocrats: "Their capital error seems to be in considering the class of artificers, manufacturers and merchants as altogether unproductive and barren." What really annoyed Stewart was the fact that Smith had in several other places accepted the substance of Physiocratic doctrines and yet had misrepresented them in his portrait of their system.

Indeed, the facts on which the above classification of productiveness was based were frequently stressed by none other than Smith himself. In the chapter "Of the Different Employments of Capital" there is an extensive discussion of the manner in which nature works along with man in agriculture and how this gives rise to a source of revenue, rent, which is not derived from human labor. Stewart notes that this grants all the Physiocrats contended for.[28]

Throughout his presentation of Physiocratic doctrines Stewart makes what can only be considered minor and tangential criticisms. In concluding his account, Stewart considers the only serious faults of the Physiocrats to be their emphasis upon the long run and their being too idealistic; their doctrines, however, contained no real errors. As for Adam Smith, the only superiority Smith possessed over the Physiocrats lay neither in analysis nor in doctrine, but in readability. Smith's real contribution lay in deducing the validity of free trade while adopting his speculations "to the present state of the world."[29] At least one student of Stewart, Francis Horner, took the superiority of the Physiocrats quite seriously, but this point was not publicly raised by any authors in the nineteenth century and Physiocracy died a quiet death.

In sum, Adam Smith's contribution to the history of economic thought was twofold: on the one hand, he presented a distorted and misleading picture of the efforts of earlier British economists; on the other hand, he performed a service in making the British more aware of the ideas of the Physiocrats, while damning their excellence with faint praise.

III

The fervour of the Whig historian very often comes from what is really the transference into the past of an enthusiasm for something in the present, an enthusiasm for . . . the liberal tradition. But the true historical fervour is the love of the past for the sake of the past.
                    Herbert Butterfield, The Whig Interpretation of History

The earliest attempt to place Adam Smith in perspective was made by Dugald Stewart in his *Memoir* on the life of Smith, written in 1793.[30] At this point Stewart was concerned largely about Smith's originality in espousing the system of free trade, which Stewart clearly considered the essence of Smith's contribution. In his *Lectures on Political Economy* some seven years later Stewart, with much help from Lord Lauderdale, showed good insight on the growth of British economic thought. Thus, he does not make the mistake, still met with today, of claiming that Smith had first separated economics from other concerns. The limitation of political economy to the "resources of a state" was present in Quesnay, Sir James Steuart,[31] "and a long list of respectable authors in this Island, both before and after the publication of Quesnay's works." This did not, however, prevent Stewart from stating explicitly the caricature of Mercantilism that had been frequently used by Smith:

> The great principle of the Mercantile system is, that money constitutes the wealth of a nation, or in other words, that a nation is rich or poor in proportion to the plenty or scarcity of the precious metals.[32]

Almost at the same time as Stewart was delivering his lectures, the Frenchman, J.B. Say was writing his own view of the history of economics in his influential *Treatise on Political Economy*.[33] In Say's judgement, Smith's great contribution had been to demonstrate that the primary source of value was the labor of man. This appears to be a reaction to the view of the Physiocrats that land was the true source of wealth. Certainly, even a slight acquaintance with earlier British economists would have shown Say that labor, or alternatively, industry, received very great emphasis. Two peoples were always held up to light in the English pamphlet literature: the Spaniards, who lost the treasures of America through sloth, and the Dutch, who, through sheer hard work, had converted a barren land into a prosperous community. It is worth noting that the earlier British economists are completely missing in the Introductory Discourse of Say's *Treatise*. As a result, Say is able to consider the principle that labor is the main source of wealth as Smith's "fruitful demonstration" and the conclusions drawn therefrom as "rigorous deductions from an unassailable principle" which only weak minds would reject.[34] "Whenever the Wealth of Nations is perused with the attention it so well merits," Say urged, "it will be perceived that until the epoch of its publication, the science of political economy did not exist." This comes close to asserting that Smith singlehandedly created the science of political economy.

The views of Dugald Stewart gained great currency through the very distinguished students who attended his lectures at Edinburgh. Among his students were some of the most important publicists of political economy in the early nineteenth century as well as several distinguished politicians: James Mill, John Ramsey McCulloch, Thomas Chalmers, the Earl of Lauderdale, Henry Brougham, Francis Horner, and Lord Palmerston are but a few of this rather exceptional class.[35] Say's Introductory Discourse did not receive as much currency in Britain and America as it could have because Say's translator, C.R. Prinsep, for some unaccountable reason, omitted this portion of Say's *Treatise* from his translation. Nonetheless, George Pryme did use it to introduce his lectures on political economy at Cambridge from 1816 onwards, a fact which must have given Say's views additional authority.[36]

The legacy of the first two attempts to view the history of economics after Adam Smith was thus not entirely fortunate. On the one hand, economists prior to Adam Smith were regarded as believing that gold and silver were the only forms of real worth and, on the other hand, they were represented as not having realized the simple fact that labor is the primary creator of wealth. Both notions were not a little mistaken, but they were to be repeated with increasing emphasis and somewhat monotonous regularity for most of the nineteenth century. And behind both of these notions there was the firm belief that political economy was really the theory of free trade, an assumption that colored their reading of Mercantilism and confirmed somewhat their condemnation of earlier writers.

Say and Stewart were not of course the only popularizers of Adam Smith. It is quite plausible that William Pitt's public approbation of him was more influential in this regard. Popular opinion in favor of Smith had already reached very great heights by 1800. In 1814 the conservative Anglican *British Critic* exclaimed: "Dr. Smith stands in the same relation to political economy that Homer holds to poetry and Newton to Physical science."[37] The *British Critic* also pinpointed Smith's fundamental principle: that security of property and the administration of justice when coupled with the greatest possible amount of individual initiative provided the speediest way to achieve economic prosperity; with this article of faith the *Critic* heartily concurred.

It is not to be expected that journals commenting on current economic issues, such as the *British Critic*, should worry about nice points of historical priority. This was properly the task of scholars, and it was one which was very cursorily done. Free trade was taken to be the fundamental position of true political economy and it acquired a quasi-theological authority in the eyes of its expounders. Contrary systems, such as Mercantilism, were seen, so to speak, as the handiwork of the devil. The French Count Hauterive fiercely condemned the mercantile system as the fount of the wars of the preceding centuries: "The theory of prohibitory laws," he announced, "is written in letters of blood in the history of all the wars which for four centuries have everywhere brought industry into conflict with powers." It was a system which, Hauterive claimed, produced "poverty, ignorance and crimes," which have made of human society, at some epochs in the history of modern nations, a picture so odious that one dare not stop to gaze at it. . ."[38]

Hauterive might conceivably have justified his excessively strong language in that French Mercantilism under Colbert did uphold some maxims which claimed that one nation would grow richer only at the expense of another. The same excuse cannot be applied to the Englishman, Nassau Senior, the first holder of the Drummond chair of Political Economy at Oxford in 1826. In two lectures devoted exclusively to the mercantile theory of wealth in 1827, Senior proceeded to seek reasons why such a simplistic theory of wealth as Mercantilism had ever gained sway.[39] Children, he noted, hear their fathers complain about money and this is one of the ways in which people come to believe that money is real wealth; by implication, economists such as John Locke, who emphasized the importance of the balance of trade, never quite outgrew this early impression. Much in the manner of Hauterive, Senior viewed Mercantilism not only as a mistaken economic system but as a propagator of evil: "To the Mercantile System . . . we may in general attribute the greatest of all human follies, the existence of war between civilized nations."[40] It was therefore his opinion that "the question of free trade is, next to the Reformation, next to the question of free religion, the most momentous that has ever been submitted to human decision."[41] Free trade has risen in status from economic theory to a messianic belief.

A more sophisticated view of the history of economics had been expounded a few years earlier by J.R. McCulloch. In the introductory portion of his Ricardo lectures, McCulloch provided a much fairer account of Mercantilism than Senior was later to do, and paid considerable attention to the ideas of such earlier economists as Dudley North, Sir Matthew Decker, and Joseph Harris. It is much to be regretted that McCulloch's views became simplified in time, because his influence grew in later years. Among the economists of the early nineteenth century, he was probably the best read in the history of economics and this of course gave added strength to his opinions. In a work called *The Literature of Political Economy*, written in 1845, which professedly attempted to review all past tracts and pamphlets of note, McCulloch combined the mistaken emphasis of both Say and Stewart to provide a biased account of British economic thought prior to Adam Smith:

> After the revival of arts and industry in modern Europe gold and silver were almost universally regarded as the only real wealth . . . This delusion was not merely general, but universal.[42]

His later comments upon economists such as Sir Josiah Child and Sir Matthew Decker are much more respectful and we are left with the paradoxical picture of the pre-Smithian economists as capable of good sense on every branch of economics, such as money, banking, or taxation, while being quite in the dark on the source of economic value.

The other aspect of Smith's economics that McCulloch emphasized was the belief, earlier expounded by Say, that labor was the true source of wealth. Having been a die-hard Ricardian for several years McCulloch gave special emphasis to this point. He considered the view that labor gives rise to value "the fundamental principle which lies at the bottom of the science of wealth"[43] and quoted extensively from John Locke to show that that philosopher had grasped this important point but had left it undeveloped. So strong was the Ricardian influence upon McCulloch even at this stage that despite an admission that the nature of commerce, of exchanges, of the division of labor, and of money and banking had all been "fully ascertained" by 1750, nonetheless the absence of the labor theory of value left the nature and sources of wealth "confused and contradictory."[44]

An interesting example of the fascination exercised by the doctrine that labor creates value is found in Charles Ganilh's *An Inquiry into the Various Systems of Political Economy* (1812). Ganilh characterizes the mercantile system as believing that wealth resides in foreign trade, the school of Quesnay as believing that it resides in land, while it was Adam Smith who first portrayed the source of wealth as labor embodied in material goods, and who thus became "as it were, the creator of science." Ganilh cannot praise this doctrine too highly:

> This theory, admirable for the greatness of the mind by which it was conceived, commands still greater respect for the profundity of the views of its author, the sagacity of his discoveries, and his concatenation of effects with causes, and of consequences with principles.[45]

Ganilh was a widely read and fair scholar. He goes on to note that Lord Lauderdale had criticized Adam Smith severely and founded a new system which derived wealth from the joint action of land, labor, and capitals. How could Ganilh react to this commonsense view and still sustain his earlier panegyrics on Smith? Ganilh evades the issue by claiming (inconsistently with his earlier remarks) that Lauderdale only modifies Smith's theory. His honesty then forces Ganilh into making a surprising admission:

> Such are the various systems concerning the sources of wealth. Though they offer different points of view, their difference is however merely nominal, and of very little importance to the science.[46]

Ganilh goes on to assert that everyone in fact took it for granted that land, labor, and capital cooperated to produce wealth, and that the only difference between systems lay in the relative emphasis given by each system. If Adam Smith's (purported) view of labor as creating wealth provided only a "nominal" difference, "of very little importance to the science," what was it that entitled Smith to be called the founder of the science?

We get a clue to Ganilh's predictions when we read how he characterizes the normative properties of a system which sees wealth as the result of labor. Four pages are filled with praise for the democratizing and civilizing virtues of labor: "Wealth, produced by labour—restores man to his primitive dignity, through the sentiment of his independence, through his obedience to laws common to all, and his sharing in the benefits of society in proportion to his services."[47] Furthermore, this system is to be especially esteemed since it encourages friendly relations between nations:

> In this system, man is no longer an obstacle to man, nations are no longer obstacles to nations. It is the interest of all to labour the one for the other, to interchange the respective produce of their labour, and to increase the domain of general wealth. The labour, industry, and commerce of every individual is useful to all, whatever portion of the globe they may inhabit; the more extensive agriculture of one country is beneficial to all laborious, manufacturing, and trading nations; it increases the produce destined for general consumption, which, in its turn, augments population; and this augmented population affords new consumers to the productions of the industry of every nation. Thus all nations share in the prosperity of each, and the portion of each is proportioned to its labour, manufactures, and commerce.[48]

Several decades later, another French economist, Blanqui, was again to rejoice in Smith's discovery of labor as the true source of value:

> there were no longer any sterile occupations, since every body was capable of giving things an exchange value, by means of labor. What an encouragement to men ill-favored by fortune and to those who did not expect the boon of an inheritance![49]

The next economist to attempt a history of economic thought was Travers Twiss, in his 1846 lectures as Drummond Professor of Political Economy at Oxford.[50] There is, however, little to distinguish Twiss' treatment of British economists prior to Adam Smith from that of McCulloch. Twiss lays the same emphasis on labor as the true source of wealth and on the mercantile belief in gold and silver as the true repositories of wealth coupled with criticisms of Smith for his definition of unproductive labor and his neglect of distribution, much as McCulloch had done. And when Nassau Senior obtained the Drummond Professorship a second time, he repeated his earlier view that Mercantilism confused gold with wealth.[51] By the 1860s this view of the history of economics had gained sufficient currency for T.H. Buckle to state blandly that after the publication of the *Wealth of Nations*, "innumerable absurdities, which had been accumulating for ages, were suddenly swept away."[52]

It is now well known that the tradition of economic history initiated by the Reverend William Cunningham rehabilitated Mercantilism by giving it a new role, that of nation-building. Cunningham was one member of a group of economists loosely referred to as the English Historical School. It would take us too far to enter into the merits and demerits of Cunningham's interpretation, but it may be noted here that the other economists of this school did not express much interest in a detailed study of pre-Smithian economics. Both Arnold Toynbee (whose method of study on any particular economic topic, say wages, was to read and criticize what all previous authorities had to say on the subject) and John Kells Ingram (who wrote a very successful *History of Political Economy*) consider the justification of protection for infant industries to be due to John Stuart Mill, whereas it was in fact staple Mercantilist fare.[53]

In reviewing the first century of the history of economic thought in Britain, the most striking feature is the great dominance of Smith's presentation of the subject in Book IV of the *Wealth of Nations*, throughout this period. The imputation of a belief in the precious metals as the major source of real wealth to the Mercantilists follows directly from Smith; while the view that labor is the true cornerstone of wealth is inferable from Smith's account, because the Mercantilists believed in gold and silver and the Physiocrats in land as the true repositories of wealth. One reason why this opinion prevailed is surely the prophetic role of Adam Smith in relation to the doctrine of free trade.

The extraordinary prestige of free trade cannot by itself account for the continuance of the Stewart-Say-McCulloch view of the history of economics. Even so historically minded an author as T.E. Cliffe-Leslie, who provided a perceptive critique of Smith's philosophical preconceptions, accepted without hesitation the Smithian view of the subject:

> It would not be difficult to trace the connection between every extant treatise prior to the "Wealth of Nations" and conditions of thought at the epoch at which it appeared. But there is the less occasion . . . to go behind the epoch of Adam Smith, that he has himself traced the systems of political economy antecedent to his own to a particular course of history.[54]

It was not until the Cunningham-Schmoller interpretation of Mercantilism as nation-building necessitated looking at the Mercantilist tracts in piecemeal fashion and in relation to the particular policies of any given time, that some justice was done to the earlier British economists; and it was not until the reaction to the state-making view stimulated the works of Eli Heckscher and Jacob Viner that the general reader was presented with a sufficient variety of evidence from the primary material to be able to form his or her own judgement on the history of British economics prior to Adam Smith.[55]

NOTES

1. E. Heckscher, *Mercantilism*, rev. edn (London: Allen & Unwin, 1955), vol. 2, 332.
2. R.S. Howey, *A Bibliography of General Histories of Economics* (Kansas: University of Kansas Press, 1982), 9.
3. Recently, scholars have paid a fair amount of attention to the question whether Smith was writing "history" or only "conjectural history." As there is no evidence in the *Wealth of Nations* that Smith meant to write anything other than "history," I shall ignore this view as a misleading historical reconstruct.
4. By comparing the thoughts of those economists whose works Smith owned or which his correspondence shows he had read it is possible to come up with a considerable list of ideas that Smith could have directly borrowed. I have provided my conjectures in "Adam Smith's Acknowledgements, Neo-plagiarism and the *Wealth of Nations*," *Journal of Libertarian Studies* (1990), **9**, 1-24.
5. Howey, *Bibliography of General Histories*, notes Smith's systematizing tendency but considers it to have been a worthwhile aspect of Smith's account. The difference between us lies in judging whether "Mercantilism" was in fact a system and, if so, how far Smith's presentation of it was fair. My own view will appear in section II of this chapter. For a recent look at Walpole's tax scheme, see W.L. Hausman and J.L. Neufeld, "Excise Anatomised: The Political Economy of Walpole's 1733 Tax Scheme," *Journal of European History* (Spring 1981), **9**, 131-44.
6. It is not possible to provide a detailed analytical treatment of Smith's views on unemployment here, but the differences between Smith and his predecessors have been frequently commented upon. See, for example, N.J. Pauling, "The Employment Problem in Pre-Classical English Economic Thought," *Economic Record* (June 1951), **27**, 52-65; W.D. Grampp, "The Liberal Elements in English Mercantilism," *Quarterly Journal of Economics* (November 1952), **66**, 465-501.
7. Adam Smith, *Wealth of Nations*, ed. R.H. Campbell and A.S. Skinner (Oxford: Clarendon Press, 1976), vol. I, 429, 430.
8. Ibid., 449.
9. Quoted by I.S. Michelman, *The Roots of Capitalism in Western Civilization* (New York: Fell, 1983), 71.
10. F. Hutcheson, *A Short Introduction to Moral Philosophy* (1747); reprinted in *Collected Works* (Darmstadt: Olms, 1969), vol. IV, 252.
11. Adam Smith, *Lecture on Jurisprudence* (Oxford: Oxford University Press, 1978), 52, 88-90.
12. B. Supple, *Commercial Crisis and Change in England, 1600-1642* (Cambridge: Cambridge University Press, 1959).
13. With the notable exception of Sir Matthew Decker. At one point Smith does contradict Decker, but his other three references to Decker, on taxes and their mode of accumulation and on the price of corn in Holland, are written in a favorable tone.
14. In view of the considerable emphasis given by Edwin Cannan to Bernard Mandeville as a source of Smith's ideas it is worth quoting W.L. Taylor's opinion that Cannan's edition of the *Wealth of Nations* "possibly more than any other major contribution, has enabled us to assess 'how firmly' Adam Smith 'stood on the shoulders of his predecessors,'"

(*Francis Hutcheson and David Hume as Precessors of Adam Smith*, Durham, N.C.: Duke University Press, 1965, 10).

15. Sir Joshua Child, *A New Discourse on Trade*, 5th edn (Glasgow, 1751), 112. In his *A History of Economic Ideas* (New York: McGraw-Hill, 1976), 634, R. Lekachman has emphasized the dependence of Smith's theory of wage differentials upon Cantillon's *Essai*.

16. John Locke, *Some Considerations of the Consequence of Lowering Interest, and Raising the Value of Money*, in *The Works of John Locke*, vol. V (London, 1823), 140. In the quote, Locke must mean "they are many way obnoxious to us."

17. S. Rashid, "The Interpretation of the 'Balance of Trade': A 'Wordy' Debate," *Research in the History of Economic Thought and Methodology* (1994), **12**, 93-111.

18. S. Rashid, "The Political Balance of Trade . . .??," *Research in the History of Economic Thought and Methodology* (1993), **11**, 73-92.

19. S. Rashid, "The Pragmatic Case for Freeing Trade from Intervention, 1660-1776," *Research in the History of Economic Thought and Methodology* (1996), **14**, 93-117.

20. L. Rothkrug, *Opposition to Louis XIV: The Political and Social Origins of the French Enlightenment* (Princeton, N.J.: Princeton University Press, 1965).

21. T.W. Hutchison, *Before Adam Smith: The Emergence of Political Economy, 1662-1776* (Oxford: Blackwell, 1988).

22. Dugald Stewart made this point in the Appendix to his Memoir of Smith (*Collected Works of Dugald Stewart*, vol. 10, Edinburgh, 1858-78).

23. Arthur Young, *Political Arithmetic* (London, 1744), ch. 3.

24. In H.S. Foxwell's copy of *Select Essays on Commerce* (London, 1754), he notes that this volume contains "The first reference to the physiocratic doctrine." I have had no luck in finding others. Certainly, if the periodicals of the day are an indication of popular interest, then there is no evidence of popular interest in the Physiocrats before 1776. After 1790, on the other hand, there was much more interest in Physiocratic ideas. See R.L. Meek, "Physiocracy and Classicism in Britain," *Economic Journal* (March 1951), **51**, 26-47.

25. *Monthly Review*, **53**, 168.

26. *Monthly Review*, **54**.

27. Dugald Stewart, *Lectures on Political Economy*, ed. Sir W.R. Hamilton (Edinburgh, 1877), vol. I, 268 (emphasis added). This is volume VIII of *The Collected Works of Dugald Stewart*, 11 vols (Edinburgh: Constable, 1858-78).

28. Ibid., 271.

29. Ibid., 298-301.

30. Dugald Stewart, *Memoir of the Life of Adam Smith* (1793); reprinted in *Collected Works*, vol. X.

31. Ibid., liv-lv.

32. Ibid., vol. IX, 23.

33. J.B. Say, *Treatise on Political Economy*, new American edn, ed. C.C. Biddle (Philadelphia: Lippincott, 1853), Introduction.

34. Ibid., xxxvii-xxxviii.

35. Stewart, *Collected Works*, vol. X, liv-lv.

36. See the extract from Say's letter in *Treatise on Political Economy*, xii fn.

37. *Critical Review* (1806); *British Critic* (Nov. 1814), 470.

38. Quoted by A. Blanqui, *History of Political Economy in Europe*, trans. E.J. Leonard (New York, 1880), 319.

39. Nassau Senior, *Three Lectures on the Transmission of the Precious Metals . . . and the Mercantile Theory of Wealth* (London, 1828), 37; reprinted in *Selected Writings on Economics* (New York: Augustus Kelley, 1966).

40. Ibid., 51.
41. Ibid., 88.
42. J.R. McCulloch, *The Literature of Political Economy* (London, 1845), 1.
43. Ibid., 3.
44. Ibid., 4.
45. C. Ganilh, *An Inquiry into the Various Systems of Political Economy*, trans. D. Boileau (London, 1812).
46. Ibid., 70.
47. Ibid., 46.
48. Ibid., 48.
49. Blanqui, *History of Political Economy*, 386.
50. Travers Twiss, *View of the Progress of Political Economy in Europe* (London, 1847; reprinted New York: Augustus Kelley, 1973).
51. N. Senior, *Four Introductory Lectures* (London, 1852), contained in the Kelley reprint referred to in n. 39. Even an otherwise unorthodox economist, H.D. McLeod, repeats many of the "orthodox" opinions in his *History of Economics* (London: Blies, Sands & Co., 1896), 96-7.
52. T.H. Buckle, *History of Civilization*, 2nd edn (New York: Appleton, 1920), 154.
53. A. Toynbee, *The Industrial Revolution of the Eighteenth Century in England*, new edn (Gloucester, Mass.: Peter Smith, 1980), ch. VII; J.K. Ingram, *History of Political Economy* (New York: Macmillan, 1893), ch. V.
54. T.E. Cliffe-Leslie, "The Political Economy of Adam Smith," *Fortnightly Review* (1870); reprinted in *Essays in Political Economy* by T.E. Cliffe-Leslie, 2nd edn (Dublin, 1888); reprinted New York: Augustus Kelley, 1969.
55. Heckscher, *Mercantilism*; J. Viner, *Studies in the Theory of International Trade* (New York: Harper & Row, 1937).

9. The Intellectual Standards of Adam Smith's Day*

I

In reviewing the contributions of Adam Smith to the growth of economics Hans Brems writes:

> Much of what Smith had to say had been said before—but in French. Academic etiquette of his day demanded no acknowledgments, and he offered none.[1]

This is an unusually clear statement of a point of view that appears to circulate through much of the profession. Adam Smith, it would appear, borrowed much without acknowledgement. Nonetheless, it is not fair to dig deeply into this issue because the mid-eighteenth century was not an age much concerned with scholarly courtesies. There does not, however, appear to be any study of the nature of scholarly expectations at this period. It has also been suggested that much of the earlier literature may have been so hard to obtain that it was simply not reasonable to expect Adam Smith to hunt out such material. This chapter aims to examine the view extant in the literature that academic etiquette of Smith's day "demanded no acknowledgments." When we find indignant charges of plagiarism raised against John Asgill in 1696 and against one M'Arthur by George Chalmers in 1803, it would require the curious circumstance for scholarly manners to have altered during the century in between. The obituarist of Sir James Steuart was already accusing (unnamed) scholars of having plagiarized Steuart's works, and the suspicion that the barbs were aimed at Smith needs to be examined.[2]

There are four main streams of economic knowledge from which Adam Smith could have drunk. First, the Classics were a staple in every educated man's diet and Smith relished, in particular, the Stoics. Secondly, the works of the Natural Law Philosophers, exemplified chiefly by Grotius and Pufendorf, were commented upon and transmitted to Scotland by Adam Smith's teachers. Thirdly, Scotland had long had close ties with France and

*I am grateful to Royall Brandis for his helpful comments.

Holland and even though there do not appear to be direct links with the Dutch, several French economists were undoubtedly familiar to Smith. Finally, the long tradition of English pamphleteering has to be considered, a literature that was generated in order to debate policy issues, but which often provided insights of permanent value. Those who assert that acknowledgements were not expected in the eighteenth century will have to establish not only that all of the above traditions are deficient in providing due acknowledgement but also that there was no such practice in other fields, such as history or literature, which were important parts of education in Adam Smith's day, and to which Smith himself paid considerable attention.

Strictly speaking, we should separate some closely related issues. Evidence from sources of a much earlier age might show that Smith was familiar with the practice of careful citation but does not tell us about the literary manners of Smith's own day. If we look at Smith's contemporaries we may be able to infer that Smith knew that *his* period required careful citation. Finally, there is the murky question of plagiarism and the attitude of scholars in economics as well as other fields towards this issue. My concern here is with the practice of citation, and I believe most of the evidence points in the same direction.

II

It is well known that the Greeks provided only very limited material on economics but even here Adam Smith did not fully escape censure.[3] In his translation of Aristotle's *Ethics and Politics*, the Scottish historian John Gillies accused Smith of borrowing the main ideas of the *Theory of Moral Sentiments*. Subsequently, Vernard Foley has dealt with Smith's use of a variety of examples—cloth and ships being the main ones—which suggest Greek inspiration, as well as the use of the contrast between a porter and a philosopher, which is suggestive of the life of Protagoras.[4] However, our interest lies not in the substantive doctrines themselves but in what Smith may have taken to be due literary courtesy so we may move on from the Greeks to the Moral Philosophers.

The writings of Hugo Grotius will serve adequately to emphasize the importance of acknowledgements, especially since most later writers were, by their own admission, commenting on Grotius. A quick look at *De Jure Belli* will serve to justify the appellation of "Miracle of Holland" that stuck to Grotius. The careful scholarship that he brings to bear on each issue is striking. To take but one example, because the principles stated have relevance to the wider issue being discussed—the fair treatment of one's predecessors—we can turn to the chapter, "On Interpretation," where the proper way to deal with treaties and promises is discussed. The first four principles stated are:

I.   How promises are outwardly binding.
II.   If other implications are lacking, words are to be understood in their ordinary sense.
III. Technical terms are to be explained according to their technical use.
IV.   Resort is to be had to conjectures in the case of ambiguous and contradictory expressions, or if conjectures naturally suggest themselves.[5]

There is manifest a desire to be "fair" to one's sources. To support these points alone we find references to Cicero, Isocrates, Livy, the Jewish scholars who wrote on *Numbers*, Procopius, Polybius, Thucydides, Ulpian, Augustine, Servitus, and the Greek rhetoricians. In another place, in order to justify Plutarch's claim that "There is no war among men which does not originate in a fault," Grotius wrote in a footnote:

> This thought is absolutely true, but men seldom reflect upon it, though it has been set forth by many admirable statements by the ancients. What harm, then, to fortify it by the sayings of others, which are not less effective?[6]

Grotius goes on to quote Athenaeus, Fabianus, Papirius, Philo, Pliny, Terome, Chrysostom, Claudian, and Agathias in support. Even in a work designed to have practical influence, as *De Jure Belli* eminently was, the love of scholarship shines abundantly.

When Adam Smith's teacher, Francis Hutcheson, came to write a short textbook, he made it very clear that he was only representing well-established notions and gave an explicit reference to Grotius and to his own teacher, Gershom Carmichael.[7] In the preface addressed "To the Students in Universities" Hutcheson is careful to note how heavily he depends upon others:

> The following books contain the elements of these several branches of moral philosophy; which if they are carefully studied may give the youth an easier access to the well known and admired works either of the ancients, Plato, Aristotle, Xenophon, Cicero; or of the moderns, Grotius, Cumberland, Pufendorf, Harrington and others, upon this branch of philosophy.
>
> The learned will at once discern how much of this compend is taken from the writings of others, from Cicero and Aristotle; and to name no other moderns, from Pufendorf's smaller work, *De Officio Hominis et Civis*.

Hutcheson was apparently not satisfied with such a general acknowledgement and indicates later how he would have liked to have elaborated on it:

> In the second impression of this book some few additions seemed necessary and several amendments. The author once intended to have made references all along to the more eminent writers, antient or modern, who treated the several subjects. But considering that this could be of no use except to those who have the cited books at hand, and that such could easily by their indexes find the corresponding place for themselves: he spared himself that disagreeable and unnecessary labour. All who have looked into such subjects know that the general doctrine and foundations of morals may be found in the antients above mentioned, and in Dr. Cumberland, and in Lord Shaftesbury: and that scarce any question of the law of nature and nations is not to be found in Grotius, Pufendorf, especially with Barbeyrac's copious notes, Harrington, Locke, or Bynkershock, to mention no more. Nay in Barbeyrac one finds the principal authors who have published large dissertations on particular heads. Such as want more full discussions of any such points, must have recourse to these authors.[8]

It is worth emphasizing that Hutcheson was so careful even in a textbook, where originality would have been a minor concern and readers would not have expected the citation pattern of a research report.

III

The authorities referred to by Adam Smith himself in the *Wealth of Nations* suggest that the eighteenth century had much higher literary standards than economists have commonly supposed. Charles Smith, whom Adam Smith called "the very-well informed author" of *Three Tracts on the Corn Trade*, provides careful references to all his sources.[9] The "sober and judicious" Adam Anderson, as he is called in the *Wealth of Nations*, is yet another author who is careful to document his work in the *Historical and Chronological Account of the Origin of Commerce*. The extent to which some of Smith's authorities took pleasure in looking up predecessors is amply indicated by the following entry for 1581 in Anderson:

> The author of this work has in his possession a most judicious pamphlet, published in this year 1581, and dedicated to Queen Elizabeth, which, in his opinion, merited this short mention, being intitled, A compendious Examination of certain ordinary Complaints of divers of our Countrymen in these our days. (By W. S.) It is in the black letter. Therein, public spirit, or zeal for the community,—the point of inclosures for pasture, then so much clamoured

against,—the dearth of provisions,—the decay of towns,—the multitude of sheep,—the coin's being worn out,—the true standard and intrinsic value of our money, compared with that of foreign nations,—wool, against its exportation,—our extravagant love of foreign wares,—and several other national points of great importance, are all handled in so masterly a manner, and in so pure a diction for the time he wrote, as to give room for conjecturing it might have been penned by the direction of that Queen's ministers, since scarcely any ordinary person, in those early days, could be furnished with so copious a fund of excellent matter.[10]

The only economist of Adam Smith's century who has acquired notoriety for plagiarism is Malachy Postlethwayt, whose works Smith appears to ignore, and who has been most fairly treated by Lucy Sutherland:

Originally based on Savary's *Dictionnaire*, this compilation [i.e. Postlethwayt's Dictionary] always contained much extra material and by the time of the enlarged 4th ed., 1774, the original material was quite swamped.[11]

Two of the pamphleteers who drew praise from Smith are "Sir Matthew Decker" and the Reverend John Smith. It will be instructive to see what sort of an example these authors set. The author of the *Essay on the Causes of the Decline of the Foreign Trade*, supposed by Adam Smith to be Sir Matthew Decker, is one of the few English pamphleteers to have gained praise from Smith for a theoretical point:

The observation of Sir Matthew Decker, that certain taxes are, in the price of certain goods, sometimes repeated and accumulated four or five times, is perfectly just with regard to taxes upon the necessaries of life.[12]

There are three other references to the same pamphlet in the *Wealth of Nations* so we may be sure that this is a pamphlet Smith had read with some care. The *Essay* displays quite modern literary standards, especially if we remember that it was a tract for the times, written by a merchant. John Locke, Charles Davenant, John de Wit, Roger Coke, *The British Merchant*, and *Britannia Languens* are repeatedly used and due acknowledgement made. When the *Essay* wishes to refute Joshua Gee's opinion on the inadvisability of free ports, it makes repeated reference to and provides adequate quotes from Gee's own work:

Objections against a free-port here having been made by *Joshua Gee*, an author of good credit, for that reason must not be left unanswer'd, in his *Tract on Trade* (p. 165), he expresses himself thus

But to think it would be an advantage for a trading nation to admit all manner of foreign commodities to be imported free from all duties, is an unaccountable notion, and still less suitable to the circumstances of our island than to the Continent; for we have no inland countries beyond us (as they have) with whom we may carry on trade by land; but what is of the utmost consequence to us, is, that by laying high duties we are always able to check the vanity of our people in their extreme fondness of wearing exotic manufactures: For were it not for this restraint, as our neighbours give much less wages to their workmen than we do, and consequently can sell cheaper, the Italians, the French and the Dutch, would have continued to pour upon us their silks, paper, hats, druggets, stuffs, ratteens, and even Spanish wool cloths.[13]

The *Essay* then proceeds with an extended refutation. Although "Decker" was only a merchant, it is noticeable how well read he is. Indeed, one finds a good portion of the *Select Tracts* that J.R. McCulloch was to reprint in the mid-nineteenth century among the authors referred to by "Decker."[14]

When we turn to an author who had more leisure and who wrote self-consciously as a scholar, we find even higher standards. We are introduced to the Reverend John Smith by Adam Smith as "the very accurate and intelligent" author of the *Memoirs of Wool*, and the book in question is indeed fully deserving of such high praise. In order to provide readers with a comprehensive view of the wool trade, John Smith provides extensive quotes from every author he uses as well as detailed references.[15] "It was judged better to be prolix," Smith tells us in the Preface, "than to omit any Thing in the least Material; and still better, than to *leave any Fact of Moment doubtful*." The Preface also provides a detailed account of all the foreign references he plans to use:

> From the Nature of *which*, many of them, it was necessary to be the more large and circumstantial, in several Quotations or Transcripts, in regard they are not *simple*, but *complicated Facts*, viz. 1. *Opinions* and *Arguments*; or, if it is allowable to use the Word on this Occasion, *Doctrines* or *Theories*. 2. *Policies* or *Measures* taken in Consequence thereof. 3. The Result or Consequence of *those Measures*. And these being contained partly in *small Tracts*, long since, out of Print; the Purport of them did not admit of being so briefly summed up, with Reference made to the *Tracts* themselves, as if they had been *more accessible Authors*; but in order to a competent Pourtrait, they required to be exhibited in their original Dress; and though not at full Length, yet in some due Proportion.
>
> It was further necessary, for the ascertaining and pointing out to Observation, several of *these Facts*, to make large Additions, occasionally, by way of *Note, &c.*; which has contributed to swell this Work to what it is, the Quantity of *Four Volumes*, altho' in the Compass of *Two*. (Emphasis in original)

In the two volumes that follow, John Smith is almost embarrassingly complete in the way he provides complete references for every view. Sir Josiah Child, Thomas Mun, Charles Davenant, John Locke, Sir Matthew Decker, and a host of lesser lights of English economic pamphleteering appear in these books, together with copious illustrations of their thought. How could one admire such an author and be unaware of the desirability of due acknowledgement?

IV

It remains to inquire whether general literary standards permitted a looser attitude to acknowledgements and borrowings. Two examples should suffice. When Samuel Johnson wrote about John Dryden in *Lives of the English Poets* he noted how Dryden had been frequently accused of borrowing:

> The perpetual accusation produced against him was that of plagiarism, against which he never attempted any vigorous defence; for though he was perhaps sometimes injuriously censured, he would, by denying part of the charge, have confessed the rest.[16]

It is of some importance to note that the issue was not one just recently raised by Johnson, but one that had been with Dryden even in the latter half of the seventeenth century.

Edward Gibbon wrote his *Decline and Fall of the Roman Empire* at the same time as Adam Smith was writing *Wealth of Nations*, and the "solemn sneer" that he cast on the rise of Christianity was immediately recognized.[17] The credentials of the historian were questioned by several, most notably by H.E. Davis of Balliol College, Oxford, who produced dozens of pages which showed, in parallel columns, the wholesale manner in which Gibbon had borrowed. In replying to Davis, Gibbon does not claim that he is being held up to new standards, nor that it was common practice to plagiarize and he should not be made an exception. Rather, his excuse is based on the very different point that, for his purposes, such borrowing did not matter.

Even the practice of Adam Smith and his friends suggest that borrowing was not considered quite so innocently. In 1752 Smith made a long and vehement speech defending his priority regarding the doctrines of natural liberty.[18] Such vigor surely had little point unless originality was valued—and, by implication, unacknowledged borrowing condemned. A few years later it was reported to Smith that Hugh Blair was using materials from his lectures on Rhetoric, and Smith replied to the effect that Blair was welcome to do so.[19] Once again, the report to Smith of Blair's purported borrowing makes little sense unless we accept the fact that literary standards then were not widely different from standards today. Adam Smith is careful to acknowledge his debts to David Hume (with the possible exception of the specie-flow mechanism). Indeed, in singling out Hume for having noted the link between commerce and liberty, Smith ignores Sir James Steuart, Lord Kames, Adam Ferguson, John Millar, and William Robertson.[20] Now Hume himself was not very careful with his acknowledgements.[21] There is the possibility that scholars have been misled about the general intellectual climate by focusing on the mutual admiration club of David Hume and Adam Smith.

In conclusion, a consideration of the standards of acknowledgement prevalent in Adam Smith's day led to the examination of several possible sources. The Moral Philosophers from whom Smith learned are found to have upheld recognizable standards of scholarship, and this is also true of those English pamphleteers with whom Adam Smith was familiar. It is scarcely possible by means of extracts and quotes to provide an adequate notion of the extent to which high scholarly standards are visible in Hugo Grotius and the Reverend John Smith. The interested reader must consult the originals to get such a feeling. The works of Samuel Johnson and Edward Gibbon show that a lack of proper acknowledgement was deemed reprehensible by both poets and historians. Several incidents from Adam Smith's own life show that originality as well as due acknowledgements were valued. If Adam Smith was indeed deficient in his acknowledgements, there is little justification for supposing that his own practice was justified by the standards of his age.

NOTES

1. Hans Brems, "Frequently Wrong but Rarely in Doubt," *Challenge* (Nov.-Dec. 1987), **30**, 55. It is certainly striking that all the "second-generation" Scottish economists—Dugald Stewart, Francis Horner and Henry Brougham—as well as Thomas Robert Malthus showed a preference for the Physiocrats.
2. Anon., *Mr. John Asgill, his Plagiarism detected* (London, 1696).
3. As reported by Dugald Stewart, "An Account of the Life and Writings of Adam Smith, LL.D.," in *The Collected Works of Dugald Stewart* (Edinburgh, 1872), vol. 10, 82-4.
4. V. Foley, *The Social Physics of Adam Smith* (West Lafayette, Ind.: Purdue University Press, 1976), 154.
5. Hugo Grotius, *The Law of War and Peace*, trans. F.W. Kelsey (Indianapolis: Bobbs-Merrill, 1925), 409-13.
6. Ibid., 80.
7. Francis Hutcheson, *A Short Introduction to Moral Philosophy* (1747; Hildsheim: George Olms, 1969), i.
8. Ibid., iv.

9. C. Smith, *Three Tracts on the Corn Trade and Corn Laws* (London, 1766).
10. Adam Anderson, *A Historical and Chronological Account of the Origin of Commerce* (London, 1801), vol. II, 151.
11. Lucy Sutherland, "The Law Merchant in England," in *Politics and Finance in the Eighteenth Century*, ed. A. Newman (London: Hambledon Press, 1984), 29.
12. Adam Smith, *An Inquiry into the Nature and Causes of the Wealth of Nations*, ed. R.H. Campbell and A.S. Skinner (Oxford: Clarendon Press, 1976), vol. II, 873 (hereafter referred to as *WN*).
13. Sir M. Decker, *An Essay on the Causes of the Decline of the Foreign Trade* (London: Brotherton, 1756), 2nd edn, as reprinted in J.R. McCulloch, *A Select Collection . . .* (London, 1856), 251.
14. On the basis of contemporary attributions, followed by George Chalmers in his *Estimate of the Comparative Strength of Great Britain* (London: Printed for John Stockdale, 1804), p. 113, note 2. I believe the author is actually William Richardson.
15. John Smith, *Chronicon Rusticum—Commerciale or Memoirs of Wool* (London, 1747), vol. I, viii.
16. Samuel Johnson, *Lives of the English Poets: A Selection* (London: Everyman's Library, 1975), 135-6.
17. G.W. Bowersock, "Gibbon's Historical Imagination," *American Scholar* (Winter 1988), **57**, 33-47.
18. Stewart, *Collected Works*, vol. 10, 67-8.
19. This aspect is covered in most biographies of Smith. The most careful journal treatment is R. Hamowy, "Adam Smith, Adam Ferguson and the Division of Labor," *Economica* (August 1968), **35**, 249-59.
20. *WN*, vol. I, 412, n. 6, where the editors draw attention to this point.
21. Laird Okie, "Ideology and Partiality in David Hume's *History of England*," *Hume Studies* (April 1985), **XI**, 1, 1-32; David Wootton, "Humes 'Of Miracles,'" in M. Stewart, ed., *Studies in the Philosophy of the Scottish Enlightenment* (Oxford: Clarendon Press, 1990), 202-3; Salim Rashid, "David Hume and Eighteenth Century Monetary Thought: A Critical Comment on Recent Views," *Hume Studies* (Nov. 1984), **X(2)**, 156-64.

10. Concluding Reflections

Economics is a study of mankind in the ordinary business of life.
Alfred Marshall

The most relevant standard for judging the *Wealth of Nations* would be that set by his contemporaries and immediate predecessors. Using this standard, I have argued that the *Wealth of Nations* provided no advance in the understanding of the market mechanism; it used facts selectively and purposefully but not with the aim of providing a well-rounded view of the economy; the *Wealth of Nations* does provide a brilliant development of the extant case for *laissez-faire* in the market for food, but the treatment of applied economics was generally a pedagogic presentation of common knowledge, as in the case of taxation. The preeminence of the *Wealth of Nations* was achieved by a combination of political support and historiographical ignorance. Smith's presentation of all competitors as stupid or misguided did wonders in educating the public. One can hardly blame Adam Smith for all this. He clearly stated that the dominant force in our lives was self-interest and his own self-interest was maximized by being recognized as the founder of the science of political economy.

Perhaps the first query raised by careful study of the *Wealth of Nations* is to wonder about the way the history of economics has been studied. How could Adam Smith have achieved such exalted status when so many generations of economists have studied the *Wealth of Nations* with meticulous care? It is one of our cherished beliefs that a multitude of scholars produces diversity and that diversity will force us closer to the truth. And yet, decade after decade, the old half-truths about Adam Smith have been confidently repeated. The sociology of historical ideas clearly deserves more attention than we have given it hitherto. What makes an idea popular? How is the popularity sustained? What does it take to dethrone an orthodoxy? While these points have received considerable attention in the case of the Keynesian Revolution and, to a lesser extent, that of the Marginal Revolution, they have yet to be applied with equal care to the work of Adam Smith.

It is a truism that everyone relies on the past, but such truisms are of no help in studying the history of ideas. The primary object of research into the history of ideas must be the effort to understand each idea in its proper context and then reach some judgement on the originality and truth of the idea. I have argued that Adam Smith did not provide a valuable synthesis of eighteenth-century economic thought and that he made matters worse by failing to acknowledge clearly his considerable debts to the past. But why would anybody want to know such facts as I have dwelt upon? In the Introduction, I tried to plead for the pursuit of historical accuracy for its own sake. Now I would like to point out some of the consequences of our generally historical study of Adam Smith.

To begin with, let me note that our current approach has fostered what can only be called the "hero view of history," which says that great men do magnificent things and put posterity in their debt. Cicero's classic description of the "Lawgiver" immediately comes to mind:

> There was a time when men wandered at large in the fields like animals and lived on wild fare; they did nothing by the guidance of reason, but relied chiefly on physical strength; there was as yet no ordered system of religious worship nor of social duties; no one had seen legitimate marriage nor had anyone looked upon children whom he knew to be his own nor had they learned the advantages of an equitable code of law . . . At this juncture a man—great and wise I am sure—became aware of the power latent in man and the wide field offered by his mind for great achievements if once he could develop this power and improve it by instruction. Men were scattered in the fields and hidden in sylvan retreats when he assembled and gathered them in accordance with a plan; he introduced them to every useful and honourable occupation, though they cried out against it at first because of its novelty, and then when because of his reason and eloquence they had listened with greater attention, he transformed them into a kind and gentle folk.[1]

Needless to say, this is not the sort of proposition that can be dismissed as being false on some *a priori* grounds. But we have gone through so many sad experiences where heroes have turned out to have feet of clay that such "hero views" should be accepted only after the most careful scrutiny. Actually, Smith's fame has gone beyond that of a hero in the common acceptance. In 1976 several individuals traveled from the United States to Kirkcaldy in order to lay wreaths on Adam Smith's grave; and even in 1983 there was a professor of economics who lectured on Adam Smith in the way Alexander Pope worshipped Newton:

> Nature and Natures Laws lay hid in night.
> God said, let Smith be, and all was light.

These are two examples known to me personally. Doubtless others could multiply such instances. When the Republicans were in power, we saw members of the President's White House staff and administration appear with "Adam Smith" ties during television interviews. The fact that such saintly status is given to Adam Smith cannot now be purely an intellectual question.

Those who adopt the hero-view implicitly argue that economics is a very difficult subject which can only make sense after we have been initiated into its mysteries. (Of course, it is the hero who first initiates us.) The fact that so many people from all walks of life: merchants, politicians, philosophers, and clergymen, could all write sensibly on economics during the "Mercantilist" age should serve to dispel such an impression. It should suggest that economic knowledge is not like pyramid building, where we can climb higher only after ascending all the lower steps, but rather it is like observing an undulating meadow which can be entered from many different sides, and the view we obtain depends very much on where we enter and how hard we look. If a hillock blocks our vision, even the most piercing eye will be unable to see through. In such a field everyone can make a little sense of what they know. To make sense of the whole, it is not brilliance but hard work and experience that are needed. The anthropologist Max Gluckman notes that during the Second World War the prices of European goods rose sharply and the prices of goods produced by the Lozi, an African tribe, rose with them. The Lozi national council were led to debate on the merits of controlling the price of fish. Here are some of the arguments provided by the councillors:

> One argued that they would have to fix differential prices within the kingdom because in centres near the European towns money was plentiful while at distant centres money was scarce: and prices of goods adjusted themselves to the supply of money. Others said that while there was a fall in the total supply of fish as more men left to work for Europeans with rising wages, and while demand remained high, prices were bound to rise. A third argued that control would be difficult to enforce, since a man who had a pressing need for fish for a feast would find it worth while to pay more, and generally he drew attention to the effect of a man's idea of marginal utility to him on prices in a seller's market. A fourth, following the same line, argued that an attempt to control would drive sales of fish into out-of-the-way places away from the normal centres of marketing.[2]

Surely basic economic truths are much too important and much too accessible for economists to monopolize them by claiming that a "true" understanding of economic principles had to wait until the year 1776?

It is ironical to note that it was Alfred Marshall, the very person who emphasized the relationship of economics to ordinary life, who argued the case for Adam Smith's having made a singular contribution to the subject:

> The next great step in advance, the greatest step that economics has ever taken, was the work, not of a school, but of an individual. . . Wherever [Adam Smith] differs from his predecessors, he is more nearly right than they; while there is scarcely any economic truth now known of which he did not get some glimpse.[3]

In view of Viner's characterization of the *Wealth of Nations* as containing "traces of every conceivable doctrine," Marshall's praise has some unintended ambiguity.

The fact that the British economy showed rapid industrial growth shortly after the publication of the *Wealth of Nations* has even led some scholars to attribute the Industrial Revolution to the influence of Adam Smith. Arnold Toynbee asserted that "*The Wealth of Nations* and the steam engine destroyed the old world and built a new one." This idea still has its proponents, as may be seen by L.A. Clarkson's refusal to accept the view that Mercantilist policies did aid British economic growth and by his use of Smith's critique of the colonial system as the basis for his refusal. More careful scholars, such as Jacob Viner, have denied any direct practical influence of the *Wealth of Nations* (as opposed to verbal support for its policies); Viner even claims that there was perhaps just as much interference after 1776 as before.[4]

The refusal to take seriously the quality of British economic thought before Adam Smith has led to an inability to appreciate the process of economic development. Smith's ideas were presented with such scant reference to their applicability to economies unlike those of England or Holland that many individuals seriously referred to the *Wealth of Nations* to justify economic policy even for places like colonial Brazil.[5] The variety of problems faced by the English between 1600 and 1776, such as the development of the Poor Law, the growth of a banking system, the regulation of the stock market and of industrial organization, none were considered to hold instructive lessons for other developing economics. There is a curious note in the Preface to Ephraim Lipson's *Economic History of England* in which he states that he had difficulty procuring copies of old economic literature because they were all being bought up by Russian and Japanese libraries. How far the Russians were influenced is not clear, but Japanese bureaucrats were substantially following the tenets of the German historical school and Wilhelm Roscher.[6] Those who took the Mercantilists seriously may even have profited!

Adam Smith popularized a basic philosophy of economics which said that:

1. all individuals seek to maximize wealth;
2. individuals know better than governments how to maximize wealth.

Combining the above, we see that individuals grow richest when governments leave them alone. If we add a third axiom:

3. national wealth is the sum of individual wealth[7]

then we can say that "Nations grow rich by leaving their people alone." The claim that such a policy had guided British prosperity was made by the Prime Minister, William Pitt, in 1791 and later in Parliamentary Reports.

Smith reserved defense, justice, and public works for the state on the grounds (not quite explicitly developed) that individuals could be both unduly selfish and myopic. However, these exceptions deny the validity of axioms 1 and 2 above. One needs fine judgement to apply Smith's ideas. Smithian economic policy prescribes only justice and public works as the domestic concerns of the state. However, if a state can be found with the integrity not to make justice a business, with the power to enforce its will, with the foresight and the benevolence to introduce only needed public works, then we can probably rely on such a government to interfere judiciously in economic affairs.

The affection of conservatives for Adam Smith is all the more touching in view of Smith's determined insistence that all value was created by labor. Both profits and rents were, according to Smith, deductions from the value arising from the efforts of labor. Karl Marx does not miss this gift.

In *Theories of Surplus Value*, Marx begins by quoting Smith's own words in Chapter 6 of Book I of the *Wealth of Nations* and then comments upon the significance of the quote:

> "The *value*," Adam continues immediately, "*which the workmen add to the materials*, therefore, resolves itself *in this case*" (when capitalist production has begun) "*into two parts, of which the one pays their wages, the other the profits of their employer upon the whole stock of materials and wages which he advanced.*" [emphasis given by Marx]
>
> Hence therefore Adam Smith explicitly states: the profit which is made on the sale of the complete manufacture originates not from the sale of the commodity *above* its value, is not profit upon alienation. The value, that is, the quantity of labour which the workmen add to the material, falls rather into two parts. One pays their wages or is paid for through their wages. By this transaction the workmen give in return only as much labour as they have received in the form of wages. The other part forms the profit of the capitalist, that is, it is a quantity of labour which he sells without having paid for it. If therefore he sells the commodity at its value, then his profit originates from the

fact that he has not *paid* for a part of the labour contained in the commodity, but has nevertheless *sold* it.[8]

It is clear that the "surplus value" of Marx is but a developed form of Smith's ideas.

The origins of Marx's views on surplus value also bear upon our reading of Adam Smith. Did Marx misread Adam Smith and find out some passages that would support his preconceived ideas? Such an interpretation is untenable in view of the fact that both Lord Lauderdale and T.R. Malthus read Smith exactly as Marx did. Francis Horner explicitly attributed the labor theory of prices to Adam Smith. Samuel Read also agreed that Smith had made an erroneous assertion. It is worth emphasizing that no monopoly or power relations are relevant. Smith is simply claiming that under competitive market conditions, the employer's return consists of a deduction from the value created by labor.[9]

How clearly did Adam Smith grasp the foundational premise of modern economics on the mutual beneficence of market exchange? Later scholars have been content to note that since Adam Smith admitted capital to be productive he could not have meant to imply the radical conclusions of a labor theory of value. However, this is to force a consistency that the rest of Smith's work appears to deny. As Alec Macfie has said (in a different context): "Consistency was not his [Smith's] shining virtue."[10] Before forming a final judgement on the validity of such an approach the neo-classical economist is asked to recollect how plentiful are the theorems showing the impossibility of forming accurate economic aggregates and how more plentiful are models making use of just such aggregates.

Marian Bowley has said of Adam Smith that:

> We too often forget that the problem which led him into wage theory initially was "why does labour not receive the whole product of labour"—treating the whole product of labour as the gross product of labour assisted by other factors.[11]

Samuel Hollander similarly states:

> The true impetus to early nineteenth-century British socialism deriving from the conception of profits and rent as "deductions from the whole produce of labor" came . . . from the *Wealth of Nations*.[12]

Paul Douglas noted this aspect of Smith in his sesquicentennial lecture and concluded that Marx had adopted his views from Smith via the Ricardian socialists. Even though Douglas did not see the conceptual difference between the Ricardian socialists and Marx's viewpoint, or refer to Marx's explicit acknowledgement in the *Theories of Surplus Value*, the conclusion drawn by Douglas still has some validity:

> There are, it seems to me, few more unfair instances in economic thought than the almost complete unanimity with which the English-speaking economists of the chair have heaped condemnation upon the overworked and poverty-stricken Marx, who worked under such great difficulties, and, save for the comments of Jevons and a few others, have heaped praises upon Smith and Ricardo. The failure was the failure not of one man but of a philosophy of value, and the roots of the ultimate contradiction made manifest to the world in the third volume of *Das Kapital* lie embedded in the first volume of the *Wealth of Nations*.[13]

How are we to reconcile such a view with the Adam Smith of the chapters on Mercantilism? Is free trade mutually beneficial in international trade and exploitative in domestic production? Does the evidence not indicate some basic indecision and inconsistency in Smith regarding the benefits of free exchange, contrary to popular wisdom and generations of textbooks?

The most remarkable feature of the renascence of Smithian hagiography is its association with Christianity.[14] The idea that secularism, or at least "secular Deism" (if one may use the phrase), dominated the Scottish Enlightenment, is but a natural by-product of the emphasis given to David Hume and Adam Smith while studying the eighteenth-century Scots. There is no doubt that some contemporaries saw the activities of the Scots literati as being anti-Christian, as in John Maclaurin's parody of the literati, where David Hume appears as "Mr. Genius":

> Satan is reliably informed that Mr. Genius is the only author of note. Greatly impressed, Satan meets Genius, observing that he has read his books. "Why, then, Sir," replies that worthy, "you are convinced, I suppose, that there is no God, no devil, and no future state;—that suicide is a duty we owe ourselves;—adultery a duty we owe to our neighbours;—that the tragedy of *Douglas* is the best play ever was written: and that *Shakespeare* and *Otway* were a couple of dunces.—This, I think, is the sum and substance of my writings." Genius departs, leaving Satan a little perplexed: "Faith, I don't know well what to think of him. Are you sure he is true blue on our side? I confess, I have some suspicion, that he is a shrewed fellow, endeavoring to convert men to Christianity, by writing nonsense against it."[15]

Such opinions should be seen from the background of the strict Calvinism of a Kirk which, for example, forbade Edinburgh ministers (but not those from out of town!) to attend public plays, and can be misleading if read out of context. It is hoped that this bias will diminish with the publication of such works as that of Richard Sher, because a failure to appreciate the force of an active Christian intellectual tradition in driving the Scottish Enlightenment has been fairly widespread. How do we account for the well-ensconced positions of David Hume and Adam Smith after 1755 if the Church did in fact *actively* see them as enemies? That Church Moderates such as Hugh Blair and William Robertson were not quite as orthodox as others is beside the point. It is worth observing that they were never charged with heresy, and, more importantly, that they themselves saw a distinct difference between their own viewpoint and that of David Hume. The pleasantry with which Hume's brilliant but wayward genius was tolerated is well reflected in a letter of Thomas Reid to Hume:

> 18 March 1763. When you have seen the whole of my performance, I shall take it as a very great favour to have your opinion on it, from which I make no doubt of receiving light, whether I receive conviction or no. Your friendly adversaries, Drs. Campbell and Gerard, as well as Dr. Gregory, return their compliments to you respectfully. A little philosophical society here, of which all three are members, is much indebted to you for its entertainment. Your company would, although we are all good Christians, be more acceptable than that of St. Athanasius; and since we cannot have you upon the bench, you are brought oftener than any other man to the bar, accused and defended with great zeal, but without bitterness. If you write no more in morals, politics, or metaphysics, I am afraid we shall be at a loss for subjects.[16]

Sir George Clark has claimed that the primary feature of a great civilization is its energy. That Calvinism contributed to awakening the latent energies of the Scots has been argued by Gordon Marshall in *Presbyteries and Profits*. The least one can say about the Scottish Church of the mid-eighteenth century is that it did not use this energy to destroy the coterie of intellectuals that made Scotland famous. This is really saying very little, and I do not believe it to be accurate. The more important question, whether Scotland would have possessed such energy with Presbyterianism, has not been adequately probed, despite the strong claims made by John Millar for the Reformation and the highlighting of the issue by modern scholars such as Anand Chitnis.[17]

Lord Keynes is among the few economists to have appreciated the contributions of several clergymen-economists. One of the clergymen Keynes missed was Archbishop King, author of the widely read *The Origin of Evil*, who provided a penetrating analysis of the ills of Ireland; the following economic principle set forth in one of King's unpublished papers is remarkable for its acumen. In defense of the right of the Irish to fishing, he states:

> The wisdom of England wou'd be (one wou'd think) to make use of the hands of all their subjects each in the works that they can best and cheapest perform.[18]

With some further development—for example, if combined with a labor theory of value—it leads to the principle of comparative advantage.

Archbishop King leads us naturally into the role played by Ireland in stimulating the Scottish Enlightenment, especially since a number of the Irish, such as the Archbishop, were motivated by their faith to examine economic issues. Francis Hutcheson first rose to prominence in Ireland—his famous refutation of Mandeville is contained in the *Hibernicus Letters*—and the role of the Irish in stimulating the Scots has been largely neglected. If we except the debates over "Private Vices, Public Benefits," incited by Mandeville in the 1720s, it is Ireland which shows the greatest concern for economic discussion between 1720 and 1740. These were years of economic depression, and the poverty of the Irish stimulated them to consider ways out of their misery. Jonathan Swift and George Berkeley are the most famous names associated with this period, but there were also a number of other able economists such as Arthur Dobbs, Thomas Prior, and Samuel Madden. It is also significant that these men organized themselves into a formal society—the Dublin Society—which was committed to the economic development of Ireland. There is a meaningful sense in which it can be said to form a "school" of economics. The pattern of the Dublin Society was later copied by several other societies, and even as late as 1761 a Scotsman could regret that the Scots were not copying the Irish.[19]

The *Querist* of Bishop Berkeley (1737) was an enormously successful pamphlet which served to demolish the notion of "money as wealth" while seeking to lay new grounds in considering the welfare of the common man as the foundation for economic policy. Ten editions were printed in Berkeley's own lifetime, and we know that Adam Smith possessed a copy in his library. The economics of the Irish was of necessity focused upon problems of poverty and development, and was far more relevant to the Scots than the contemporary English literature. Robert Wallace, a noted civic republican, picked up Berkeley's ideas and propounded them at some length in his *Characteristics* (1758). One of the figures he combats is David Hume, whose views on money were quite different from those of Berkeley and Wallace.[20] Nonetheless, prejudice and ignorance still combine to give some remarkable accounts of the influence of Christianity in Adam Smith's day:

The *Wealth of Nations* offered a remarkable cognitive vision. The broad sweep of the book launched economics on the road to becoming *the* social science. A wide range of social phenomena was approached with a unifying analysis. It was the perception of man introduced in the writings of the Scottish philosophers that provided coherence and structure to such a broad examination of social arrangements. This perception offers an understanding of man that contrasts with the Christian tradition in philosophy and theology. The Christian tradition, expressed by Christian theology and Marxian doctrine, offers two conflicting but essentially metaphysical views of man that pervasively shape our political thinking. Man is seen either as basically evil, requiring constraints or properly conceived authoritarian institutions imposing suitable guidance, or as inherently good and noble, deserving liberation from institutions repressing his "natural humanity." . . .

The Scottish philosophers broke with this religious tradition, and Adam Smith's work opened the door to a social science.[21]

What then were the contributions of the Scots-Presbyterian milieu to the economic views of the Scots? Let us take the principal concept discussed by modern libertarians such as Hayek: the idea that beneficence and coherence can be obtained through actions undertaken with no such good intentions. In sermons preached during and after the Jacobite rebellion of 1745, both Adam Ferguson and Hugh Blair emphasize just this point. Ferguson tells his troops in December 1745 of the Jacobites and French that "they are only made Tools to serve Purposes very different from the Ends they propose to themselves." In May 1746, Hugh Blair reports of the same events that God "makes the unruly Passions of bad Men work in a secret way, towards Ends, by them altogether unseen."

Whether or not Ferguson and Blair believed such things, they clearly expected their congregations to believe them.[22] The tradition of seeing God thus wring good out of evil and produce beneficence where none was intended is no doubt most prominent in Puritan times but it has much earlier origins. St Thomas Aquinas already considers it an established view when he writes: "even God uses all sins for some good end: he draws some good out of every evil."[23]

Theological analyses of coherence in societies of selfish individuals was even more pronounced among the Jansenists, and Smith was well conversant with French intellectual trends. A historian of economic thought with the widest erudition, Jacob Viner, wrote that *laissez-faire* was simply the application to economics of concepts long familiar to theologians and moral philosophers. While some work has been done, notably by Milton Myers, in elaborating upon this important statement, it needs emphasis that such thought patterns appear to have been *commonplace* among Scots-Presbyterian congregations. Viner also noted that the "Invisible Hand" could only have meant the invisible hand of God to eighteenth-century readers, who used a variety of ways to avoid addressing the Deity directly. Readers in Brazil, however, did not hesitate on this issue. In his Introduction to *Studies of the Common Good and Political Economy*, Silva Lisboa, an important Brazilian economist and politician of the early nineteenth century, wrote:

> Smith, my principal mentor in Political Economy, first showed that the production of goods is proportional to market expansion and that through free trade the invisible hand of the Creator could extract the General Good among the particular interests . . .[24]

Because Smith is hailed as the founder of individualistic economics and perhaps because the "Invisible Hand" can be thought of as the directing hand of the Deity, Smith has always had a special fascination for Christians. In the half-century following the publication of Newton's *Principia* several prominent Anglicans worked hard to fashion a theory of society using the Newtonian model of gravitation. Adam Smith was able to draw upon this existing metaphysic of ideas when he wrote, and later Christians in turn drew upon Adam Smith. The Reverend Richard Whately, Drummond Professor of Political Economy at Oxford, the most influential populariser of the subject in the mid-eighteenth century, explicitly argued that the coherence achieved by free competition was a proof of the existence of God. Adam Smith's argument had demonstrated that free trade led to the maximization of economic growth; it was Richard Whately who explicitly extended the virtues of free trade to consumption and consumer satisfaction. Free trade, Whately demonstrated, produced an outcome superior to any human planning. Since man was not the planner, God must be.[25]

The identification of free trade with the will of God became less fashionable as the nineteenth century wore on but has now begun to experience a revival. The fact that Smith removed, in later editions, the only explicitly Christian reference in *The Theory of Moral Sentiments* hints at his true beliefs.[26] Even stronger evidence comes from Smith's repeated quotes from Hume's anti-Christian *History of England*, including a long passage mockingly describing the variety of religious sects as "ghostly practitioners." And Smith's epitaph on Hume, that he had been one of the best and most virtuous men alive, sufficiently shows how far he sympathized with Hume's virulent opposition to Christianity. All this is entirely consistent with Smith's well-known admiration for Rousseau and Voltaire. The only wonder is that scholars have not taken more note of Alexander Dalrymple's report that Smith had told him in private that "Christianity debased the human mind."[27] That sincere Christians would see fit to consider Smith a friendly figure is just another indication of the want of care in examination with which historical ideas have been hitherto accepted.

I have argued that the great fame of Adam Smith has become a barrier to sound historical understanding. Scholars do us no service when they elevate Smith's abilities without careful attention to the rich and varied writings of Smith's predecessors and contemporaries. This superficial attitude was begun by Adam Smith himself, probably because he was jealous about gaining priority for expounding the system of natural liberty. For almost a century economists did not look carefully into the Smithian view of the past, but this situation was patiently remedied between 1900 and 1950. Nonetheless, the recent literature has gone back to the well-worn paths of Smithian hagiography. Why they have chosen to do so is a sociological question whose answer I have attempted to guess at. Whatever the explanation, the popular adoration of Adam Smith should not be allowed to continue unchallenged. Such a view mocks historical scholarship and promotes general views of economics as a discipline and of the field of economic development in particular that have little historical foundation. In view of the great importance of the new free market economics in Britain and the USA, it behooves us to know exactly where the patron saint of this movement stands.

NOTES

1. As quoted by Richard Tuck, *Natural Rights Theories* (Cambridge: Cambridge University Press, 1979), 33.
2. M. Gluckman, *Politics, Law and Ritual in Tribal Society* (New York: New American Library, 1965), 99.
3. Alfred Marshall, *Principles of Economics*, vol. I, ed. C.W. Guilleband (London: Macmillan, 1961), 757.
4. L.A. Clarkson, *The Pre-industrial Economy in England, 1500-1750* (London: Batsford, 1971); J. Viner, *Studies in the Theory of International Trade* (New York: Augustus Kelley, 1965), 109-10.
5. E.B. Burns, "The Enlightenment in Two Colonial Brazilian Libraries," *Journal of the History of Ideas* (July 1964), **25**, 430-38.
6. E. Lipson, *Economic History of England* (London: Black, 1929-31), 3 vols; K.B. Pyle, "Advantages of Followership: German Economics and Japanese Bureaucrats, 1890-1925," *Journal of Japanese Studies* (1983), **9**, 127-64. For the influence of List on Russia, see T.H. von Lane, *Sergei Witte and the Industrialization of Russia* (New York: Ethen Allen, 1969).
7. Elaborated most clearly by Wesley Mitchell, *Types of Economic Theory* (New York: Augustus Kelley, 1965), vol. I.
8. Karl Marx, *Theories of Surplus Value* (Moscow: Progress Publishers, 1966), vol. I, 79.
9. James Maitland, Earl of Lauderdale, *An Inquiry into the Nature and Origin of Public Wealth* (London, 1804), 157-8; T.R. Malthus, *Principles of Political Economy*, 2nd edn

(London, 1836), 76; Francis Horner, *The Economic Writings of Francis Horner*, ed. F.W. Fetter (London: London School of Economics, 1957), 60.

10. Alec Macfie, "Adam Smith's *Moral Sentiments* as Foundation for his *Wealth of Nations*," *Oxford Economic Papers* (1959), **11**, 217.

11. Marian Bowley, *Studies in the History of Economic Thought before 1870* (London: Macmillan, 1973), 193-9.

12. Samuel Hollander, *Classical Economics* (Oxford: Blackwell, 1987), 415.

13. Paul Douglas, "Smith's Theory of Value and Distribution," in *Adam Smith, 1776-1926* (Chicago: University of Chicago Press, 1928), 77-115. It should be noted that a reliable edition of the *Theories of Surplus Value* was not available at the time of Douglas's essay.

14. For example, John Chamberlain, *The Roots of Capitalism* (Indianapolis: Liberty Press, 1976). In an almost pathetic attempt to enlist Smith in a "theological" course, Dr Bendj Kenadjian offers the following explanation, which he obtained through ESP, for Smith's decision to burn his works before his death: "Toward the end of his life, Adam Smith became convinced that reincarnation was an indisputable fact of life. Since this made him feel that many of his arguments were no longer valid, he decided to burn his works" (*Economics of the New Age*, Philadelphia: Dorrance, 1973, 29).

15. As quoted by D.D. McElroy, *Scotland's Age of Improvement* (Pullman, Wash.: Washington State University Press, 1969), 65.

16. Ibid., 47. The freedom of out-of-town clergy is described by Alexander Carlyle, *Anecdotes and Characters of the Times* (Oxford: Oxford University Press, 1973), 163.

17. A. Chitnis, *The Scottish Enlightenment* (London: Croom Helm, 1976); Gordon Marshall, *Presbyteries and Profits* (Oxford: Clarendon Press, 1980).

18. P. Kelley, "A Pamphlet Attributed to John Toland and an Unpublished Reply by Archbishop William King," *Topoi* (1985), **4**, 81-90, esp. 86.

19. S. Rashid, "The Irish School of Economic Development," *The Manchester School of Social and Economic Studies*, **56**, 345-69.

20. S. Rashid, "Berkeley's *Querist* and its Influence," *Journal of the History of Economic Thought* (Spring 1990), **2**, 38-60. One of the distinguishing features of Hume in this regard is that his outlook is not Scottish at all, but English. The cosmopolitanism, the desire for moderate luxury, the intellectual pleasantry, all take us back to Addison and the *Spectator*. Perhaps this is one reason for the great popularity of the *Essays*: they reviewed the elegant appreciation of civil life over which Mandeville had cast a shadow.

21. K. Brunner, "Milton Friedman in our Time," in *Economics and Social Institutions*, ed. K. Brunner (The Hague: Martinus Nijhoff, 1979), 30-1.

22. Richard Sher, *Church and University in the Scottish Enlightenment* (Edinburgh: Edinburgh University Press, 1985), 42-3.

23. R. Lekachman, *The Varieties of Economics* (Boston, Mass.: Peter Smith, 1977), vol. I, 57.

24. I have not seen the original and owe the reference to Ricardo Gazel.

25. S. Rashid, "Richard Whately and the Struggle for Rational Christianity in the Mid-Nineteenth Century," *Historical Magazine of the Protestant Episcopal Church* (September 1978), **47**, 293-312. Even while accepting *laissez-faire* for its providentialist implications, a substantial portion of the clergymen-economists were actively defending the poor—e.g., Bishop Woodward, David Davies, John Howlett. This tension was a constant feature of the Christian reaction to political economy.

26. This point is well described by D.D. Raphael in an Appendix to the Glasgow edition of the *Theory of Moral Sentiments* (Oxford: Oxford University Press, 1976).

27. Alexander Dalrymple, *Thoughts of an Old Man . . .* (London, 1801).

Index